The Cracker Jack® Collection

Baseball's Prized Players

The Cracker Jack Collection

Baseball's Prized Players

Tom Zappala & Ellen Zappala

with John Molori & Jim Davis

FOREWORD AND CONTRIBUTIONS BY JOE ORLANDO

100TH ANNIVERSARY COMMEMORATIVE EDITION

Peter E. Randall Publisher
Portsmouth, New Hampshire
2013

ISBN 13: 978-1-931807-24-1

Library of Congress Control Number: 2013933911

Produced by Peter E. Randall Publisher

Box 4726, Portsmouth, NH 03802

www.perpublisher.com

Book design: Grace Peirce

Photography credit:

© Images Anthony Dube/White Point Imaging 2013

www.whitepointimaging.com

Cracker Jack® memorabilia provided by the Harriet Joyce Collection.

Cracker Jack® player card images throughout book provided by Professional Sports Authenticator PSA.

www.psacard.com

Cracker Jack® player card images for front cover provided by 707 Sportscards.

www.707sportscards.com

Cracker Jack® Ball Players advertising piece image provided by Robert Edward Auctions.

www.robertedwardauctions.com

Vintage baseball equipment provided by Brett Lowman of Play OK Antiques.

www.playokantiques.com

"Take Me Out to the Ball Game" by Albert Von Tilzer, composer, and Jack Norworth, lyricist.
(New York: The New York Music Co., 1908.) Public domain.

Additional copies available from:

www.crackerjackplayers.com

Printed in China

To Lucy, Emmie, Anna Rose,
and all of our future mini Cracker Jack All-Stars

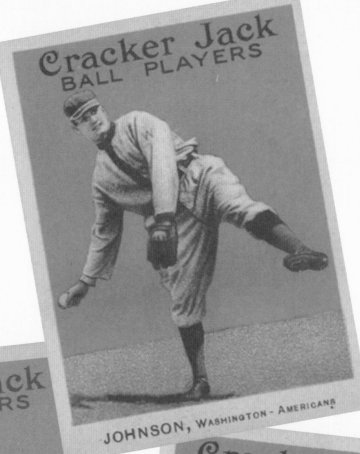

Cracker Jack
BALL PLAYERS

JOHNSON, WASHINGTON - AMERICANS

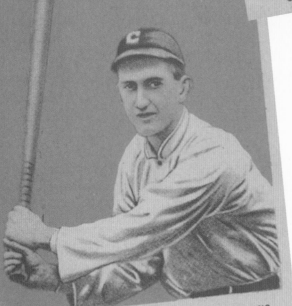

Cracker Jack
BALL PLAYERS

JOE JACKSON, CLEVELAND - AMERICANS

Cracker Jack
BALL PLAYERS

MATHEWSON, NEW YORK - NATIONALS

CONTENTS

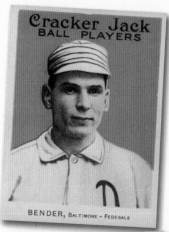

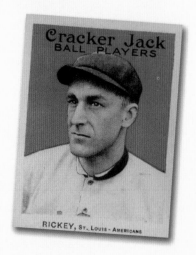

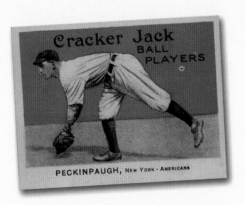

FOREWORD

CRACKER JACK, THE STICKY-SWEET candy treat, will be a part of our National Pastime forever . . . and we are reminded of its place in baseball history during the seventh-inning stretch of every game:

Take me out to the ball game.

Take me out with the crowd.

Buy me some peanuts and Cracker Jack,

I don't care if I never get back,

Let me root, root, root for the home team,

If they don't win it's a shame.

For it's one, two, three strikes, you're out,

At the old ball game.

Most of us have vivid memories of going to baseball games in our youth and devouring boxes of these caramel-covered treats, leaving our hands so sticky that we felt like Spider-Man for a couple of hours. No, you might not have been able to scale walls like the web-slinging superhero, but the Cracker Jack residue could help you snare a foul ball if one was headed your way. It was also helpful when turning the pages of your baseball program at the game.

While many baseball fans can recall the look and taste of the candy, along with the tiny wrapped gift inside each box, most of us were not around when original baseball cards were included in every package. In 1914, Cracker Jack would produce the first of two classic sets. Each inserted card from the 144-card set could be found nestled amongst the syrupy concoction that kids couldn't wait to get their hands on.

Therefore, each card that found its way into the Cracker Jack boxes was subjected to a host of condition obstacles. The cards bounced around inside the box, covered by an avalanche of candied corn and peanuts. As the temperature rose, the contents became stickier and more hazardous to the trading cards enclosed with the sweet and gooey treats. As a result, the 1914 Cracker Jack issue is terribly difficult to find in high-grade today. How some of these cards survived in presentable

condition is beyond me, but it is clear that some of the best examples must have escaped being imprisoned in their candy cages. This is also true of other candy and tobacco issues from the first half of the 20th century. Absent rare finds of unblemished examples, ones that were never placed into the product packages, most of these types of cards are found in mid-to-lower grades.

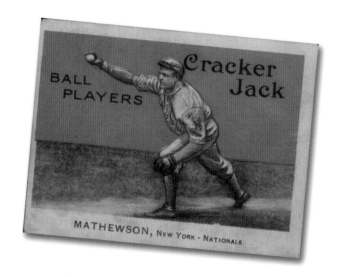

In 1915, Cracker Jack continued planting Shoeless Joes, Ty Cobbs, Christy Mathewsons and the like inside their boxes, but they also offered the public an opportunity to acquire a complete set with an accompanying album, in exchange for coupons, to house the cards that avoided the minefield of sugar. This offer, the first major "factory set" offer of its kind, has helped to ensure that beautiful specimens could reach collectors today.

It is virtually impossible to locate high-grade copies from the 1914 set. However, while still challenging and larger at 176 cards, the 1915 Cracker Jack set is one that collectors can actually assemble in top condition if they possess the financial wherewithal to do so. Ironically, despite being technically easier to find in high grade, the 1915 cards actually sold for more than their 1914 counterparts for a long time. Many collectors dared not try to collect the 1914 set. The difficulty operated as a deterrent. In turn, more collectors flocked towards the technically more attainable 1915 set.

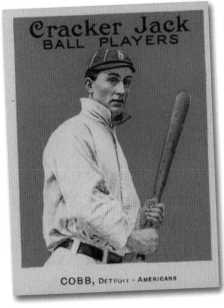

It was only recently, perhaps the last several years, that collectors began fully appreciating the great disparity in scarcity. As a result, collectors began paying stronger prices for the 1914 Cracker Jack cards across the board. There were always great price premiums paid for the key cards, such as the 1914 Christy Mathewson (pitching pose) card, but the premiums now apply to all the cards in the set.

At the time of this writing, the legendary 1914 and 1915 Cracker Jack baseball card issues were approaching their 100th anniversary. While not considered part of *The Big Three* baseball sets in the hobby, which includes the classic 1909–1911 T206, 1933 Goudey and 1952 Topps issues, the Cracker Jack cards would arguably round out *The Big Four* if the list was expanded. Some would argue the Cracker Jack issue should be part of *The Big Three*. One thing is certain; the cards have always been desirable.

The Cracker Jack issue, which is loaded with great stars from the period, is one of the most eye-appealing releases ever manufactured. The distinct poses, which lie against the rich, red background, provide some of the best visuals ever captured on cardboard. From the ferocity in Ty Cobb's gaze to the regal portrait of Christy Mathewson to the joyous look on Shoeless Joe Jackson's face prior to the Black Sox scandal, many collectors feel that this set provides some of the finest-looking cards known of many of its featured figures.

There was one major star who could have been included in the 1915 release but didn't make the cut. This man was a young pitcher for the Boston Red Sox who made his debut in 1914. He became the most dominant left-hander on the mound, but once he was sent to the New York Yankees in 1920, he became the most dangerous hitter at the plate. Yes, you guessed it, Babe Ruth. Falling under the heading of "what could have been," a mainstream Babe Ruth rookie card could have appeared in the set, but it wasn't meant to be.

If the Cracker Jack Ruth rookie card had ever been made, there is no doubt it would be one of the most coveted and valuable cards in the entire hobby. Prior to 1948, there weren't what most collectors would describe as "mainstream sets" produced each year. Many great players like Jimmie Foxx and Lou Gehrig did not have official rookie cards, at least the way we define rookie cards today. There are two rookie-era Ruth cards and both are worth a tremendous amount of money. In 1914, Ruth appeared on a Minor League card as a member of the Baltimore Orioles. This Baltimore News card has fetched well into six figures with the highest price ever paid reaching $575,000 in 2012 for a PSA Good 2.

Ruth's first appearance as a Major Leaguer came in the black-and-white M101-5 and M101-4 Sporting News sets, which are now both believed to have been released in 1916. Several copies of that Ruth card, in various grades, have sold for in excess of $100,000 during the past several years. The Cracker Jack Babe Ruth rookie card may not exist, but as collectors, we can still dream.

As long as the hobby exists, Cracker Jack baseball cards will remain a part of the collecting fabric. Their link to the classic American confection, their stunning eye-appeal and fantastic player selection have made these tiny time capsules one of the most desired card productions of all time.

As you dive into the pages ahead like you would a box of tasty Cracker Jack, you will learn more about the

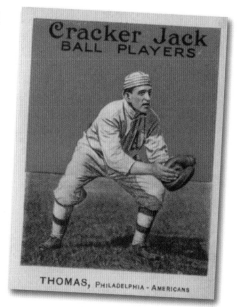

dominant stars, the tragic figures and lesser-known players of the era who helped shape the National Pastime just prior to the emergence of The Great Bambino.

AUTHORS' NOTE

◆ All of the card images, Cracker Jack prize images and baseball memorabilia used in this book are originals and not reproductions.

◆ As this book discusses the Cracker Jack Collection as a whole, we have included narratives on the four players who were included in the 1914 release but were not part of the 1915 set. Those players are Nixey Callahan, Jay Cashion, Frank Chance, and Harry Lord.

◆ We have included both the 1914 and 1915 cards for Christy Mathewson and Del Pratt as their 1914 card featured a pitching pose while the 1915 card featured a portrait. In addition, we have included both Rollie Zeider card poses. Zeider had two cards in the 1914 set, but just one in the 1915 set.

◆ This book is organized in chapters by position. Player narratives are included in the chapter for the position they played. Utility players are listed by the position they played the majority of times during their careers.

◆ The players included in the Cracker Jack All-Star Team chapter were selected by the authors, and reflect the subjective opinion of the authors. One could argue that several other extraordinary players could have been included instead.

◆ The individuals included in the chapter entitled "The Front Office" were all working in administrative positions in 1915. Although there are others in the collection that had important careers as managers, they were included with the chapter on their position if they were an active player or player-manager in 1915.

◆ Catcher Frank Owens is referred to in some circles as "Yip." We list him as Frank as it is our belief that Yip was the nickname of the pitcher Frank Owen who played from 1903 to 1909 for the Chicago White Sox. This player was born in Ypsilanti, Michigan, thus the nickname. The catcher featured in the Cracker Jack Collection was born in Toronto, Canada. Interestingly, both Owens the catcher and Owen the pitcher played for the White Sox in 1909, which may have caused the name confusion.

◆ The Jimmy Austin Cracker Jack player card lists his team affiliation as Pittsburgh of the Federal League, but there are no records that he actually played in the Federal League. The card depicts him in a St. Louis Browns uniform. As reported in the March 6, 1915, edition of *Sporting News*, Austin had signed with Pittsburgh of the Federal League, but jumped back to St. Louis before spring training when they matched the salary offered by the Feds.

ACKNOWLEDGMENTS

THE DECISION TO WRITE THIS BOOK AS A follow up to our first book, *The T206 Collection: The Players & Their Stories,* was an easy one, especially since we are very intrigued by the Deadball Era and all that went along with it. Research on the great players, mediocre players, rule changes, the outbreak of World War I, and the incarnation of the short-lived Federal League all made this a fun project.

First and foremost, we would like to thank our good friend and colleague, Joe Orlando, president of Professional Sports Authenticator (PSA) and editor of Sports Market Report (SMR), for taking the time out of his busy schedule to work with us again. Joe is the "go-to" guy in the card collecting world, and his knowledge is unsurpassed.

We would also like to thank Jim Davis, one of the foremost Cracker Jack historians in the world, for his exhaustive research on the history of both the Cracker Jack® product as well as the prizes found in every box. A shout out also goes to Wes Johnson, Harriet Joyce, Alex Jaramillo, Gail Sullivan, Barbara Hastings and Judy Thornton for assisting Jim in his research and writing.

The Cracker Jack® prizes that you see throughout this book come from the Harriet Joyce Collection. Many thanks to Harriet for giving us carte blanche on selecting the wonderful memorabilia to illustrate this book. We would be hard-pressed to find a finer collection anywhere.

Special thanks to Tony Dube of White Point Imaging. His exceptional photography is seen throughout this publication. Tony is one of the most talented collectibles photographers in the country, and we are very fortunate to have worked with him on this project as well as our T206 book.

Levi Bleam and Jim Fleck of 707 Sportscards provided the original cards shown on the cover of this book. These two gentlemen were very kind to supply these beautiful cardboard gems for the photo shoot.

Thank you to Professional Sports Authenticator (PSA) for providing the Cracker Jack player card images used throughout the book and to Robert Edward Auctions for providing the Cracker Jack Ball Players advertising piece image shown in Chapter 11.

The vintage baseball equipment that you see in this book, as well as our T206 book, was provided by Brett Lowman from Play OK Antiques in Connecticut. We are pleased to once again have the opportunity to showcase some of his incredible collection.

A huge thank you to Deidre Randall, Grace Peirce, Zak Johnson and the staff at Peter E. Randall Publisher for design, layout, editing, and their fine attention to detail, all making this a book to be proud of.

Very special thanks to our friend, the talented John Molori, for his efforts in helping with researching and writing about various players. His keen wit contributed to making the player narratives interesting as well as informative.

Thanks to all of you for encouraging us to write this book and for loving both the game of baseball as well as the hobby of collecting.

Lastly, special thanks to the players of the Cracker Jack Collection. From the greats like Mathewson, Speaker and Plank to the commons like Strunk, Lavender and Knetzer. You all contributed to making the game of baseball the only game in town.

INTRODUCTION

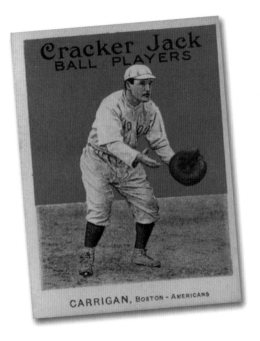

AS A KID GROWING UP IN A MILL CITY IN Massachusetts, I spent a lot of time during the hot summer days in a vacant parking lot across the street from my home with my pal Wayne, pretending that we were Major League pitchers. We would take turns pitching to each other, calling balls and strikes. I would try to imitate the herky-jerky motion of Luis Tiant, who pitched for Cleveland at the time, and Wayne pretended to be Bill Monbouquette, a pretty good pitcher for the Red Sox. After about three innings of throwing a hard rubber baseball, we would take a step back in time, and I would become Cy Young and Wayne would become Smokey Joe Wood, both great Sox pitchers. For some reason those two guys seemed like gods to us, although we never saw footage of either one of them, only photographs. In retrospect, I think it was the uniforms that we liked. I was eleven and Wayne was ten . . . very impressionable.

After pitching until our arms were ready to fall off, we would wander down to Eddie's Variety Store and buy two things: a popsicle and a box of Cracker Jack. The Cracker Jack was a staple, because it was the only thing we could split evenly and

it would also last for a while. The problem occurred when we would dig through the sweet popcorn and peanuts in search of The Prize. Once we would find that little treasure, the two of us would barter. Who was going to get The Prize this time? I would relinquish to Wayne more often than not, so I could get my favorite when it appeared in that box of Cracker Jack. I had to have the tattoo. Not the stick-on things you get today, but rather those wonderful little pieces of artwork that you could transfer onto your skin by licking it, and holding it face down for about twenty seconds before slowly lifting it. You would have a perfect grown-up tattoo on your forearm. I would let Wayne keep the little tops, plastic rings and stuff like that. I wanted the tattoo. Maybe I'm getting sentimental as I get older, but there is a sense of comfort that comes over me when I think back to those hot summer days, sitting on my front stoop, cooling off with a popsicle and munching on Cracker Jack with Wayne.

Over the years, the prizes that have been inserted in Cracker Jack® boxes have

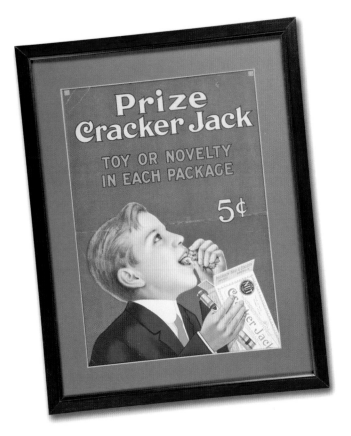

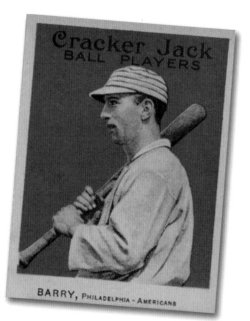

history of the product and its prizes, we discuss the stories behind each player, and Joe takes it full circle and talks about the differences between the 1914 and 1915 sets and also sheds some light on the history of the cards as well as how scarce they really are today. Like the T206 Collection, the stories are fascinating. Some of these players are Hall of Famers and some were up for the proverbial cup of coffee, but every one of them contributed to laying the foundation for the greatest game in the world. In this collection, we have players in American League uniforms, National League uniforms, Federal League uniforms, and management business suits.

Sit back, break open a box of Cracker Jack, kick your feet up, and travel back to a time and place where baseball was really our National Pastime. Shoeless Joe, Mack, the enigmatic Cobb, and my all-time favorite Tris Speaker (my Boston provincialism always rears its head) lead this great cast of characters. By the way, if you find a stick-on tattoo in your box, would you kindly send it to me? My grandchildren would get a hoot out of seeing it on my arm. Enjoy!

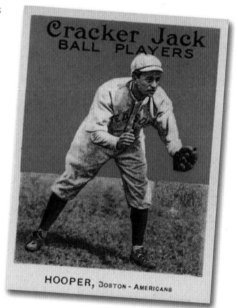

varied greatly. Everything from spinning tops, to paper fans, to toy figures, has been inserted along with the caramel corn and peanuts. The very best prizes, however, were inserted in those boxes long before Wayne and I were throwing balls and strikes in that parking lot. These were not tattoos or plastic rings, but rather paper images of baseball greats like Joe Jackson, Ty Cobb, and Connie Mack. These paper gems found their way into the hands of kids and adults across the country as Cracker Jack® prizes decades before I was trying to perfect the Tiant fadeaway pitch. The cards were not covered with tobacco stains or found in packages of cigarettes. They were carefully placed in boxes of Cracker Jack so that people could put together full sets, or simply hope to get their favorite player. Although people loved the idea when the set was introduced in 1914, they complained that many of the cards were stained by the sugary contents of the box. Cracker Jack solved the problem in 1915 by offering the public the opportunity to send away for the whole collection. These cards never saw the inside of a Cracker Jack box, and were in pristine condition.

The players that make up this set, like the T206 Collection (the subject of our first book, *The T206 Collection: The Players & Their Stories*) were the founding fathers of our National Pastime. Like our first book, we decided to offer narratives on the stories behind each of the players. There is some information on the back of the original Cracker Jack cards, but not a heck of a lot.

With the help of our good friends Joe Orlando and Jim Davis, we decided to take it a little further. Jim discusses the

A LITTLE CRACKER JACK© HISTORY

GRIFFITH, Washington - Americans

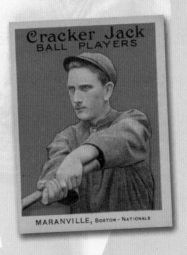

HUGGINS, St. Louis - Nationals

Before we get into the player stories, we thought it would be a good idea to give a short history on both the Cracker Jack® product as well as the prizes that were inserted into every box of those tasty little treats. Noted historian James H. "Jim" Davis takes us on a guided tour through the annals of Cracker Jack® history from the birth of the company after the Great Chicago Fire of 1871 through the various transitions that took it to its present ownership by Frito-Lay. He also looks at the history of a very successful marketing campaign launched by the fledgling company, the Cracker Jack prizes, and the connection of those prizes with baseball. Little did the Rueckheim brothers know that their product would one day become synonymous with our National Pastime and the seventh-inning stretch.

MARANVILLE, Boston - Nationals

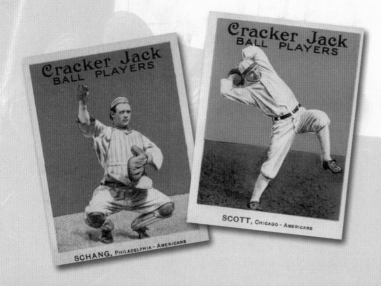

SCHANG, Philadelphia - Americans

SCOTT, Chicago - Americans

CLAUDE HENDRIX, Chicago - Federals

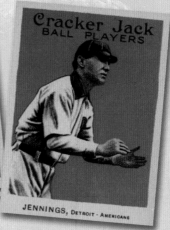

JENNINGS, Detroit - Americans

A Company is Born

A German immigrant who came to the land of opportunity almost 150 years ago saw his American dream fulfilled and in so doing created a product that has become an icon of quality and creative marketing ingenuity.

Frederick William Rueckheim, the 23-year-old son of a tailor and Austro-Prussian War veteran, came to America in 1869 from his home in Hamburg, Germany. After working on his uncle's small farm just south of Chicago for a couple of years, Rueckheim moved to Chicago to help clean-up the debris caused by the Great Chicago Fire of 1871.

With $200 he saved from the $150 his uncle had paid him annually, he went into business with William Brinkmeyer, a friend whose popcorn and confectionery business had been burned out by the fire. They equipped a rented back room with a hand popper and a molasses kettle, and soon opened a stand in Chicago's Loop area. The popcorn business did well that first year, but the popcorn partnership did not. When Frederick's younger brother

Louis joined the company in 1872 (some records state 1873), Brinkmeyer sold his share of the business and F. W. Rueckheim & Bro. was born.

The business flourished. Louis handled the manufacturing side of the operation, becoming a master at candy making, while Frederick managed the business and marketing components. In 1874 they expanded their product line to include candy and marshmallows after purchasing equipment from a Dutch confectioner who returned to Holland. "Reliable Confections" became their trademark with a big red "R" in a circle as the company logo.

Rapid growth necessitated expansion into larger and larger facilities, with four moves in ten years from the original plant on East Van Buren Street. By 1885 the firm occupied a three-story brick factory on Desplaines Street, but in 1887 the factory experienced Chicago's earlier fate. The plant burned to the ground and all equipment was destroyed. Like the city, the Rueckheim phoenix rose from those

"That's a crackerjack!"

very ashes. In just two weeks the brothers were back in business at a temporary site and in only six months the factory was reconstructed and reoccupied. In 1895, the company expanded again and increased production by replacing the hand work, iron kettles, and open furnaces of the past with automatic systems, new candy-making machinery, and steam jacketed copper kettles. To avoid another catastrophe, a modern sprinkler system was installed in the new facility.

As the business grew, so too did the city...so much so that Chicago was chosen to host the 1893 World's Columbian Exposition. Over twenty-seven million travelers from all over the world converged in Chicago, giving the Rueckheim brothers an unprecedented opportunity to introduce their Reliable Confections. Legend has it that they sold a precursor to Cracker Jack at the Exposition. Legend notwithstanding, no documentation has surfaced to substantiate that the Rueckheim brothers were even at the Expo.

F. W. Rueckheim & Bro.'s application for a trademark patent states that its popcorn confection was first called "Cracker Jack" in late January 1896. As the story goes, salesman Jack Berg tasted a new version of the product developed by Louis to solve the problem of the candied

A Little Music, A Little Marketing

> *"The more you eat, the more you want"*

Before the end of its first year, the popcorn confection appeared on the music scene. The "Cracker Jack Two-Step," an instrumental piece for piano composed by Niu-Va, was published by S. Brainard's Sons Co. of Chicago in 1896. The illustration on the cover of the sheet music, labeled "The Cracker Jack Party," shows children gathered around the table with the familiar red, white, and blue packages with the diagonal wording and the Reliable red circle clearly depicted on the table and floor. The cover states that "Cracker Jack" was used "by permission of F. W. Rueckheim & Bro." and that the music was also copyrighted in England; thus Cracker Jack was already known abroad within its inaugural year.

In 1899, H. G. Eckstein, a friend of the Rueckheim brothers, joined the enterprise, bringing with him an outsider's perspective to the operation. Eckstein's eventual contribution to the success of Cracker Jack cannot be overestimated. He realized the huge sales potential, if only a way could be found to preserve the freshness and crispness of the product and prevent it from sticking together.

After some experimentation, he came up with the idea of a "waxed sealed package" to reduce moisture. In 1902, Eckstein further refined the process with the development of the triple-sealed, moisture-proof package. An expanded shelf life meant the product could be shipped throughout the country with contents as fresh as the day it was packaged, and it would never again become a soggy block. So significant were Eckstein's contributions that he was made a partner and the name of the company was changed to Rueckheim Bros. & Eckstein.

The company created a phenomenal array of candy and confections along with popcorn products, which over time included Favorite Candy Pulls, Chocolate Creams and Chocolate Assorted Nuts, Toasted Yum Yums, Hunky Dory Chocolate Confection, Fireside Hard Candies, Pastime Crystal Jelly Wafers, Assorted Tarties, Iced Nougats, New Wrinkle, Trisum, Black Crook Cocoanut Candy, Big Ben Bars, and Reliable Menthol Cough Drops and Lemon Drops, just to name a very few.

Molded candies were sold in myriad

popcorn sticking together. The salesman's reaction was "That's a crackerjack!" and that inspired the name. A customer's favorable comment that "the more you eat, the more you want" gave the product its slogan.

According to children's books given with the purchase of F. W. Rueckheim & Bro. Popcorn Bricks in 1897, a few hundred pounds of Cracker Jack® were produced the first week after it was introduced on January 28, 1896. This increased to a ton a day the second week, and two tons a day the third week, leading to the rental of a four-story building to manufacture the instant-hit confection. Within two weeks, equipment had been installed and the company was making six tons of Cracker Jack a day. In May 1896, twenty-four railroad cars loaded with the new product were shipped to New York, and a carload per week was arriving in St. Louis. Chicago consumed thirty carloads in one month. In addition to the tons of Cracker Jack sold in bulk that first year, almost seven million five-cent packages were sold. In May 1897, five carloads were shipped to Liverpool and a customer in Norway who initially purchased fifty cases quickly telegraphed for one hundred more. Soon, the "Famous Pop Corn Confection" was being "sold in nearly every country on the globe."

forms, including hearts, stars, anchors, crosses, pocket watches, violins, baskets, spoons, saws, hatchets, monkey wrenches, pistols, bananas (single, in bunches, and peeled), pineapples, strawberries with wire stems, fish, alligators, rats on a stick, hens, roosters, chicks emerging from eggs, corn-fed hogs, rabbits, monkeys, organ grinders, angels, Santa Claus, "Charlies" resembling Chaplain, ice-cream cones, baby dolls, "Sure Catch" baseball gloves with ball, and several baseball players, including a bear cub with bat.

There were Cracker Jack Peanuts with Puffed Rice, and Prosit Parched Corn was promoted with glasses of beer in the background of the ad. In addition to popcorn bricks and popcorn balls, the firm also sold its own popping corn, marketed under such names as Pop-It, Bingo, Party Favor, and Volley. Marshmallows were another product in the company line, including the "sister" to Sailor Jack, Angelus, as well as Reliable, Fairy, Recipe, and Starlight brands, and after buying a leading competitor's product, Campfire marshmallows. The various products were packed in paper boxes, tins, glass jars, tubes, bail buckets, and wooden crates.

The 1908 publication of a ballad about Katie Casey immortalized Cracker Jack• and inexorably connected it with our National Pastime. Though few are familiar with the song's stanzas, the refrain with Katie's insistence to her beau, "Take Me Out to the Ball-Game," has become baseball's unofficial anthem; and its rendition is a tradition during the seventh-inning stretch. The lyrics were written by Jack Norworth, inspired by a sign he read during a subway ride announcing "Baseball Today – Polo Grounds," and were set to music by Albert Von Tilzer. Interestingly, neither of the two would see their first professional baseball games until decades later, and in the 1927 copyrighted version of the song, Katie had become Nelly Kelly.

Expansion and Acquisition

By 1910, the plant covered almost a city block at a new location on Harrison, Peoria, and Sangamon Streets. A newspaper ad proclaimed the company's "normal output 40 tons of candy daily." A second facility to serve eastern and foreign customers was opened in 1914 in Brooklyn, New York, but manufacturing was discontinued in 1923 when production was centralized in Chicago. The New York subsidiary then served only as a sales agency until 1932. Still, the company had come a long way from the days when peddlers with their wagons delivered Cracker Jack to stores just in the Chicago vicinity.

After a half century in business, in recognition of the success, popularity, and dominance of its signature popcorn confection, the organization changed its name to The Cracker Jack Company. This took place at the beginning of its Golden Year, 1922, which saw publication of the company's celebratory history, *Fifty Years*. By the following year, the plant was producing more than 138 million boxes annually. By the end of July 1925, Cracker Jack and Angelus marshmallows were the biggest sellers, prompting the company to discontinue all other confectionery production in order to concentrate on popcorn products and marshmallows. In 1930, the operation moved into a 233,000-square-foot factory on Cicero Avenue in the Clearing Industrial Section. For the next 34 years, the Cracker Jack Company churned out product, and in 1964 it was finally sold to Borden Inc. as a separate division.

Administration and marketing moved to the Columbus, Ohio, headquarters in 1982; and in 1986 production moved from the Cicero location to a 250,000-square-foot facility in the northern Chicago suburb of Northbrook. In 1997 Cracker Jack was purchased by corporate giant Frito-Lay, headquartered in Plano, Texas. Frito-Lay has maintained the Cracker Jack branding and has established an excellent relationship with Major League parks across the country.

Let's Talk About The Prizes

It is not known precisely when prizes were first inserted in boxes of Cracker Jack, or what the first prize may have been, but giving a free novelty as a sales incentive was not a new concept to the Rueckheims when Cracker Jack came along. Sometime between 1885 and 1895, paper dolls were given away with the purchase of a Happy Family Candy stick.

Among the earliest prizes found in Cracker Jack® boxes was a series of "pretty lady" pinback buttons. Pins of the exact type, made by Whitehead and Hoag, were used as tobacco premiums in 1905. The paper inserts with the Cracker Jack name on the back of the pins are often found with stains, suggesting that they were packaged inside rather than given out as point-of-sale premiums.

Another early premium series was a set of 16 Cracker Jack bears postcards, dated 1907. Absence of stains on these cards indicate that they were given out with purchase and not inserted in the boxes. One example of a postcard that was actually used to mail a message tells the recipient that the sender got the card at Lincoln Park *on* a package of Cracker Jack. A complete postcard set, which tells a continuing story in verse of the two bears' adventures, could be obtained free by sending ten sides from Cracker Jack packages or for ten cents with the side of one package. Cards received through this offer were printed without the instructions for ordering the set. Of particular note, card no. 12 in the series depicts the two bears playing baseball, with one bear at-bat while the other in catcher's gear uses a carton of Cracker Jack as his mitt. Apparently, this is the first baseball-related premium marked Cracker Jack.

The use of coupons as sales incentives began somewhere around 1910 or 1911. Either inserted in the Cracker Jack package or printed on the side panel, coupons could be redeemed for a variety of items listed in catalogs. The first catalog was designated "A," with additional alphabetically identified editions of the catalog issued at least through "E." A 116-page "E" catalog published in 1912 offered an amazing array of over 500 items including clothing, silverware, toys, jewelry, sports equipment, books, sewing machines, and "many other useful household items." Coupons were also issued in Angelus marshmallow containers and could be added with the Cracker Jack coupons to accumulate the amount required to redeem the desired catalog item.

Although one company publication stated, "It was in 1908 that the company started putting a toy or novelty for the children in each box of Cracker Jack," 1912 seems to be the date more widely accepted for the Cracker Jack prize insertion. However, coupon incentives continued for several years because Frederick wanted to give customers time to save coupons for the larger items. There was no coupon offer for a complete set of the 1914 Cracker Jack Ball Players cards, but according to the information on the back of the cards, all 176 of the 1915 set could be obtained with 100 coupons, or with one coupon and a quarter; and the album for displaying the cards was available for 50 coupons, or for one coupon and a dime.

The company itself had other products which included prizes as premiums. From the onset, popcorn bricks were sold by F. W. Rueckheim and Bro. which were popular at circuses, amusement parks, and county fairs. Eventually, these blocks of candied popcorn wrapped in colorful tissue were banded with labels that enwrapped a paper horn, a balloon, or an expanding fan. Some of the candies had a prize inside, such as a tin "Novelty Whistle," and some were contained in a prize. A fried-egg candy came in a miniature tin skillet and an ice-cream candy was molded into a tin dish, complete with a little tin spoon. Miniature tin garden tools with wooden handles served as the sticks for some candies. All Day Suckers had a flag at the other end of the stick. Pillow Top Sticks

1915 CRACKER JACK BALL PLAYERS CARD DISPLAY ALBUM

came rolled in cloth squares with sports themes, one with a baseball motif, a ball in one corner, crossed bats in another. Silk Banner Taffee featured various floral silks as part of the wrapping.

Pot-metal rocking horses, trumpets, or binocular charms were embedded in candy casings. Candy steins were sold with a miniature metal stein with a celluloid insert inside. Likewise, tiny pipes with celluloid inserts were contained within larger candy pipes. "Whistling Rufus" had a tin "Novelty Whistle" embedded in his mouth. Rings were inset into candy jewelry boxes and placed around barber-pole candy sticks.

The company also added other confections with prizes in the packages to its line-up, including Sur-Prize Candy, Honey Boy with Novelty, Mother Goose Prize Package, and Lik Rish Jacks with Toy or Novelty. "All the Rage Prize" promised "a beautiful candy chain and locket in each package." Other products with a prize in the box were Chums Prize Package, small Penny Packages, Toy Penny Popcorn and eventually, even Checkers. The company bought this primary competing popcorn product

with prize from Shotwell Manufacturing Company in 1926. Prizes can be found that are identical except for being labeled as a Cracker Jack or a Checkers prize. Some have both labels, and still others are labeled Angelus. Eventually, these other products with prizes fell by the wayside as Cracker Jack dominated sales.

Cracker Jack® ads included a sailor boy and his loyal dog a few years before Sailor Jack and Bingo appeared on the package in 1918. Sailor Jack is said to have been modeled after Frederick's grandson, Robert, who died at the age of eight of pneumonia. The saluting young sailor boy carrying Cracker Jack boxes of his own under his arm added a patriotic touch to the package as American soldiers were fighting in the Great War. Just as the Morton Salt girl has changed, the look of Sailor Jack and Bingo has evolved over time. Even the spot on Bingo's eye changed from one side to the other and back again. Still on the package today, they are among the most recognizable of American product icons.

Cracker Jack® has remained in existence for over a century not only because of the quality of the confection, but also due to

the toys and novelties. Billions of prizes have been distributed since the promise of one in every box. Throughout the decades, the prizes have reflected the times, such as patriotic prizes during World War II. Cleverly, prizes have been issued in series encouraging continued sales to complete prize sets. Periodically additional mail-in offers have required proofs of purchase or even prizes themselves to qualify for the special premium.

Throughout its prize history, the company has issued novelties made of paper, wood, cast metal, tin, terra cotta, Bakelite, chenille, rubber, felt, straw, cellophane, fiber, papier-mâché, cloth, string, wire, candy, aluminum, celluloid, ceramic, rattan, and even glass. The development of the injection molding process in the late 1940s saw a proliferation of plastic prizes in a rainbow of colors including an assortment of tiny models and other snap-apart and put-together prizes distributed into the 1970s.

Eventually child product safety laws brought the use of prizes with small parts to a halt. Even the inks and paper for printed prizes and prize wrappers had to pass safety tests, greatly restricting the parameters of prize production. Safety concerns were nothing new to Cracker Jack. In 1925, a Chicago doctor reported treating a child who had swallowed a small metal disk from a paper cigarette whistle, and those were discontinued. Threatened legislation also led the company to enclose tin whistles and small metal toys in envelopes to avoid potential danger.

In 1981, one prize wouldn't fit in the box: one lucky customer found a message that he was now the owner of a Winnebago. The lucky winner was a serviceman stationed in Germany, and the company shipped the RV to him.

Suppliers have included American companies with recognizable names such as Makatoy, Gold Premiums, Chein, Tootsietoy, and Eppy, as well as prize suppliers from Germany, Japan, Australia, Czechoslovakia, Taiwan, and Mexico. The actual prize designers have remained relatively unknown, with a few exceptions. Probably the most prolific of the artists, C. Carey Cloud, would likely be the first inductee into a Cracker Jack prize designer hall of fame, having designed and produced scores of prizes from the late 1930s to the 1960s. John C. "Wally" Walworth designed many put-together Cracker Jack prizes for the Gold Premium Company in the 1960s. In the 1980s, artist John Craig, who created classic album covers for Rod Stewart and more recently the famous *Mellon Collie and the Infinite Sadness* cover for the Smashing Pumpkins, designed many Cracker Jack prizes for Makatoy and other suppliers.

The popularity of some types of prizes has resulted in their cyclical recurrence. Through the years, spin tops, whistles, magnifying glasses, drawing and tracing books, puzzles, dexterity games, team pennants, rings, tattoos, plates and dishes, craft kits, jigsaw puzzles, banks, marbles, stand-up figurines, tricks, story books, decals and iron-on transfers, pinball games, toy tools, baseball cards, riddle and joke books, miniature vehicles, trains, boats, paint books, and planes have been used repeatedly. U.S. President coins, cards, books, and pinbacks were issued as well as popular comic characters depicted on metal stand-up plaques, plastic rings, and ceramic figurines. There have been some one-time oddities as well, including a pencil sharpener with an exposed metal blade and a sex detector to predict the gender of an unborn child.

Not all prizes were exclusive to Cracker Jack. For example, Tootsietoy packaged some of the same cast metal pieces, wire puzzles, tin whistles, clickers, and spin tops used by Cracker Jack in its own Junior Playtime boxes. Eppy plastic charms on silk cord were used as bread wrapper ties and as a little something for the children around the necks of liquor bottles. They were also sold separately from store display cards as good luck charms to accompany letters to World War II soldiers. Some of the prizes in boxes of Guess What? taffy candy were Swiss Warbler Bird Calls, the same as found in Cracker Jack.

From early on, the packaging itself served as toys. One series of small 1¢ boxes were made to resemble cameras, complete with pretend photographs. Another series of little boxes were illustrated as miniature furniture and kitchen items. Other such packages included the One Cent Boys Tool Chests

In 1981, one prize wouldn't fit in the box: one lucky customer found a message that he was now the owner of a Winnebago.

and Poultry Show chicken coop boxes. In the 1930s, the Mystery Cracker Jack box with a large question mark on the end contained a prize compartment which held the prize, and for a period of time, also held an edible treat such as candy peanuts, suckers, licorice whistles, jawbreakers, peppermint sticks, and Cracker Jack Gum. Though the cardboard insert functionally separated the Cracker Jack product from the prizes, some of these inserted trays served as an extra prize. These forty "slugs" printed with tricks, puzzles, and brainteasers, some with color variations, are highly collectible. The entire package also became the freight of a special toy premium. For ten cents, a metal Wyandotte truck could be purchased along with a box of Cracker Jack with a bed designed so that a Mystery box fit perfectly. Based on an ad in the Wrigley Field Official Score Card for the 1937 season, the Mystery boxes were still being used; and an entry form for a 1940 contest also shows the Mystery box.

Some of the company's product during World War II did not contain Cracker Jack or a prize. In 1943, Cracker Jack Company workers were recognized for "Excellence in War Production and backing up our soldiers on the foreign fronts" for packaging eight different types of rations sent overseas. Even without a prize inside, patriotism was packed in every box.

Some of the most memorable Cracker Jack prizes have been those inserted by consumers themselves. Many a marriage proposal has followed the clandestine hiding of a real diamond ring in a box to be found by the bride-to-be. Conversely, Cracker Jack rings have found their way into actual jewelry boxes as temporary substitutes for real engagement rings.

Cracker Jack and our National Pastime

Since the Cracker Jack bears postcard of 1907 and the Ball Players sets of 1914 and 1915, there has been a strong connection with baseball through the numerous baseball-related prizes found in boxes of Cracker Jack. An early "Cracker Jack Movies" pull-tab prize changes from a batter to an umpire. Another prize depicted an umpire whose face is animated with the pull of a tab. Cast metal button studs labeled with various field positions are highly sought after. A "Big League Base-Ball at Home" spin dial game was issued twice in different sizes. The series of twenty-five pinback buttons of baseball players has become highly collectible. A scorecard with dials for spectators to track innings and runs was issued. An advertising fan entitled "A Double Play," depicted a little baseball player hugging one girlfriend from the side while holding the hand of

another sweetheart behind him. A series of paint with water prizes included a detailed scene of a runner sliding into home with the umpire calling him out. An iron-on transfer had a fielder leaping up for a fly. In 1940, a mail-in contest even offered official Wilson baseballs, Billy Herman fielders mitts, and Joe DiMaggio bats as prizes.

Many hard-plastic baseball stand-up figurines were part of prize series. A set of flexible plastic baseball players representing each position on the field plus an umpire was released. These were issued in two colors, blue and gray, so that a full set of opposing teams could be collected. Another series of miniature flexible-plastic athletes included several baseball players. "Champ Home Run Hitter" loving cups and two "Strike Out King" figures were part of two plastic put-together trophy series. Wiggle pictures, or tilt card lenticulars, included a batter swinging as well as visual instructions on how to throw a curve ball and a slider. Baseball spin top games, stickers, pennants, and rings have served as Cracker Jack prizes as well as baseball pinball and dexterity games. In 1991, a mail-in "Hero Sport Card Offer" made it possible for children of all ages to order a set of 20 baseball cards with their picture on one side and their statistics on the back. At the beginning of this century, the "Catch the Baseball Bug!" campaign included plastic baseball cap, glove, and ball whistles and telescopes. One whistle was a baseball diamond, and there was also a bat telescope given out on opening day at ball parks and at special promotional events. These

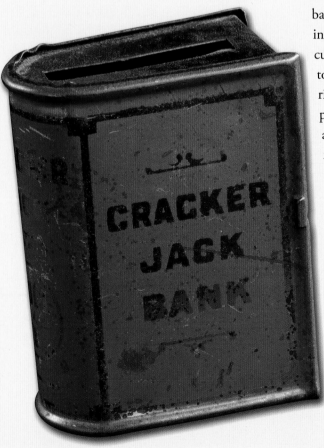

constitute only a few of the many prizes issued that relate to our National Pastime.

The Cracker Jack Company became even more involved in baseball when it directly sent "An Open Letter to Mr. Wrigley" through *The Chicago Tribune* during the Cubs' slump in 1930. Besides the fact that Rogers Hornsby and Hack Wilson were both in mild hitting slumps, Cracker Jack suggested that the team was jinxed because their product was not available at the stadium: "The fans are missing the very thing that gives them enthusiasm, pep and a happy mood to yell their heads off and back up the boys." Apparently the letter worked and sales of Cracker Jack at the games were resumed, for soon another ad appeared proclaiming

> *Besides the fact that Rogers Hornsby and Hack Wilson were both in mild hitting slumps, Cracker Jack suggested that the team was jinxed because their product was not available at the stadium.*

"Perhaps the jinx is killed! The Cubs have won every game since we wrote you our Cracker Jack letter."

As Yogi Berra said of the back-to-back home runs of Mickey Mantle and Roger Maris in the early 1960s, it was "*déjà vu* all over again" in the 1990s, only this time it was the fans who insisted that Cracker Jack be returned to the stadiums. Articles in newspapers across the country reported that fans were raising their voices in protest that Cracker Jack® was no longer available. They loudly and forcefully objected to the substitution of Cracker Jack with some other product, and one without a prize at that. "How could they do such a thing? It's a tradition!" Indeed, with Cracker Jack as the original sponsor of the Old Timers Baseball Classic, how had things come to this? It wasn't long before Cracker Jack was again being pitched by hawkers among the rows of appeased spectators.

In 1982, there was a mail-in offer for two uncut sheets of Topps "All Time Baseball Greats" cards, one for the American League and one for the National League, including such players as Mickey Mantle, Ernie Banks, Whitey Ford, and Willie Mays. Of more recent vintage, beginning in 1991, there are Topps and Donruss baseball mini-card sets, mini-replicas of the original Cracker Jack baseball player cards, baseball stadium cards, pop-up team cards, and ballpark legends. Of course, the Ball Player cards featured in this book inserted into Cracker Jack boxes during 1914 and 1915 represent the pinnacle in terms of value when it comes to discussing all Cracker Jack prizes.

No doubt, baseball will remain a recurring theme as Cracker Jack® begins its second century of a prize in every box. Hopefully, future waves of creativity in prize design along with a commitment to the rich prize heritage will continue the tradition of unique and entertaining prizes. As we celebrate the anniversary of the Cracker Jack Ball Players a century after their issue, we look forward to new prizes that will be well worth collecting a hundred years from now. After all, we hunger for both the surprise as well as the product.

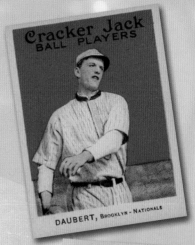

DAUBERT, Brooklyn - Nationals

2

THE CRACKER JACK ALL-STARS

COLLINS, Chicago - Americans

BAKER, Philadelphia - Americans

The great debate about the all-time All-Star Team will go on forever. Is it Berra behind the plate, or is it Bench? Does Mays crack the starting lineup or do we go with Ruth, Cobb and Williams? What about Jackie Robinson vs. Eddie Collins, vs. Rogers Hornsby? This discussion has always been a hot topic among baseball fans and historians alike. With the Cracker Jack Collection, the same holds true. The players in the collection represent only a snapshot of time in baseball history, and pose the same type of difficult choices. Should the infamous Hal Chase be the choice at first? What about Heinie Zimmerman at third? How can one possibly leave Big Ed Walsh, "Three Finger" Mordecai Brown, or the great Rube Marquard off the list? It is certainly open to debate. That is exactly what we want. We have made our choices. Agree or disagree? You make yours.

Here is our Cracker Jack All-Star Team.

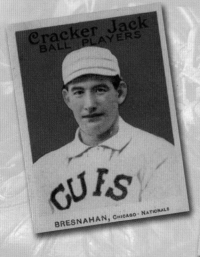

BRESNAHAN, Chicago - Nationals

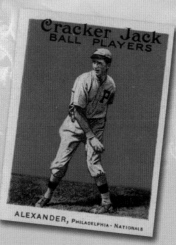

ALEXANDER, Philadelphia - Nationals

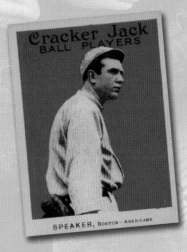

SPEAKER, Boston - Americans

Jake Daubert

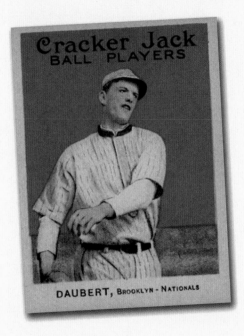

DAUBERT, BROOKLYN - NATIONALS

A whiz both offensively and defensively, Jake Daubert was considered one of the best first basemen of the Deadball Era. His career .991 fielding percentage is amazing given the playing conditions at the time. As an 11-year-old kid, he went to work in the coal mines. His ticket out was landing a spot on a semi-pro baseball team where he caught the eye of Major League scouts. As Daubert became more successful he never forgot his roots, which made him popular.

One of the real gentlemen of the game, he was a favorite of players, sportswriters and fans. Daubert had a great year in 1913 when he batted a lofty, league-leading .350 and banged out 178 hits. He had ten .300 seasons and averaged 187 hits over the course of his great career. *Baseball Magazine* chose Daubert as their All-Star first baseman in 1911, and awarded him this honor for seven years in a row from 1913 to 1919. His outstanding play in 1913 earned him the Chalmers Award as most valuable player, and he was later elected vice president of the Baseball Players Fraternity. After a salary dispute with Brooklyn, Daubert was sold to the Reds where, as captain, he led them to their first World Championship in 1919.

Off the field, he had keen business acumen and wisely invested in several businesses near his hometown, including a cigar business, pool hall, and a semi-pro baseball team. It is said he did so well in business that he did not need to play baseball, but he continued on as first baseman for the Reds. After he suffered a beaning in 1924, Daubert developed headaches and an overall malaise. In his weakened state, a hereditary spleen condition flared up. The operation recommended by the doctors was unsuccessful and Daubert died a few days later at the young age of 40.

If you look at his stats closely, it is hard to fathom why Jake Daubert has been bypassed by the Hall of Fame. He is, however, the starting first baseman on our Cracker Jack elite team. We are honored that he has his place on our team alongside Wagner, Collins and the rest.

> *One of the real gentlemen of the game, he was a favorite of players, sportwriters and fans.*

Jacob Ellsworth Daubert

Born:
April 17, 1884
Shamokin, PA

Died:
October 9, 1924
Cincinnati, OH

▷ Batted: LH

▷ Threw: LH

▷ Position: 1B

▷ Career BA: .303

Teams:
Brooklyn Superbas/Robins NL (1910–1918)
Cincinnati Reds NL (1919–1924)

Eddie Collins

There have been many great second basemen over the annals of baseball history; Jackie Robinson and Rogers Hornsby to name a few. When you take a hard look at the numbers, it becomes difficult not to name Eddie Collins as possibly the greatest of all time. He gets our vote, hands down, as the best second baseman in this group.

The pride of Millerton, New York, Eddie Collins' contributions to the game were immense as a player, manager and general manager. As a player, his statistics and records are truly amazing. With a .333 lifetime batting average and 3,315 hits, Collins holds the MLB record for career games (2,650), assists (7,630), and total chances (14,591) at second base. He was also the first Major League ballplayer to steal 80 bases in a season. In 1914 he received the Chalmers Award as the American League's Most Valuable

Possibly the greatest second baseman of all time.

SECOND BASE

Player. As part of the A's famous $100,000 infield, Collins helped the Athletics to four pennants and three World Series Championships between 1910 and 1914.

Nicknamed "Cocky" because of his obvious self-confidence, the Columbia University grad was actually very superstitious. He always wore the same game socks during a winning streak, and needed someone to spit on his hat for luck before each game. Collins won the World Series with the White Sox in 1917 and joined the U.S. Navy late in the 1918 season to serve in World War I. One of the "clean" players during the Black Sox debacle, Collins continued on with Chicago serving as player-manager from 1924 through 1926. He then returned to the A's, playing on the 1929 and 1930 World Series Champs teams.

Collins coached for the A's in 1931 and 1932, before Tom Yawkey recruited him in 1933 as vice president and general manager of the Red Sox. He served as GM through 1947 and stayed on as vice president until his death in 1951. One of the original 13 players to be elected to the Hall of Fame in 1939, Eddie is still in the top 10 in career games, walks, stolen bases, hits, on base percentage, and total bases. The greatest second baseman of all time? Maybe. If not, pretty darn close!

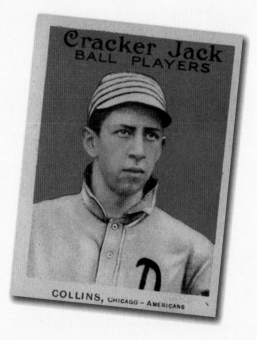

Edward Trowbridge Collins Sr.

Teams:

Philadelphia Athletics AL (1906–1914, 1927–1930)

Chicago White Sox AL (1915–1923; player-manager: 1924–1926)

Boston Red Sox AL (general manager-vice president: 1933–1951)

Born:
May 2, 1887
Millerton, NY

Died:
March 25, 1951
Boston, MA

▷ Batted: LH

▷ Threw: RH

▷ Position: 2B

▷ Career BA: .333

▷ Managerial Record: 174–160

Home Run Baker

As part of the A's $100,000 infield along with Stuffy McInnis, Eddie Collins and Black Jack Barry, Frank "Home Run" Baker was an exceptional third baseman and an outstanding hitter whose place in the Hall of Fame is well deserved. Initially, it was thought that the young Baker would not make the grade in Major League baseball. However, Buck Herzog, a friend who was already playing in the majors, convinced a few people to take a shot on the gifted third baseman.

Baker did not disappoint, as he batted .305 in 1909, his rookie season with the A's and set a record for triples by a rookie, which still stands. That season, Baker was the first to hit the ball over the right field fence at the new Shibe Park, but he earned the nickname "Home Run" by going deep on two occasions during the 1911 World Series. Baker played in four World Series with the A's and led the league in round-trippers over four consecutive seasons from 1911 to 1914. He credited his power-hitting ability to

Considered the best third baseman of the pre-war era.

his work on the family farm, and kept in shape by chopping wood in the offseason.

Considered the best third baseman of the pre-war era, Baker went on to bat over .300 six times, and twice led the league in RBI. As a third baseman, he led the league in putouts seven times. Due to a salary dispute, Baker returned to his farm for the 1915 season. He was traded to the Yankees in 1916 where he had several good seasons before tragedy struck in 1920. Baker lost his wife to scarlet fever. Grief stricken, he took time off to care for

John Franklin Baker

his family, but returned to the Yankees in 1921 in time to play in two more World Series. Later, while managing in the Eastern Shore Baseball League, Baker discovered a pretty good ballplayer and recommended him to Connie Mack. That player was the great Jimmy Foxx. Frank "Home Run" Baker was elected to the Hall of Fame in 1955. He remains one of the greatest third basemen of all time, and is definitely our choice at the hot corner.

Teams:
Philadelphia Athletics AL (1908–1914)
New York Yankees AL (1916–1919, 1921–1922)

Born:
March 13, 1886
Trappe, MD

Died:
June 28, 1963
Trappe, MD

▷ Batted: LH

▷ Threw: RH

▷ Position: 3B

▷ Career BA: .307

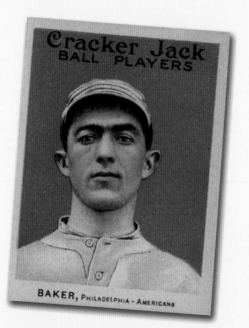

Honus Wagner

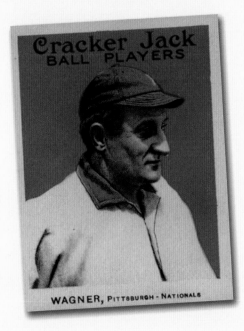

WAGNER, PITTSBURGH · NATIONALS

It is very hard not just to consider Honus Wagner as the best shortstop in the Cracker Jack Collection, but rather the greatest shortstop of all time. One of the first heroes of the game, "The Flying Dutchman" was a great batsman, superb defensively, and one of the fastest players in the league. Wagner's name is sure to appear on any short list of the 10 greatest players of all time. With eight batting titles and a .328 lifetime batting average, Wagner also banged out more than 3,400 hits over his brilliant career.

A powerfully built man with large hands and bowed legs, Wagner was not graceful, but he was speedy on the basepaths, stealing 723 bases during his career. In 1908 he led the league with a .354 batting average and in most other categories as well. His offensive winning percentage that year was .880; a single season league record that stood until 2001. Although he played on only one Pittsburgh World Series Champion team (1909), we could write volumes on his individual accomplishments. Among contemporaries like Mathewson and Cobb, he was considered the best. Although there are stories about his rivalry with Cobb, they actually spent time together hunting during the offseason.

At the end of his career, Wagner managed the Pirates for a brief period before retiring as a player. He became a successful businessman in Carnegie, Pennsylvania, coached locally, and raised his family. After his business ventures were hard hit by the Depression, Wagner returned to the Pirates to coach from 1933 until 1951. Elected to the Hall of Fame in its inaugural year, Wagner was truly one of the greats. Of course the famous Wagner T206 card has also added to the legend of "The Flying Dutchman." In the whole scheme of things, however, the legacy of the great Honus Wagner stands on its own merit.

*A*mong contemporaries like Mathewson and Cobb he was considered the best.

Born:
February 24, 1874
Chartiers, PA

Died:
December 6, 1955
Carnegie, PA

▷ Batted: RH

▷ Threw: RH

▷ Position: SS

▷ Career BA: .328

▷ Managerial Record: 1–4

Johannes Peter Wagner

Teams:
Louisville Colonels NL (1897–1899)
Pittsburgh Pirates NL (1900–1916; player-manager: 1917)

Ty Cobb

Probably the most gifted athlete of the early twentieth century, Ty Cobb was an incredible hitter, the best base stealer of his era, and superb defensively. He was the dominant player in the American League during the Deadball Era, but his aggressive, competitive style of play led to controversy throughout his career.

The superstar of his day, Cobb was not well-liked by players, even those on his team. His reckless base running intimidated the competition, giving him the edge, but it certainly didn't earn many friendships. Ty Cobb became the highest paid player in baseball during the second half of his playing career. As a businessman he was a genius, amassing a fortune with investments in companies such as Coca Cola and General Motors, but as a player he continued to be surrounded by controversy. Cobb became player-manager of the Tigers in 1921, continuing on in that role for six seasons. Although not pennant contenders, the

OUTFIELD

team did fairly well under his leadership. He retired in 1926 due to allegations of a game fix in 1919...allegations made by a player who had a grudge against Cobb. After he was cleared of any wrong doing, Connie Mack recruited him for the A's where he finished out his career.

Considered mean spirited and racist, Cobb was actually quietly philanthropic later in life, helping out many indigent ballplayers. Whatever the assessment is of Cobb, it is our consensus that, as a player, he belongs at the top of our list as the Best of the Best. "The Georgia Peach" won an incredible 11 batting titles, batted *under* .320 only once in his career, and still holds the record for highest career batting average. With 4,191 hits, along with 892 stolen bases, Cobb stands near or at the top of the all-time list. One of the first to be elected to the Hall of Fame, he is the overwhelming choice for our Cracker Jack All-Star Team.

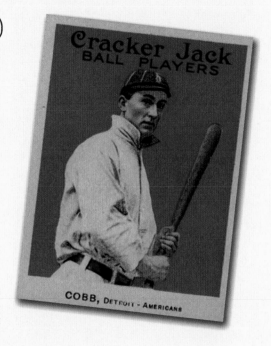

Tyrus Raymond Cobb

Teams:

Detroit Tigers AL (1905–1920; player-manager: 1921–1926)

Philadelphia Athletics AL (1927–1928)

The dominant player in the American League during the Deadball Era.

Born:
December 18, 1886
Narrows, GA

Died:
July 17, 1961
Atlanta, GA

▷ Batted: LH

▷ Threw: RH

▷ Position: OF

▷ Career BA: .367

▷ Managerial Record: 479–444

Tris Speaker

A standout both offensively and defensively, "The Grey Eagle" can certainly be included in any discussion as one of the all-time greats. With a lifetime batting average of .345 along with over 3,500 hits, Tris Speaker either sits near the top or leads the league in a number of categories, nearly 100 years later. With most career doubles, fifth in career hits, most career outfield assists, and 1,529 career runs batted in, Speaker is considered one of the five or six greatest outfielders along with the likes of Ruth, Cobb, Williams, Mays, Musial, Clemente or whomever else you would like to include. In 1912, his greatest year, Speaker wowed Boston by amassing 53 doubles, 222 hits, a league-leading 10 home runs, and 52 steals along with a .383 average, earning the Chalmers Award for Most Valuable Player.

A darling of the Boston fans, Speaker became known as "Spoke." He was given the nickname by teammate Bill Carrigan who would shout out "Speaker spoke" whenever Tris got a hit. His 1912 and 1915 Boston teams were World

OUTFIELD

Champions. Although successful on the field, there were tensions in the clubhouse and with management. After a salary dispute, Speaker was traded to the Indians where he continued to excel, beating Cobb for the batting title in 1916. Beloved by Cleveland fans, he went on to bat over .350 for seven seasons. He had a very successful career as a manager for the Indians from 1919 to 1926, leading them to a World Series Championship in 1920 with his inspirational play in centerfield.

After his Major League career, "The Grey Eagle" was part-owner of the Kansas City Blues before returning to the Indians as a scout and a broadcaster. In 1947 Speaker again donned the Indians uniform as a coach working with young players. He was inducted into the Hall of Fame in 1937. The list of his accomplishments goes on and on. However one thing is certain. Tris Speaker definitely makes the cut to be included in our dream Cracker Jack outfield.

> "*The Grey Eagle*" can certainly be included in any discussion as one of the all-time greats.

Tristram E. Speaker

Teams:

Boston Americans/Red Sox AL (1907–1915)

Cleveland Indians AL (1916–1918; player-manager: 1919–1926)

Washington Senators AL (1927)

Philadelphia Athletics AL (1928)

Born:
April 4, 1888
Hubbard, TX

Died:
December 8, 1958
Lake Whitney, TX

▷ Batted: LH

▷ Threw: LH

▷ Position: OF

▷ Career BA: .345

▷ Managerial Record: 617–520

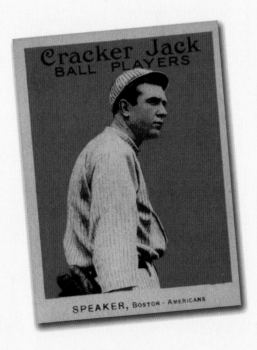

Shoeless Joe Jackson

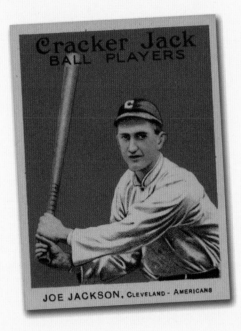

Cracker Jack
BALL PLAYERS

JOE JACKSON, CLEVELAND - AMERICANS

Putting the whole Black Sox scandal off to the side, and looking at pure skills, "Shoeless Joe" Jackson makes our team. Still considered one of the greatest natural hitting talents of the game, Jackson ranks third all time with his .356 career batting average. Defensively, he was superb with good speed.

Jackson came up to the majors as a 19-year-old kid with six years of experience playing organized ball. The oldest of eight children, he started working in textile mills at the young age of seven, and never had the opportunity to learn to read or write. He started playing on the Brandon Mill team at age 13, and quickly moved on to star in Carolina Association semi-pro clubs. There he earned the nickname "Shoeless Joe" when he played a game barefoot because his new baseball shoes weren't comfortable yet. When Connie Mack brought him up to the majors, Jackson had a difficult time adjusting to big city life. He was homesick and was teased by his teammates for his illiteracy and country ways. After bouncing between Philly and the Carolina league for a few years, Jackson was sold to Cleveland where he blossomed. The smaller city and teammates from the Southern Leagues made him feel at home.

In 1911, his first full year in the majors, Jackson hit an astounding .408 which still stands as a Major League rookie record. Following his .408 season, "Shoeless Joe" batted .395 and .373, banging out 656 hits over those three years. Jackson became such a superstar

*O*ne of the greatest natural hitting talents of the game.

that when he was sold to Chicago, it was the highest paid deal up to that point in baseball. The 1919 Black Sox scandal put a sad end to Jackson's career when Baseball Commissioner Kenesaw Mountain Landis banned him for life, along with seven of his teammates. Jackson went on to play and manage several semi-pro teams, and became a businessman in his hometown of Greenville. We are not here to judge the guilt or innocence of Shoeless Joe Jackson. We simply want to give him his just due as a great ballplayer. "Say it ain't so" Joe Jackson makes the cut and is welcome on our Cracker Jack All-Star Team.

Born:
July 16, 1887
Pickens County, SC

Died:
December 5, 1951
Greenville, SC

▷ Batted: LH

▷ Threw: RH

▷ Position: OF

▷ Career BA: .356

Joseph Jefferson Jackson

Teams:
Philadelphia Athletics AL (1908–1909)
Cleveland Naps/Indians AL (1910–1915)
Chicago White Sox AL (1915–1920)

Roger Bresnahan

Not just the first great catcher in baseball history, Roger Bresnahan, the "Duke of Tralee," is also known for his innovations in protective gear. After injuries due to home plate collisions and beanings, he developed shin guards for catchers, experimented with batting helmets, and added leather strips to wire catchers masks to make them more comfortable. As a player, Bresnahan was very good. He began his MLB career as an outfielder and later switched to the catcher position. A solid hitter, Bresnahan batted a lofty .350 working centerfield for the Giants in 1903. He was moved to the position of starting catcher in 1905 and became part of one of the most famous pitcher-catcher teams of all time with batterymate Christy Mathewson.

Defensively, he was the best in the business at the time. Some could argue that Ray Schalk should be our starting catcher, but although similar defensively,

> *Defensively, he was the best in the business at the time.*

CATCHER

Bresnahan was more skilled offensively. Bresnahan was dubbed the "Duke of Tralee" in the early days of his career when the public mistakenly thought he was born in Tralee, Ireland. Although of Irish descent, he was born and raised in Toledo, Ohio, and started his career in the Ohio State League. After he made his mark in New York, Bresnahan was recruited by St. Louis as player-manager. He didn't see eye-to-eye with the new Cards management in 1912 and took advantage of a hefty signing bonus to move to the Cubs, where he finished out his Major League career as manager in 1915.

Bresnahan later purchased the Toledo Mud Hens of the American Association and helped many MLB players on the downside of their careers by bringing them aboard. He coached for the Giants from 1925 to 1928 and for the Tigers in the early 1930s. Financially devastated in 1929 by the stock market crash, Bresnahan worked as a security guard and later as a laborer during the Depression. He got back on his feet by landing a sales job for a brewing company. The "Duke of Tralee" died in 1944 at the age of 65 and was elected to the Hall the following year. Roger Bresnahan was truly one of baseball's pioneers and is worthy as the All-Star catcher on our Cracker Jack Dream Team.

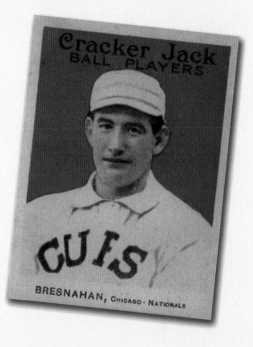

Roger Philip Bresnahan

Teams:

Washington Senators NL (1897)

Chicago Orphans/Cubs NL (1900, 1913–1914; player-manager: 1915)

Baltimore Orioles AL (1901–1902)

New York Giants NL (1902–1908)

St. Louis Cardinals NL (player-manager: 1909–1912)

Born:
June 11, 1879
Toledo, OH

Died:
December 4, 1944
Toledo, OH

▷ Batted: RH

▷ Threw: RH

▷ Position: C

▷ Career BA: .279

▷ Managerial Record: 328–432

Walter Johnson

When it comes to the best of the best, look no further than "The Big Train." In our opinion, Walter Johnson is the greatest pitcher that ever lived. The all-time leader in shutouts with 110, Johnson compiled 417 career wins as well as 3,509 career strikeouts. It's hard to find a better pitcher. Although Cy Young had more wins, Johnson was more dominant. Johnson's fastball was overpowering to begin with, and his sidearm motion made it even tougher for batters to pick up the ball.

Nicknamed "The Big Train" because of the amazing speed of his fastball, Johnson won at least 20 games 12 times. Today his single-season 1.14 earned-run average is the sixth lowest ever. Named American League MVP in 1913 and 1924, Johnson won the Triple Crown in 1913, 1918, and 1924. He led the league in strikeouts 12 times, shutouts 7 times, wins 6 times, ERA 5 times, and the list goes on and on. Interestingly enough, Johnson pitched on quite a few losing teams. Finally, in 1924 the Senators won the World

> When it comes to the best of the best, look no further than "The Big Train."

Championship due, in large part, to Johnson's pitching prowess.

One of the truly nice guys in the game, Walter Johnson was respected among his peers and admired by fans. During the rough and tumble early days of baseball, he stood out because of his modesty and dignity. Ty Cobb referred to Johnson as "the greatest of the great." After his playing days were over, Johnson managed both Washington and Cleveland for several years. He went back to the

PITCHER

Senators as broadcaster in 1939 and later made an unsuccessful run for Congress. Johnson always stayed close to the game he loved, even pitching in war bond exhibition games during World War II. He was recognized as part of the inaugural class of the Hall of Fame in 1936. After suffering from a brain tumor for several months, Walter Johnson died in 1946 at age 59. "The Big Train" gets our vote as the Best of the Best.

Teams:

Washington Senators AL (1907–1927; manager: 1929–1932)

Cleveland Indians AL (manager: 1933–1935)

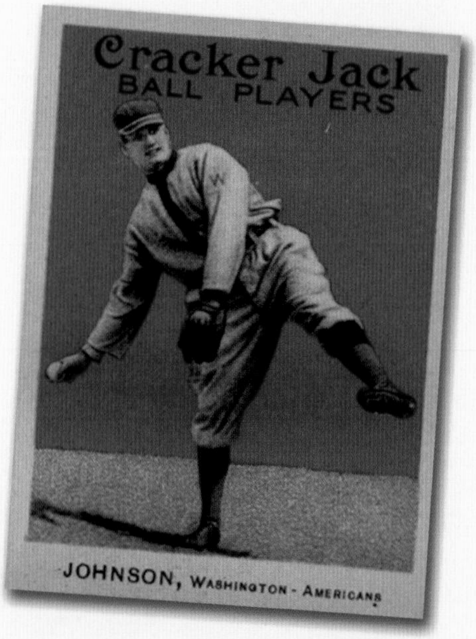

JOHNSON, WASHINGTON - AMERICANS

Walter Perry Johnson

Born:
November 6, 1887
Humboldt, KS

Died:
December 10, 1946
Washington, D.C.

▷ Batted: RH

▷ Threw: RH

▷ Position: P

▷ MLB Pitching Record: 417–279

▷ ERA: 2.17

▷ Managerial Record: 529–432

Christy Mathewson

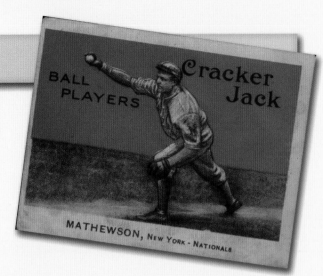

MATHEWSON, NEW YORK - NATIONALS

PITCHER

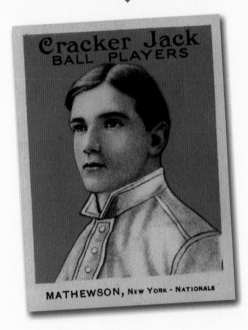

MATHEWSON, NEW YORK - NATIONALS

An easy choice for our elite team, Christy Mathewson, the pride of Bucknell College, ranks right behind Walter Johnson as the best pitcher of the era, and one of the top five or six greatest pitchers of all time. With an amazing record of 373–188, 13 twenty-plus win seasons and a 2.13 lifetime earned-run average, Matty could do it all. He actually won 20 or more for twelve straight seasons. Incredible. Christy Mathewson led the league in strikeouts and earned-run average five different times. In 1903 he won 30 games followed by 33 and 31 win seasons the next two years.

Although he played baseball in college, football and basketball were his main sports. Popular and handsome, Mathewson was class president and a member of two fraternities. The summer after his sophomore year at Bucknell, Mathewson pitched in the Virginia League and became an immediate star with his 20 wins by July. The Major Leagues came calling, and Mathewson had a choice between New York and Philly. After a rocky start over his first few seasons, Mathewson settled in and honed his skills. He was known for pitching with control and ease, and was a master of the "fadeaway," a pitch that is now known as a screwball. Mathewson held the National League pitching title five times between 1905 and 1913, achieving the Triple Crown in 1905 and 1908.

After his stint as manager of the Reds, he enlisted in the United States Army. In 1918, while serving in France, Mathewson was accidently gassed in a training exercise and developed tuberculosis. Although he struggled physically, Mathewson returned to baseball as assistant manager of the Giants. He was hired by owner Judge Emil Fuchs to run the Boston Braves but his health deteriorated and he was forced to return to the tuberculosis hospital. He died soon after in 1925 at the age of 45. Christy Mathewson was part of the first Hall of Fame class of 1936. To this day, he is regarded as the standard for all that is good in our National Pastime. "Big Six" as he was nicknamed was as good as it gets.

Born:
August 12, 1880
Factoryville, PA

Died:
October 7, 1925
Saranac Lake, NY

▷ Batted: RH

▷ Threw: RH

▷ Position: P

▷ MLB Pitching Record: 373–188

▷ ERA: 2.13

▷ Managerial Record: 164–176

Christopher Mathewson

Teams:

New York Giants NL (1900–1916)

Cincinnati Reds NL (player-manager: 1916; manager: 1917–1918)

To this day, he is regarded as the standard for all that is good in our National Pastime.

Pete Alexander

How good was Grover "Old Pete" Alexander? He won 28 as a rookie, and had 373 wins over his career. League leader in strikeouts six times, Alexander struck out 2,198 batters and had a 2.56 career ERA. He also led the league on many occasions in shutouts and complete games. That is exactly why "Old Pete" makes it into our rotation of the four best pitchers in the Collection.

Alexander ranks right behind the legendary Cy Young and Walter Johnson in wins, and has always been considered in the top 10 pitchers of all time. With the Phillies, Alexander had three 20-win seasons, three 30-win seasons, and won the National League Pitcher's Triple Crown in 1915 and 1916 before he was sold to the Cubs out of fear that he would be drafted into service for World War I, which he was. In 1918, while serving in France, Alexander experienced injuries to his ears and to his right arm, was plagued with shell shock, and developed epilepsy.

All of this, combined with the fact that he became a heavy drinker, caused problems when he returned to the mound. As a matter of fact, it has been reported that "Old Pete" sometimes took the mound in an inebriated state. He managed to have several good seasons with the Cubs, winning the Triple Crown again in 1920, but there were problems with behavior both on and off the field.

He was finally sold to the Cards. Alexander pitched two complete game wins (Games 2 and 6) for the Cards in the 1926 World Series, and then in Game 7 he was sent in as a relief pitcher in the seventh inning. It is purported that Alexander was in tough shape from drinking heavily the previous night, but he held the Yanks scoreless for the final two innings. He had one more 20-win season, and was then out of baseball, pitching for the House of David for several years. Grover Cleveland Alexander was voted into the Hall of Fame in 1938.

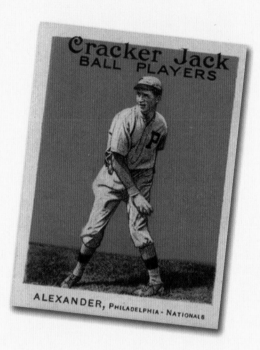

Cracker Jack BALL PLAYERS

ALEXANDER, PHILADELPHIA - NATIONALS

PITCHER

Born:
February 26, 1887
Elba, NE

Died:
November 4, 1950
St. Paul, NE

▷ Batted: RH

▷ Threw: RH

▷ Position: P

▷ MLB Pitching Record: 373–208

▷ ERA: 2.56

Alexander has always been considered in the top 10 pitchers of all time.

Grover Cleveland Alexander

Teams:
Philadelphia Phillies NL (1911–1917; 1930)
Chicago Cubs NL (1918–1926)
St. Louis Cardinals NL (1926–1929)

Eddie Plank

Considered one of the greatest pitchers of all time, "Gettysburg Eddie" Plank was a crafty lefty with stuff that was not overpowering. A sidearm pitcher with a big sweeping curveball and excellent control, Eddie was a master of stall tactics. He was extremely slow and deliberate on the mound, frustrating hitters, fans, and even his own outfielders.

The first lefthander to win 300 games, Plank amassed 2,246 strikeouts over his illustrious career, and had some phenomenal seasons, winning 20 games on eight occasions. His career 326 wins ranks 13th in MLB history.

Arguably, his best year was in 1912 for the A's when he went 26–6 with a 2.22 ERA. He played on two World Series Champion A's teams (1911, 1913) and on three pennant winners in 1902, 1905 and 1914. Plank pitched a 13-inning shutout against Boston pitcher Cy Young in 1904. In April of 1909, as starting pitcher for the Shibe Park dedication game, Plank beat Boston 8–1, but the game ended tragically. Catcher Doc Powers collided with the new park's cement wall while chasing a foul popup and died soon

PITCHER

after. However, the most notable game of Plank's career was Game 5 of the 1913 World Series. Matched against the great Christy Mathewson, "Gettysburg Eddie" threw a 2-hitter to defeat the Giants 3–1, clinching a World Series win for the A's.

Plank is the all-time leader in complete games for lefties and his 69 shutouts remain a southpaw record. He had a 20-win season for the St. Louis Terriers in the Federal League in 1915 before returning to the American League to finish out his career with the Browns. Plank announced his retirement in 1917, but was still in demand at age 42. The Yankees tried to work a trade for him but "Gettysburg Eddie" had no desire to go to New York. Instead, Plank retired to his Gettysburg farm, operated a Buick dealership, and was known to give tours of the battlefield at Gettysburg. In 1926 he suffered a stroke and died soon after at the age of 50. Elected to the Hall of Fame in 1946, Eddie Plank certainly deserves a place in our starting rotation.

His 69 shutouts remain a southpaw record.

Edward Stewart Plank

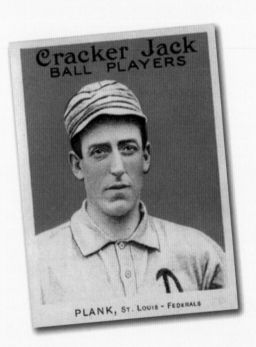

Cracker Jack
BALL PLAYERS

PLANK, St. Louis - Federals

Teams:
Philadelphia Athletics AL (1901–1914)
St. Louis Terriers FL (1915)
St. Louis Browns AL (1916–1917)

Born:
August 31, 1875
Gettysburg, PA
Died:
February 24, 1926
Gettysburg, PA
▷ Batted: LH
▷ Threw: LH
▷ Position: P
▷ MLB Pitching Record: 326–194
▷ ERA: 2.35

John "Stuffy" McInnis

"Stuffy" McInnis

"Stuffy" McInnis, one of the Athletic stars Connie Mack sold to Boston when he broke up a famous infield combination, holds the American League record for the best fielding percentage at first base. It was .9993, made in 1921, when he played 152 games for Boston with only one error. He accepted 1,625 chances between that and his next, in 1922.

ege stars. His
e to a million
to right) John
er, Massachusett
ollins who bega
umbia Universi
ivan; Jack Barr
klin (Home Ru
ms ruled from 1
which period they won four pennants and
the run (1912) they failed to f
with the finest outfield ever

3

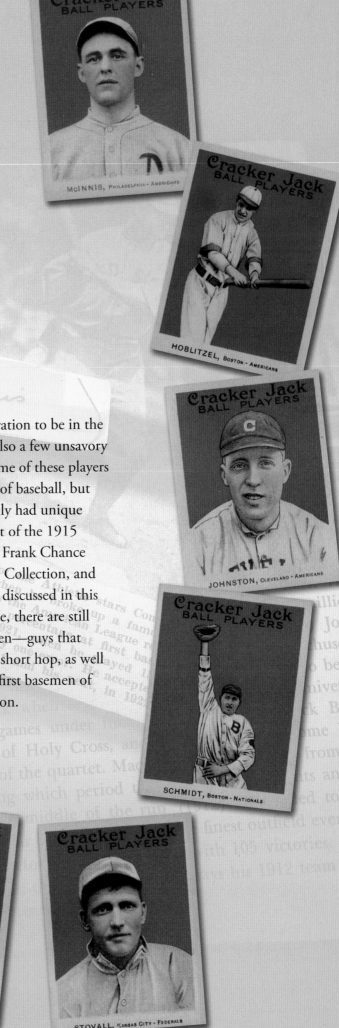

THE STRETCH

The baseball landscape has been dotted with some truly great first sackers over the years. With every passing decade, a new phenom enters the picture. At the time of this printing, the great Alex Pujols leads a list of exceptional players. On the other hand, there have been some mediocre and downright awful first basemen throughout baseball history. Dick "Dr. Strangeglove" Stuart comes to mind, although he was a pretty good hitter. The crop of first basemen in the Cracker Jack Collection is impressive. Even though there are no Hall of Famers in the 1915 group, there are some outstanding first sackers that

certainly deserve consideration to be in the Hall of Fame. There are also a few unsavory characters on this list. Some of these players almost toppled the game of baseball, but as ballplayers they certainly had unique talents. Although not part of the 1915 Collection, first baseman Frank Chance was included in the 1914 Collection, and is the only Hall of Famer discussed in this chapter. Putting him aside, there are still quite a few solid glove men—guys that could hit and handle the short hop, as well as the tag play. Meet the first basemen of the Cracker Jack Collection.

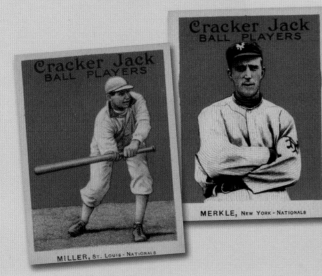

Frank Chance

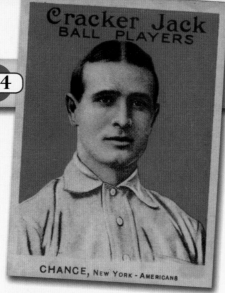

CHANCE, NEW YORK - AMERICANS

Frank Chance stands alone as a true immortal, yet he is more widely known as part of a trio, somewhat overshadowing his amazing individual talents. Chance was forever cast in literary stone as the third man in the Tinker to Evers to Chance triumvirate of F. P. Adams poem "Baseball's Sad Lexicon." Speaking from the point of view of a New York Giants' fan, Adams lamented the sublime Cubs double play combo of shortstop Joe Tinker, second sacker Johnny Evers, and first baseman Chance.

Strangely, Chance never played organized baseball until he arrived at the University of California to study dentistry. He quickly made the leap from root canals to runs scored, when he joined the Cubs in 1898. Chance's breakout season was in 1903 when he led the National League in steals with 67, had 144 hits, and posted a .327 batting average. The would-be orthodontist specialized in OBP, leading the league in 1905 and consistently approached or surpassed the magical .400 mark during his 17-year career. As fleet of foot as he was, Chance's greatest physical attribute may have been his keen eye. He struck out just 320 times in 4,299 at-bats, and drew 556 walks.

The Fresno, California native was known as "Husk" because of his stocky build and "The Peerless Leader" because of his belligerent personality and leadership

skills. The latter trait fueled Chance as player-manager of the Cubs from 1905–1912 as he piloted the Baby Bears to World Series titles in 1907 and 1908. Cubs' owner Charles Webb Murphy was so impressed with Chance that he gave him an ownership stake in the team.

Revered in the Windy City, Chance was reviled by opponents. In short, Chance was a brawler, and eventually suffered blood clots in his brain that were not only due to the many beanings he incurred at the plate. He even boxed as an amateur, gaining the praise of ring legends Jim Corbett and John L. Sullivan. Chance retired as the Cubs' all-time leader in stolen bases, and posted a .664 winning percentage as the team's manager. Frank Chance died in 1924 and was inducted into the Hall of Fame in 1946 alongside, you guessed it, Joe Tinker and Johnny Evers, eternally baseball's most famous power trio.

Frank Leroy Chance

Teams:

Chicago Orphans/Cubs NL (1898–1904; player-manager: 1905–1912)

New York Yankees AL (player-manager: 1913–1914)

Boston Red Sox AL (manager: 1923)

Born:
September 9, 1876
Fresno, CA

Died:
September 15, 1924
Los Angeles, CA

▷ Batted: RH

▷ Threw: RH

▷ Position: 1B

▷ Career BA: .296

▷ Managerial Record: 946–648

Hal Chase

Hal Chase was given careful consideration as the starting first baseman on our Cracker Jack All-Star Team. Although he is one of the most infamous characters to ever wear a baseball uniform, his numbers certainly warrant attention. One of the first stars of baseball, Chase batted over .300 six times, and won the National League batting crown in 1916 with his .339 average. A truly gifted player, Chase was a whiz defensively, pioneering some of the first base techniques that are used today. He perfected the art of playing off the bag and charging weakly hit balls. He also spent hours working on bare-handing and perfecting his sweep motion in order to tag runners out.

Offensively "Prince Hal" was a very good hitter whose best year was in the Federal League where he batted .347 playing for Buffalo. There is no doubt that Hal Chase was a great ballplayer. On the other hand, Hal Chase was as corrupt a ballplayer as ever existed. Quite frankly, he became the proverbial "black eye" to the game. During his time in New York,

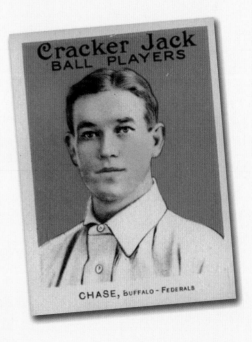

CHASE, BUFFALO - FEDERALS

Harold Homer Chase

Chase became known as a troublemaker and a show-off. He was well aware of his ability and some say he felt fans were privileged to see him strut his stuff.

Chase ran with a fast crowd of Broadway entertainers and gamblers. He thought nothing of betting either on or against his own team throughout his career. In 1918 he was suspended from the Reds for offering bribes to opponents and teammates to fix the outcomes of games he had bet on. After being implicated as a middleman in the 1919 Black Sox scandal, Chase would never again play in the majors. "Prince Hal" lived out his years playing for semi-pro teams and living in obscurity on his sister's ranch. The game of baseball would have been better off without Hal Chase.

Teams:
New York Highlanders/Yankees AL (1905–1913; player-manager: 1910–1911)
Chicago White Sox AL (1913–1914)
Buffalo Buffeds/Blues FL (1914–1915)
Cincinnati Reds NL (1916–1918)
New York Giants NL (1919)

Born:
February 13, 1883
Los Gatos, CA
Died:
May 18, 1947
Colusa, CA
▷ Batted: RH
▷ Threw: LH
▷ Position: 1B
▷ Career BA: .291
▷ Managerial Record: 86–80

Chick Gandil

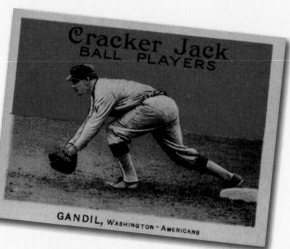

GANDIL, WASHINGTON - AMERICANS

An excellent defensive first baseman and a solid overall ballplayer, "Chick" Gandil is best known for tarnishing the game of baseball, along with his own reputation. Considered the ringleader of the infamous Black Sox scandal, Gandil wisely retired before he could be banned from baseball. This early retirement was made possible by the $35,000 in cash payoff that was the result of fixing the 1919 World Series. As a matter of fact, while playing in the Pacific Coast League in 1909, Gandil was accused of stealing money from his Minor League team.

Early in his Major League career, Gandil had the reputation of a hard-working and talented first baseman. In 1913 he batted .318 and banged out 175 hits for the Senators. Following the 1915 season, he made a brief one-season stop in Cleveland, and then proceeded to the White Sox. After a couple of fairly good years with the Sox, Gandil became irate when salaries were cut by management.

It is believed that Gandil came up with the idea to fix the 1919 World Series and that he got notorious gambler Sport Sullivan involved. Gandil was also the middleman between his old teammate Sleepy Bill Burns and Abe Attell, who represented another group of gamblers. Evidently, Gandil kept the bulk of the payoff money. He retired the next season, went on to play for various semi-pro teams, and later worked as a plumber in Calistoga, California. Over

Charles Arnold Gandil

the years, Gandil consistently denied any involvement in throwing games. He died at the age of 82, always professing his innocence. Although he was solid with the bat, and led the league in fielding percentage and assists on several occasions, Chick Gandil, like Hal Chase, almost ruined the game.

Born:
January 19, 1888
St. Paul, MN
Died:
December 13, 1970
Calistoga, CA
▷ Batted: RH
▷ Threw: RH
▷ Position: 1B
▷ Career BA: .277

Teams:
Chicago White Sox AL (1910, 1917–1919)
Washington Senators AL (1912–1915)
Cleveland Indians AL (1916)

Dick Hoblitzell

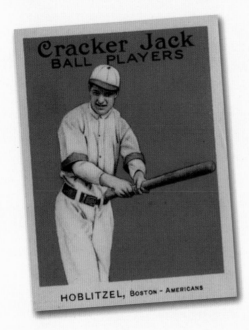

Dick Hoblitzell was born in Waverly, West Virginia, in 1888, and attended the University of Pittsburgh. He carried the blue-collar work ethic of these regions to the baseball field in his 11 Major League seasons. A left-handed-hitting first baseman, Hoblitzell began his career with the Cincinnati Reds in 1908 and quickly became a staple in the Cincy lineup. Known as "Hobby," he logged a league-leading 611 and 622 at-bats in 1910 and 1911, respectively. Hoblitzell also led the National League in games played in 1911 with 158. Respected by teammates for his intelligence, Hoblitzell was consistently productive in the Queen City between 1908 and 1913. In that time span, he hit .284 with 383 RBI and averaged just over 20 doubles per season.

In 1914, Hoblitzell was nearly traded to the Yankees, but instead, was claimed by the Red Sox off the waiver wire for a reported $1,500. While his Cincinnati teams were predominantly mediocre, Hoblitzell would become a key contributor to Boston's early 1900s dynasty. He batted .319 over the latter portion of the 1914 season for the second place Red Sox, smacking 73 hits in 69 games. Amazingly, Hoblitzell managed to show up on time for 468 games for Boston between 1914 and 1918 despite rooming on road trips with the notorious man about town Babe Ruth. In truth, Hoblitzell was the anti-Ruth, a humble and reliable teammate reflective of his simple upbringing.

By 1915, Hoblitzell had become the starting first baseman for the Red Sox. Moreover, he was a postseason stalwart, batting .313 in the 1915 World Series won by Boston in five games over the Philadelphia Phillies. In the 1916 Series, Hoblitzell walked the walk, literally, with a .435 on base percentage, buoyed by six base on balls. The Red Sox again won the crown, this time beating the

Richard Carleton Hoblitzell

Brooklyn Robins (formerly, and again later, the Dodgers) in five games. In 1918, Hoblitzell slumped and was unseated at first base by his old pal Ruth. That spring, at the age of 29, he left the Red Sox and his big-league career for good to enlist in the U.S. Army Dental Corps. He would eventually sink his teeth into a career as a sportswriter, radio personality and community activist in West Virginia. On the field and off, we applaud Dick Hoblitzell's consistency as a player, leader, and teammate.

Teams:

Cincinnati Reds NL (1908–1914)
Boston Red Sox AL (1914–1918)

Born:
October 26, 1888
Waverly, WV
Died:
November 14, 1962
Parkersburg, WV

▷ Batted: LH

▷ Threw: RH

▷ Position: 1B

▷ Career BA: .278

Doc Johnston

Wheeler "Doc" Johnston was a good all-around first baseman who was an outstanding defensive player. His most productive years were with the Indians. Johnston wasn't quite ready for the big leagues when the Reds purchased him from Chattanooga in the Southern League. After going "ofer" ten in three games, he found himself back in Chattanooga. A few more years of Minor League play honed his skills and after posting a .308 batting average in 1912 for New Orleans, he was back in the Bigs, playing first base for Cleveland. After the Pirates purchased him for $7,500 in 1915, Johnston had a great defensive season compiling a .991 fielding percentage and committing only 13 errors in 1,514 chances.

In 1916, after batting only .213 for the Steel City, he was sent down to the minors to make room at first base for the aging Honus Wagner. Johnston went back to Cleveland in 1918, where he enjoyed four very productive years. In 1920, he batted .292 and his .992 fielding percentage was good for second in the league among first basemen. The Indians made it to the World Series that year, bringing sibling rivalry to a new level. His brother Jimmy played third base for the Brooklyn Robins in the Series, but only posted a .214 BA to Doc's .273 BA for Series play. Cleveland won the Series, and big brother Doc beat his kid brother. Johnston left the Indians after the next season to spend his final Major League year with the A's before calling it quits.

When you take a close look at his defensive numbers, Doc Johnston goes down as one of the best-fielding first basemen of the Deadball Era. His .989 fielding percentage is simply amazing given the playing conditions at the time. Johnston went on to manage in the minors for a few years, mentoring young players on the fine art of fielding. All in all, Doc Johnston had a career that he could be proud of, and was a solid contributor to our National Pastime. He is what we refer to as a gamer, and a credit to any team.

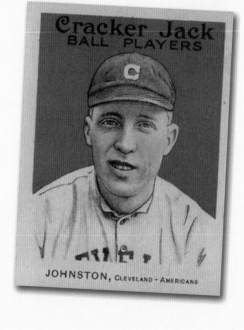

JOHNSTON, CLEVELAND - AMERICANS

Wheeler Roger Johnston

Teams:

Cincinnati Reds NL (1909)

Cleveland Naps/Indians AL (1912–1914, 1918–1921)

Pittsburgh Pirates NL (1915–1916)

Philadelphia Athletics AL (1922)

Born:
September 9, 1887
Cleveland, TN

Died:
February 17, 1961
Chattanooga, TN

▷ Batted: LH

▷ Threw: LH

▷ Position: 1B

▷ Career BA: .263

Ed Konetchy

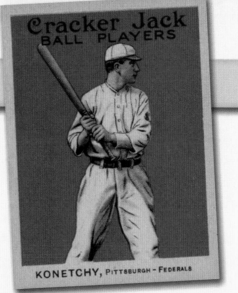

KONETCHY, PITTSBURGH - FEDERALS

There are a number of darn good first basemen in the storied Cracker Jack Collection, and Ed "Koney" Konetchy is near the top of the list. Also known as the "Candy Kid" and the "Big Bohemian," Konetchy banged out over 2,100 hits to go along with a solid .281 batting average over his stellar career. Considered a prodigy in the minors, Ed dominated in the majors. Some predicted he would become the greatest first baseman of that era. Konetchy left school at age 14 to work in the local candy factory. After working 10 hours a day, he brought his sweetness out to the ball field, and played until dark.

When Konetchy got to the big leagues, he became one of the most respected players in the game. Although he got paid pretty good money to play, he had a genuine passion for baseball. Between salary disputes and being traded for multiple players on a few occasions, Konetchy played on six different teams including a stint with the Federal League's Pittsburgh Rebels. A hard negotiator, the story goes that Konetchy met Cardinal's manager Roger Bresnahan in a barroom to negotiate his contract, and the two proceeded to drink all day. After seven hours of imbibing, they finally came to an agreement and the contract was

signed. One of the good guys of baseball, Konetchy, along with Bresnahan, is credited with saving many lives in a train wreck that occurred on a Cardinals' trip in 1911. Both men carried passengers to safety and cared for the injured until help arrived.

Besides batting over .300 four different times, Ed had 255 stolen bases and a spectacular fielding percentage of .990, superb numbers. He once had 10 consecutive hits over a three-game period. The epitome of a dedicated ballplayer, Konetchy was well-liked and respected by teammates and opponents. He had some great seasons in the minors after his MLB tour. While playing for the Fort Worth Panthers in 1925, he led the Texas League with 41 homers. After his playing days, Konetchy returned home to manage the La Crosse team and won the Wisconsin State League championship in 1940. He later went into the restaurant business, the chicken farm business, and scouted for the Cardinals.

Born:
September 3, 1885
La Crosse, WI

Died:
May 27, 1947
Fort Worth, TX

▷ Batted: RH

▷ Threw: RH

▷ Position: 1B

▷ Career BA: .281

Edward Joseph Konetchy

Teams:
St. Louis Cardinals NL (1907–1913)
Pittsburgh Pirates NL (1914)
Pittsburgh Rebels FL (1915)
Boston Braves NL (1916–1918)
Brooklyn Robins NL (1919–1921)
Philadelphia Phillies NL (1921)

Fred Luderus

Fred Luderus had no fancy or folksy nickname. His lifetime batting average was .277. In 1911, he finished 27th in MVP voting while batting .301 with 16 homers and 99 RBI for the Philadelphia Phillies. Over his 12-year big-league career he led the National League in a grand total of one category: games played, with 155 in 1913. All in all, Luderus was a pretty good ballplayer, nothing spectacular or remarkable about him, except that is, for one glorious run in the 1915 World Series against the Boston Red Sox. In those five games, Luderus went from just plain Fred to just plain fantastic. He batted .438 with seven hits in 16 at-bats, and knocked in six runs with one homer and two doubles to boot. He was nearly unstoppable. Unfortunately for Fred, the Phillies were not. The Sons of Brotherly Love lost to the BoSox in five games, and his .500 OBP, .750 slugging and 1.250 OPS went for naught.

Still, that Series was the highlight of an astonishingly consistent career. Between 1911 and 1919, the Philadelphia faithful could pretty much pencil Luderus in for 30 doubles, 60 to 80 RBI and a .270 plus average. While Luderus sometimes

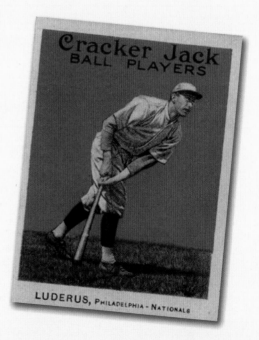

LUDERUS, PHILADELPHIA - NATIONALS

Frederick William Luderus

showed the sweet swing of a sublime slugger, his glove often hit a sour note. On four occasions, he led all National League first basemen in errors. Luderus was born in Milwaukee, and his fielding made some wonder if he sampled the many beers of his native city between innings. As a Cub in 1909 and 1910, Luderus hit but one round-tripper, an inside the park job against his future team, the Phillies. He would hit 83 more Major League homers benefitting from the baby band box Baker Bowl, the Phillies' slugger-friendly home stadium. Outside of playing first base and being of German descent, Luderus could never be confused with Lou Gehrig, however, he did set the Major League record for consecutive games played in 1919, appearing in his 479th straight game on August 3. His Iron Man string would run until Opening Day of the 1920 season stretching 533 games. Luderus retired in 1920 to dabble in home building, not a bad choice for a guy who constructed a fairly solid big-league career.

Teams:
Chicago Cubs NL (1909–1910)
Philadelphia Phillies NL (1910–1920)

Born:
September 12, 1885
Milwaukee, WI
Died:
January 5, 1961
Three Lakes, WI
▷ Batted: LH
▷ Threw: RH
▷ Position: 1B
▷ Career BA: .277

Stuffy McInnis

John Phalen McInnis

An excellent defensive first baseman with a .307 lifetime batting average as well as 2,405 hits over his great 18-season career, John "Stuffy" McInnis' numbers are better than some current members of baseball's most elite club. Besides being a solid hitter, McInnis was one of the best defensive first basemen in the game. In 1921, with the Red Sox, he committed only one error in 1,651 chances over 152 games; and his 1,300 errorless chances at first base set a league record. To top that, between May 31, 1921, and June 2, 1922, he raised the bar with 1,700 chances without an error over 163 games. These records would stand the test of time until 2007.

Nicknamed during his Minor League days, when fans would shout "That's the stuff, kid!" after his sensational plays, McInnis was signed by Connie Mack when he was only 18 years old. As first baseman for some of the great A's teams, he was part of the famed $100,000 infield along with Eddie Collins, Home Run Baker and Black Jack Barry. Over his storied career, McInnis played on five pennant-winning teams and four World Series Champs. Offensively, his best year was in 1912, when he batted .327 for the A's, but McInnis had some other great years batting .315 for the Braves and .307 for the Red Sox. All in all, he batted over

.300 on twelve different occasions, but is known more for his excellent fielding at first base. His one-handed style combined with the "knee reach" and use of the new claw-type first baseman's glove was cutting edge at the time.

McInnis ended his pro career with an unsuccessful one-year stint as manager of the Phillies. He later coached baseball at Norwich University and Cornell before moving on to coach six seasons at Harvard. In our opinion, John "Stuffy" McInnis should be a candidate for the Hall of Fame. Cooperstown should take a hard look at this guy. As a matter of fact, he was given close consideration for the Cracker Jack All-Star Team, but was nosed out by Jake Daubert, another guy who belongs in the Hall.

Teams:
Philadelphia Athletics AL (1909–1917)
Boston Red Sox AL (1918–1921)
Cleveland Indians AL (1922)
Boston Braves NL (1923–1924)
Pittsburgh Pirates NL (1925–1926)
Philadelphia Phillies NL (manager: 1927)

Born:
September 19, 1890
Gloucester, MA
Died:
February 16, 1960
Ipswich, MA
▷ Batted: RH
▷ Threw: RH
▷ Position: 1B
▷ Career BA: .307
▷ Managerial Record: 51–103

Fred Merkle

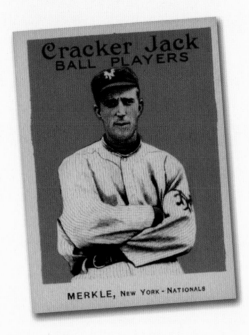

Cracker Jack
BALL PLAYERS

MERKLE, NEW YORK - NATIONALS

If we told you that a player broke into the Major Leagues at age 18 and enjoyed a 16-year career, you'd probably say the guy had talent. If we mentioned that this same player compiled a respectable .273 career batting average with 1,580 hits, you would justifiably be impressed. If we then related that in 1911 and 1912, this player hit a combined 23 home runs, 168 RBI, and batted .296 finishing 7th and 18th respectively in MVP voting; you'd no doubt say he was a pretty darn fine ballplayer. However, if we told you this man's nickname was "Bonehead," you'd let out a sigh and put your hands to your face. Such is the cross that Carl Fredrick Rudolf Merkle had to bear until his passing at the age of 67 in 1956.

Merkle lives in that thankless baseball neighborhood of good ballplayers who made one bad move. On his street reside the likes of Bill Buckner and Ralph Branca. Merkle's mistake was not as bad as his history makes it seem. In September of 1908 with Merkle's Giants battling the Cubs in a pennant race, Merkle lined a two-out, bottom-of-the-ninth single to right field sending teammate Moose McCormick to third. Al Bridwell then hit one up the middle, scoring McCormick with what fans thought was the winning run. Merkle stopped short of second base on Bridwell's hit and headed to the Giants' clubhouse thinking the game was finished. Cubs' centerfielder Artie Hofman had fielded Bridwell's hit and tossed it to second baseman Johnny Evers. For some reason, Giants pitcher Joe McGinnity got hold of the ball and tossed it into the crowd in celebration. Evers apparently found another baseball and argued that Merkle was out on a force play because he had never touched second. That claim was upheld, and the game ended in a 1–1 tie because the jubilant Giants' crowd could not be cleared from the Polo Grounds field. The tie, in theory, cost New York the 1908 pennant. If that play had occurred after the dawn of television replay, Merkle would enjoy a kinder fate. Instead, we place Fred Merkle in a kind of baseball Twilight Zone, deified for consistent play and perseverance, and vilified for a single baseball brain blip.

Carl Frederick Rudolf Merkle

Teams:

New York Giants NL (1907–1916)
Brooklyn Robins NL (1916–1917)
Chicago Cubs NL (1917–1920)
New York Yankees AL (1925–1926)

Born:
December 20, 1888
Watertown, WI
Died:
March 2, 1956
Daytona Beach, FL
▷ Batted: RH
▷ Threw: RH
▷ Position: 1B
▷ Career BA: .273

Dots Miller

John "Dots" Miller enjoyed an exceptional rookie year, helping the Pirates win the World Series in 1909. Miller took over the second base position from Ed Abbaticchio and became the great Honus Wagner's double-play partner. The combo clicked so well that the rookie led National League second basemen in assists and chances that year, and was second in fielding percentage. Because of their shared German heritage, Miller and Wagner also became close friends.

How did he get the nickname Dots? Evidently one day a reporter walked up to Honus Wagner, and asked who the new kid was. With his German accent, Wagner replied, "Dots Miller." In reality he was saying, "That's Miller." At that very instant, a neat nickname was given to the young ballplayer. A steady batsman and decent fielder, Miller's best year was 1914 when he batted a solid .290 during his first year with the Cards. He finished in the top 10 in National League MVP voting in 1913 and 1914. Miller banged out 1,526 hits during his 12 years in the big leagues. Although he is included

with the Cracker Jack first basemen, Miller was primarily a utility player over his successful career, playing 737 games at first base, 681 at second, 68 at third, and 111 as shortstop. As a matter of fact, many considered him the best utility man in the game at the time.

His baseball career was interrupted when Miller joined the Marines in 1918 and fought overseas as a sharpshooter. He returned to the Cards in 1919, a bit rusty, and batted .231. Miller finished out his Major League career in Philadelphia after he was purchased by the Phillies in 1920. He retired after the 1921 season, and in 1922, as a 35-year-old rookie manager, Miller managed the San Francisco Seals of the Pacific Coast League to the league championship. Unfortunately, like so many other people at that time, Dots Miller died at the early age of 36 after contracting tuberculosis, cutting short his promising career as a Minor League manager.

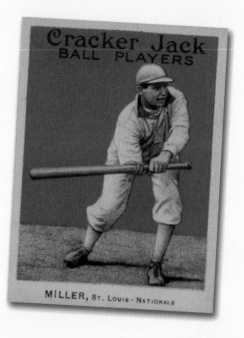

MILLER, St. Louis - Nationals

John Barney Miller

Teams:

Pittsburgh Pirates NL (1909–1913)

St. Louis Cardinals NL (1914–1919)

Philadelphia Phillies NL (1920–1921)

Born:
September 9, 1886
Kearny, NJ

Died:
September 5, 1923
Saranac Lake, NY

▷ Batted: RH

▷ Threw: RH

▷ Position: 1B/2B/SS/3B

▷ Career BA: .263

Vic Saier

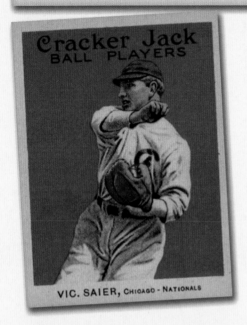

VIC. SAIER, CHICAGO - NATIONALS

We can definitely file Chicago Cubs first sacker Vic Saier in the "What Might Have Been" category. He was fast, as evidenced by his league-leading 21 triples in 1913, and his 19 steals without being caught in 1914. He could hit for average, batting .288 and .289 in 1912 and 1913. He could get on base, posting an OBP of over .350 in four of his eight big-league seasons. He also had power, clubbing 18 home runs in 1914. What Saier did not have was luck. In the prime of his career, he was actually being compared with Ty Cobb and other diamond deities, but in 1915, Saier suffered a leg injury that drastically marred a budding career.

In his watershed 1913 campaign, Saier was the total package for player-manager Johnny Evers' Cubbies. He led all starters in hits and homers. Among the Windy

City regulars, only third baseman Heine Zimmerman had more RBI and hit for a higher batting average. Michigan born and bred, Saier had a cup of coffee with a local club, the Oldsmobile Nine, and played for the Lansing Senators in the Southern Michigan League. He joined the Cubs in 1911 and eventually solidified the first base position after Frank Chance was forced to retire due to a series of beanings. Saier also used his head, but not as violently. He was enrolled at St. Mary's Business School when baseball became his vocation. As a player, he brought a cerebral and business-like approach to the game.

Not one for superstar arrogance, Saier was a true gamer who fought through his injuries to play 147 games in 1916. His skills, however, were obviously diminished, most notably, his speed. Saier managed to pilfer 20 bases that year, but was nabbed 17 times. In 1917, bad luck found Saier again. He shattered his leg in a home plate collision, and eventually quit the game after the 1919 season. Vic Saier might as well have raised black cats under a ladder surrounded by broken mirrors. To say that his once promising career was snake bitten would be an understatement. His biography says that Vic was short for Victor. In our view, it was short for victim.

Victor Sylvester Saier

Teams:

Chicago Cubs NL (1911–1917)

Pittsburgh Pirates NL (1919)

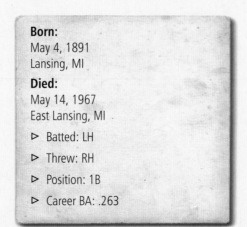

Born:
May 4, 1891
Lansing, MI
Died:
May 14, 1967
East Lansing, MI

▷ Batted: LH

▷ Threw: RH

▷ Position: 1B

▷ Career BA: .263

Butch Schmidt

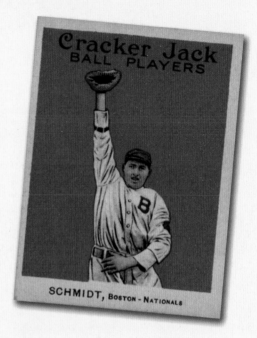

SCHMIDT, BOSTON - NATIONALS

Charles "Butch" Schmidt, also known as "Butcher Boy," had a very short career in the majors, but it was time well spent. His Major League debut took place in 1909 when he was called up from the minors by the New York Highlanders and appeared in one game with two at-bats. He promptly went back to the minors where he played for the Baltimore Orioles in the Eastern League and Rochester Hustlers in the International League. Schmidt's contract was finally purchased by the Boston Braves in late August of 1913. Brought up to play first base for the rest of the season, Butch did well with his first 78 Major League at-bats, averaging .308 that year, which was good enough to earn him the starting first baseman position for the following season.

The 1914 Braves team, managed by George Stallings, climbed from dead last place in July to win the pennant and defeat the Philadelphia Athletics in the World Series. Dubbed "The Miracle Braves" they put together one of the

Charles John Schmidt

biggest comebacks in baseball history, steamrolling over the first place New York Giants to take the National League pennant and marching on to sweep the A's in four straight games—the first sweep in World Series history. Schmidt had a good year, batting .285 for the Braves. More importantly, he was part of the best middle infield in baseball that year, along with Johnny Evers at second base and Rabbit Maranville at shortstop.

Interestingly enough, the Braves were so bad in July that they hit a new low, losing an exhibition game to the Buffalo, New York, Minor League team. It is said that veteran player Johnny Evers rallied the team and that the embarrassing loss in Buffalo became the catalyst for the Braves' inspired winning streak. Schmidt moved on from baseball after one more solid season where he batted .251 for the Braves. He returned home to run the family wholesale butcher business in Baltimore. "Butcher Boy" Schmidt carved out a pretty good baseball career.

Teams:

New York Highlanders AL (1909)
Boston Braves NL (1913–1915)

Born:
July 19, 1886
Baltimore, MD
Died:
September 4, 1952
Baltimore, MD
▷ Batted: LH
▷ Threw: LH
▷ Position: 1B
▷ Career BA: .272

George Stovall

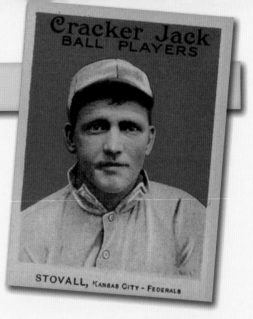

STOVALL, KANSAS CITY - FEDERALS

Slick-fielding first baseman, George Stovall, had a couple of unusual nicknames. He was referred to as "Brother George" because of the kind way he mentored the illiterate Joe Jackson and other young ballplayers. He later earned the nickname "Firebrand" when he led the charge to the upstart Federal League. Some even referred to him as the "Jesse James" of the Federal League. Stovall was very outspoken, a trait that caused run-ins with managers, owners, and umpires over the years. Yet he was well-liked by his contemporaries because of his convictions. He just would not back down.

A farm boy from the Kansas City area, George hit his first home run in the majors off his brother, Detroit pitcher Jesse Stovall, in 1904. With the Cleveland Naps for most of his career, Stovall's best season was in 1908 when he batted .292 and banged out 156 hits. Recognizing that his true talent was leadership, Cleveland owner Charles Somers named Stovall player-manager in 1911. A real team guy, Stovall orchestrated a one-day strike in 1911 so his team could attend the funeral of pitching great Addie Joss. This was just one of the many times he was to butt heads with ownership throughout his career. Just as he was hitting his stride as manager, Stovall was sold to the Browns in 1912 where he was player-manager for two years.

After a contract dispute, he jumped ship to the Federal League to become player-manager of the Kansas City Packers. The first big star to move to the Federal League, Stovall actively recruited other MLB players to join the league. A true players' rights activist, Stovall was eventually named president of the Association of Professional Ballplayers. After retiring in 1915 at age 38, he managed in the Pacific Coast League before joining the war effort in the shipbuilding industry in 1918. He then managed in the Florida State League, coached for Loyola and scouted for Pittsburgh. During the 1930s Stovall organized several "old timers" exhibition games to raise money for indigent players. During WWII he returned to the shipbuilding trade as a foreman. A true patriot and activist, "Brother George" Stovall steered the ship through a very productive, full life.

George Thomas Stovall

Born:
November 23, 1877
Leeds, MO
Died:
November 5, 1951
Burlington, IA
▷ Batted: RH
▷ Threw: RH
▷ Position: 1B
▷ Career BA: .265
▷ Managerial Record: 313–376

Teams:

Cleveland Naps AL (1904–1910; player-manager: 1911)
St. Louis Browns AL (player-manager: 1912–1913)
Kansas City Packers FL (player-manager: 1914–1915)

J. C. DELEHANTY, Brooklyn - Federals

THE KEYSTONE SACK

Cracker Jack BALL PLAYERS

DUGEY, Philadelphia - Nationals

T he key to a quality second baseman is quick hands and feet, and the ability to get rid of the ball quickly. It is also important that the player be able to make the pivot and have good range getting to the ball. The second baseman is primarily looked upon for his defensive capabilities rather than his offensive prowess. In this group of Cracker Jack players, we get the best of both worlds.

Most of the players in this chapter were very good both offensively and defensively. We have two that deserve special attention because both left their indelible marks on the game: Johnny Evers and Nap Lajoie. The rest were talented ballplayers who made their contributions.

Meet the guardians of the keystone sack, your Cracker Jack second basemen.

Cracker Jack BALL PLAYERS

EVERS, Boston - Nationals

Cracker Jack BALL PLAYERS

LAJOIE, Philadelphia - Americans

Cracker Jack BALL PLAYERS

KNABE, Baltimore - Federals

Cracker Jack BALL PLAYERS

PRATT, St. Louis - Americans

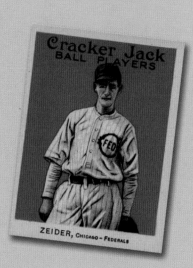

Cracker Jack BALL PLAYERS

ZEIDER, Chicago - Federals

Jim Delahanty

The second youngest of the five baseball-playing Delahanty brothers, Jim was probably the most well-traveled. He bounced around the minors before, during and after his Major League tour. In the majors, Delahanty was often used as trade bait to get several players in return. As a result, he traveled the circuit, playing for eight different teams over a span of 13 years.

A utility player at the beginning of his career, Delahanty settled in at second base in 1907 when he joined the Senators. After two solid seasons that were unfortunately tarnished by injury and controversy, Delahanty was traded to Detroit in August of 1909. He helped the Tigers to a pennant that year, and was a solid contributor in the World Series, appearing in all seven games and batting .346. His best career season was 1911 when he batted a lofty .339 for the Tigers. Despite that performance, Delahanty was released by Detroit the following season. Officially the release was for injury and illness, but some say his involvement in the 1912 players' strike in support of

James Christopher Delahanty

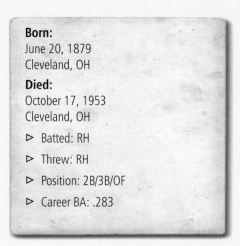

Born:
June 20, 1879
Cleveland, OH

Died:
October 17, 1953
Cleveland, OH

▷ Batted: RH

▷ Threw: RH

▷ Position: 2B/3B/OF

▷ Career BA: .283

Ty Cobb was the real cause. Delahanty jumped to the fledgling, short-lived Federal League where he played for the Brooklyn Tip-Tops. He finished out the 1915 season with the Hartford Senators of the Colonial League and then managed the Beaumont Oilers of the Texas League before calling it quits.

Although he was a dependable second baseman, Jim's achievements were overshadowed by those of his famous older brother Ed Delahanty. After traveling the circuit for many years, Delahanty finally left baseball in 1916 at age 37 and settled down to family life in his native Cleveland where he worked for the city as a truck driver.

Teams:
Chicago Orphans NL (1901)
New York Giants NL (1902)
Boston Beaneaters NL (1904–1905)
Cincinnati Reds NL (1906)
St. Louis Browns AL (1907)
Washington Senators AL (1907–1909)
Detroit Tigers AL (1909–1912)
Brooklyn Tip-Tops FL (1914–1915)

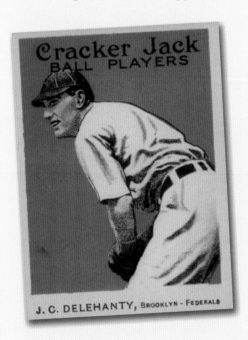

J. C. DELAHANTY, Brooklyn - Federals

Larry Doyle

DOYLE, New York - Nationals

One of the best second basemen of the era, "Laughing Larry" Doyle could do it all. Known for his outgoing personality and happy disposition, he was well-liked by manager John McGraw and his Giants teammates. The former coal miner was no standout when he first arrived in the Major Leagues, but McGraw stood by his highly paid rookie, giving him the opportunity to develop into an outstanding player.

Doyle eventually became captain of the Giants and one of baseball's biggest stars,

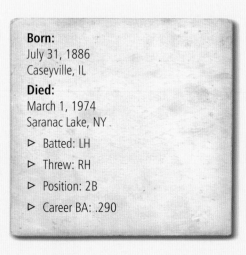

Born:
July 31, 1886
Caseyville, IL

Died:
March 1, 1974
Saranac Lake, NY

▷ Batted: LH

▷ Threw: RH

▷ Position: 2B

▷ Career BA: .290

Lawrence Joseph Doyle

leading the National League in several offensive and defensive categories. Besides being on three pennant winners as team captain, he led the National League with 172 hits in 1909 and 25 triples in 1911. Doyle's 184 hits and .330 batting average earned him the Chalmers Award (National League MVP) in 1912, and his trophy was a brand new Chalmers automobile. He won the batting title in 1915 with a sparkling .320 average, and led the league in hits, singles and doubles as well that year. At the height of his career, the second sacker was paid a salary of $8,000 which was almost as much earned by his famous roommate, Christy Mathewson.

A shrewd businessman, Doyle dabbled in the stock market and in real estate, and did quite well for himself. In 1913 Doyle turned down a $27,000 contract from the Federal League out of loyalty to the National League. He was one of those players who did everything right. Doyle finished out his career as player-manager in the minors and retired in 1922. After his playing days, he worked in various capacities for the Giants. His coal-mining background and heavy smoking caught up with Doyle in 1942 when he was diagnosed with tuberculosis. He was treated at Saranac Lake, the same sanitarium that treated Christy Mathewson. Laughing Larry had the last laugh though. He fully recovered and lived to be 87 years old, even outliving the sanitarium. Larry Doyle was one heck of a player and surely warrants another look by Cooperstown.

Teams:
New York Giants NL (1907–1916, 1918–1920)
Chicago Cubs NL (1916–1917)

Oscar Dugey

Oscar Joseph Dugey

What Oscar Dugey lacked in pure baseball talent, he made up for in knowledge and intelligence. These traits were most likely inherited from his father, a prominent businessman in Palestine, Texas. Because his dad's name was also Oscar, the family took to calling little Oscar by the nickname Jake. In 1913, as a rookie with the Boston Braves, Dugey had two hits in eight at-bats posting a career-best .250 batting average. He had a decent .339 on-base percentage in 1916 with the Phillies, but would only play two more big-league seasons, returning to the Braves for his final season in 1920.

Statistics, however, do not tell the whole story of Dugey's baseball acumen. Known mainly as a backup second baseman to future Hall of Famer Johnny Evers, Dugey was a "*Jake*-of-all-trades" for the 1914 Braves managed by George Stallings. According to reports, Stallings was obsessive about keeping the Braves' dugout clean. Opposing players would toss peanut shells into the Braves' dugout just to goad Stallings. Dugey was in charge of keeping the pigeons away. Legend has it that he ruined his arm by constantly tossing rocks at the birds. The Braves won the World Series in 1914 in a sweep of the Philadelphia Athletics. In 1915, Dugey would find himself in the City of Brotherly Love playing for the Phillies. As a player and trusted advisor to manager Pat Moran, Dugey would once again reach the World Series as the Phils lost to the Red Sox.

Ever the thinker, Dugey gained a

reputation around the big leagues as an expert sign stealer. As a coach for the Braves and Cubs, he could tell what a pitcher would be throwing just by eyeing the grip. Dugey was also known for antagonizing and inciting opponents to the point of brawling. He was, in today's parlance, a good baseball man, a smart and feisty grinder whom we would take on our team any day.

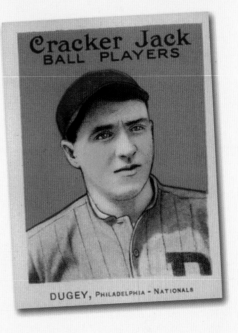

DUGEY, PHILADELPHIA - NATIONALS

Teams:
Boston Braves NL (1913–1914, 1920)
Philadelphia Phillies NL (1915–1917)

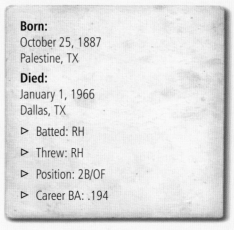

Born:
October 25, 1887
Palestine, TX
Died:
January 1, 1966
Dallas, TX
▷ Batted: RH
▷ Threw: RH
▷ Position: 2B/OF
▷ Career BA: .194

Johnny Evers

Buck Herzog

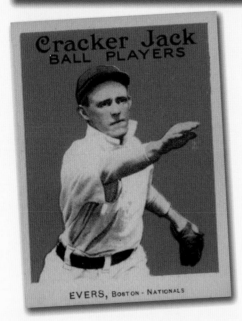

EVERS, BOSTON - NATIONALS

Nicknamed "The Crab" because of the unusual crablike stance he used to scoop up ground balls, Johnny Evers (pronounced *Eevers*) was well known as part of the greatest double-play combination of all time as immortalized in the poem written by newspaper columnist Franklin Pierce Adams entitled *Baseball's Sad Lexicon*.

A wiry 125 pounds, Evers was a solid second baseman who played on the great Cubs teams from 1902 through 1913 and appeared in four World Series, winning two of them. Later traded to the Boston Braves, he not only won another World Series, but also won the Chalmers Award

(MVP) in 1914. A real sparkplug for his size, Evers was tossed out of nine games during the 1914 season. He became known for arguing with teammates, opponents and officials, which gave his nickname, "The Crab," a new meaning.

Evers was very high-energy and temperamental. As part of that famous double-play combo with Frank Chance and Joe Tinker, he was superb on the field. On the other hand, off the field, Johnny Evers and Joe Tinker never spoke. Evers once even stated that they truly hated each other. The two did not speak for 30 years. Some say it was because Tinker fired a baseball at Evers from a very close distance and injured Evers' hand. Others claim that it was a result of a fight the two got into in 1905. In any event, the two remained passionate about the Cubs and never let their relationship interfere with their stellar play.

Johnny Evers batted a respectable .270 over his career and stole 324 bases. He later managed both the Cubs and White Sox and served as a scout for the Braves. He was elected to the Hall of Fame in 1946. Evers was also involved in the famous 1908 "Merkle Boner" play, calling out the fact that Fred Merkle never touched second base and was heading back to the clubhouse. This set off a chain of events that became one of the more bizarre stories in baseball history.

A talented infielder, Buck Herzog played second base, shortstop and third. He is included with the Cracker Jack second sackers because he played a few more games at that position than the other two. Herzog goes down in the annals of baseball history as one of the most colorful and controversial players of all time. Displaying a fiery temper both as a player and manager, Buck is often compared to former player and manager for the Yankees, Billy Martin.

Incredibly versatile at any infield position, Herzog was also a pretty good hitter. He batted .290 in 1911, helping the Giants to the pennant. As a Giant, Herzog and his manager, the legendary John McGraw, often tangled with each other. Their relationship was similar to that of Martin and his star, Reggie Jackson. Herzog, like Jackson, was the anchor on those great pennant-winning Giants teams of 1911, 1912, 1913 and 1917. As a matter of fact, Herzog was dealt away on two occasions only to be brought back to shore up the Giants' infield. As player-manager of the Reds, Herzog consistently fought with the front office, but despite his fiery temper the Giants wanted him back and named him captain upon his return.

Born:
July 21, 1881
Troy, NY

Died:
March 28, 1947
Albany, NY

▷ Batted: LH

▷ Threw: RH

▷ Position: 2B

▷ Career BA: .270

▷ Managerial Record: 180–192

John Joseph Evers

Teams:
Chicago Orphans/Cubs NL (1902–1912, player-manager: 1913, manager: 1921)

Boston Braves NL (1914–1917, 1929)

Philadelphia Phillies NL (1917)

Chicago White Sox AL (1922, manager: 1924)

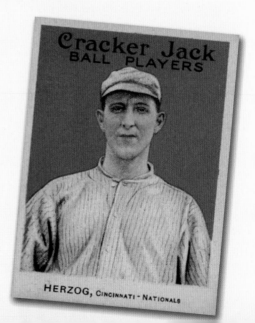

HERZOG, CINCINNATI - NATIONALS

Charles Lincoln Herzog

One of the greatest brawls of all time took place between Herzog and Ty Cobb when Cobb slid into third with spikes high and injured Herzog. The two battled on the field and, after the game, they continued the fight in Cobb's hotel room. Cobb proceeded to thrash Herzog soundly. On a couple of occasions there was speculation that Herzog had been laying down on games where money was wagered. The most serious accusation was in 1920 while he was with the Cubs. Although there was no evidence of his participation, Herzog was released with several other accused teammates. Herzog went on to play and manage in the minors through 1924. He later coached at the Naval Academy and worked for the B&O Railroad for many years. In 1953 Herzog's baseball friends found out that he was penniless, homeless, and sick with tuberculosis. Although they tried to help, it was too late. Herzog died that year at the age of 67. A sad ending to a good player.

Teams:

New York Giants NL (1908–1909, 1911–1913, 1916–1917)

Boston Doves/Rustlers/Braves NL (1910–1911, 1918–1919)

Cincinnati Reds NL (player-manager: 1914–1916)

Chicago Cubs NL (1919–1920)

Born:
July 9, 1885
Baltimore, MD

Died:
September 4, 1953
Baltimore, MD

▷ Batted: RH

▷ Threw: RH

▷ Position: 2B/3B/SS

▷ Career BA: .259

▷ Managerial Record: 165–226

Miller Huggins

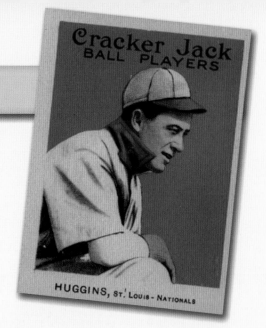

As both a slick-fielding second baseman and legendary manager, Miller "Mighty Mite" Huggins definitely left his mark on our National Pastime. The diminutive 5-foot, 6-inch Huggins was bitten by the baseball bug while attending the University of Cincinnati. Although he graduated with a law degree, Huggins never practiced law, opting for a baseball career instead. Huggins proved to be fleet-footed, stealing 324 bases over his playing career, and was adept at getting on base. The perfect lead-off hitter, Huggins led the league in walks four times. He became a steady influence at the pivot position for both his Reds and Cardinals teams.

Even though he was a skilled second baseman, Huggins found his true calling as a manager. He became player-manager of the Cards, and had some success in St. Louis but his teams never finished higher than third place. It is said that Huggins tried to buy the franchise when it was for sale in 1918, but his offer was rejected. Huggins then left the Cards, but Jake Rupert, owner of the Yankees, saw something in his management style, and the rest is history. Once in New York, Huggins took a group of undisciplined carousers and turned them into a spectacular baseball team. He systematically rebuilt the Yankees by bringing in new talent. Huggins corralled the great Babe Ruth, and recruited future stars Lou Gehrig, Tony Lazzeri and Earle Combs. His 1927 "Murderer's Row" team is considered one of the best of all time.

Huggins led the Yankees to World Series wins in 1923, 1927 and 1928, and to the pennant in 1921, 1922 and 1926.

Some consider Huggins the greatest manager of all time. In any event, he is right up there with the best. Tragically, Miller Huggins died in 1929 from an infection. He had stepped down as manager of his beloved Yankees only five days earlier due to illness. Thousands of shocked and saddened fans poured into Yankee Stadium to view his casket and pay their respects. "Mighty Mite" was inducted into the Hall of Fame in 1964. Some say that good things come in small packages. Miller Huggins is certainly a good example of that.

Teams:

Cincinnati Reds NL (1904–1909)

St. Louis Cardinals NL (1910–1912; player-manager: 1913–1916; manager: 1917)

New York Yankees AL (manager: 1918–1929)

Miller James Huggins

Born:
March 27, 1878
Cincinnati, OH

Died:
September 25, 1929
New York, NY

▷ Batted: Switch

▷ Threw: RH

▷ Position: 2B

▷ Career BA: .265

▷ Managerial Record: 1,413–1,134

John Hummel

Otto Knabe

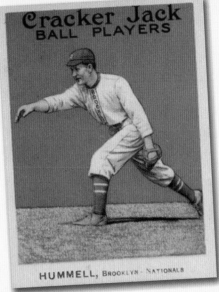

led the National League in whiffs in 1910. He had over 140 hits in the 1908, 1909 and 1910 seasons, but that offensive consistency was in direct contrast to his defense. With 548 games at second, 293 in the outfield, 160 games at first base, and just for fun, another 74 at shortstop, Hummel wasn't just versatile, he was a one-man roster. In the field, Hummel had as much quality as quantity. He registered a combined career fielding percentage of .969 and led all second sackers in that statistic in 1910 (.965) and 1911 (.972).

Known as a loner, Hummel was sometimes hard to figure. He was quiet, unassuming and nearly aloof, yet had a reputation for his violent slides on the base paths, spikes high with bad intentions. In 1909, he was ejected from games on three different occasions. Maybe Hummel did it on purpose. The Superbas lost 98 games that season. In fact, Hummel's Brooklyn clubs lost over 500 games over the course of his first six seasons. We include Hummel in our group of second basemen, but his all-around skills are a testament to a man who, for 12 seasons, talked softly and carried a big glove.

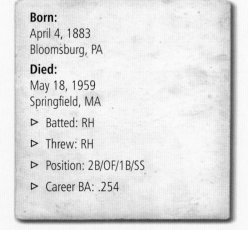

John Hummel must have loved cities that began with the letter B. He was born and raised in Bloomsburg, PA, and remained there to study at the University of Bloomsburg. Eventually, he would play 11 seasons with Brooklyn on teams known as the Superbas, Dodgers and Robins from 1905–1915. Known as "Silent John," Hummel let his play do the talking over a 12-year career that ended with the Yankees in 1918.

A dependable doubles and RBI man, Hummel was a bit of a free swinger who

On October 3, 1905, a 21-year-old Otto "Dutch" Knabe came up to the majors for a cup of coffee with the Pirates. Appearing in just three games at third base for Pittsburgh, Knabe handled himself well, coming up with three hits in 10 at-bats and drawing three walks. Despite that performance, Knabe was back in the minors by December. He made it back to the big leagues in 1907 and quickly solidified his position as the Phillies star second baseman.

Known for his roughhouse style of play, Knabe would not hesitate to mix it up with an opposing player. A good infielder, Knabe and shortstop Mickey Doolin made a formidable and tough tandem. Over his seven years with the Phillies, Knabe averaged about 120 hits per year, and led the league in sacrifice hits in 1907, 1908, 1910 and 1913. His best year offensively was 1913 when he batted a respectable .263 and banged out 150 hits. His .957 fielding percentage was quite good considering the conditions and equipment of his day.

Given his star status and solid position

John Edwin Hummel

Born:
April 4, 1883
Bloomsburg, PA

Died:
May 18, 1959
Springfield, MA

▷ Batted: RH

▷ Threw: RH

▷ Position: 2B/OF/1B/SS

▷ Career BA: .254

Teams:

Brooklyn Superbas/Dodgers/Robins NL (1905–1915)
New York Yankees AL (1918)

Franz Otto Knabe

in Philadelphia, it was a shock to all when Knabe jumped to the Federal League for the princely sum of $10,000 a season to become player-manager for the Baltimore Terrapins. The story was featured prominently in the press as it was considered a real coup for the new league to acquire Knabe. There was also speculation that he would sign Phillies teammates Gavvy Cravath and Sherry Magee to lucrative contracts, but that never materialized. Knabe had mixed results in Baltimore, finishing third in 1914 with 84 wins, but losing a whopping 107 games in 1915, coming in eighth place. His tenure as manager of the Terrapins was cut short by the demise of the Federal League, and Knabe found himself back in Pittsburgh for another short stint with the Pirates. He was traded in July 1916 to the Cubs, where he finished out his last Major League season. Overall, Dutch was a tough and capable Major Leaguer over his career.

Teams:
Pittsburgh Pirates NL (1905, 1916)
Philadelphia Phillies NL (1907–1913)
Baltimore Terrapins FL (player-manager: 1914–1915)
Chicago Cubs NL (1916)

Born:
June 12, 1884
Carrick, PA
Died:
May 17, 1961
Philadelphia, PA
▷ Batted: RH
▷ Threw: RH
▷ Position: 2B
▷ Career BA: .247
▷ Managerial Record: 131–177

Nap Lajoie

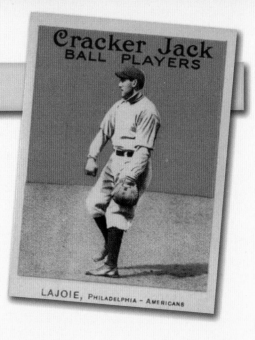

LAJOIE, PHILADELPHIA - AMERICANS

Napoleon Lajoie

Leaving Nap "Larry" Lajoie off the Cracker Jack All-Star Team may seem ludicrous. After all, how many players get teams named after them? Nap Lajoie was a truly great ballplayer. There is no debate there. As a matter of fact, he was once walked intentionally—*with the bases loaded*. It is said that he could hit so hard that it actually tore the cover right off the ball on a few occasions. In 1901, Nap batted an amazing .426 with 232 hits. During his 21 seasons in the majors, he batted over .300 sixteen times.

Probably the greatest and most controversial batting race in history took place in 1910 between Nap Lajoie and Ty Cobb. The race was tight, but Cobb had the advantage. Lajoie would need a hit in every at-bat in his final game of the season to win. The Naps faced the St. Louis Browns that historic day. The Browns disliked Cobb so much that they helped Lajoie by playing their third baseman in shallow left field, even though Lajoie was laying down bunts. Lajoie went 8-for-8, securing the title with the aid of the opposing team. A week later, Ban Johnson, the American League president, declared Cobb the winner by a .000860 margin. By his figures, Lajoie finished at .384 to Cobb's .385 BA. However, both Cobb and Lajoie were awarded a new Chalmers automobile as they were essentially tied. The 1910 contest is still controversial to this day, with some sources showing Cobb the winner, and some showing Lajoie as batting champ.

Defensively Lajoie was stellar at second base, leading the league in assists three times, putouts five times, and fielding percentage seven times. When he was traded to the Cleveland Bronchos in 1902, the team was so ecstatic that they renamed themselves the Naps at the end of the season. Lajoie was part of the second class elected to the Hall of Fame and lived to the ripe old age of 89. With a .338 lifetime batting average, over 3,200 hits, three uncontested batting titles, a Triple Crown, as well as solid defensive play, Nap Lajoie could be considered one of the three or four greatest second basemen of all time.

Teams:
Philadelphia Phillies NL (1896–1900)
Philadelphia Athletics AL (1901–1902, 1915–1916)
Cleveland Bronchos/Naps AL (1902–1914; player-manager: 1905–1909)

Born:
September 5, 1874
Woonsocket, RI
Died:
February 7, 1959
Daytona Beach, FL
▷ Batted: RH
▷ Threw: RH
▷ Position: 2B
▷ Career BA: .338
▷ Managerial Record: 377–309

Frank LaPorte

Danny Murphy

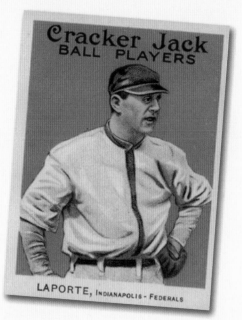

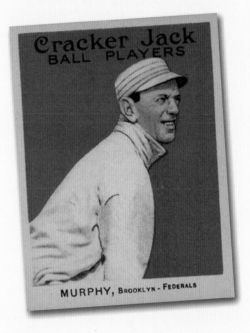

A capable ballplayer, Frank LaPorte never really lived up to the expectations of the scouts. He was pegged as a future top-tier player while with the Buffalo Bisons under manager George Stallings, where he posted a .331 batting average in 1905. As a rookie, he did not disappoint, batting .400 in his first 40 Major League at-bats with the Highlanders. LaPorte turned out to be a decent second baseman who was valued more for his hitting than his fielding. He had some solid seasons with his best being in 1911 when he batted .314 for the St. Louis Browns. After jumping to the Federal League, LaPorte had another fine season as team captain of the Indianapolis Hoosiers when he batted .311, posted a league-leading 107 RBI, and led his team to the pennant in 1914.

One of the knocks on LaPorte was that he would take himself out of the lineup for even the slightest of injuries. He just would not play unless he was 100% healthy. Evidently he did not have much of a personality either, as some managers and teammates referred to him as quiet or boring. Between his work ethic and his personality, LaPorte was not a good fit with most teams and as a result was

traded regularly. As a fielder LaPorte was fairly consistent. He was primarily a starter for most of his career, but there were occasions where he was relegated to a utility role. After the 1915 season, LaPorte moved back to Ohio where he took up farming and later worked as a foreman for a tool company, both professions more suited to his quiet personality than baseball.

Frank Breyfogle LaPorte

Teams:

New York Highlanders AL (1905–1907, 1908–1910)
Boston Red Sox AL (1908)
St. Louis Browns AL (1911–1912)
Washington Senators AL (1912–1913)
Indianapolis Hoosiers FL (1914)
Newark Peppers FL (1915)

Danny Murphy was both a very good second baseman as well as outfielder. We include him with our second sackers because he played the better part of his career at that position. Considered a power hitter, Murphy had some very good offensive years. On August 25, 1910, he hit for the cycle, an extremely difficult feat for that era, and in 1911 he batted a lofty .329 with 167 hits. That year Murphy played the outfield position and led the league in assists.

Prior to his lengthy A's career, Danny spent two Major League seasons playing for the Giants in the National League. Murphy's contract was purchased by Connie Mack and he made his debut for the A's on July 8, 1902, going 6-for-6 with a home run. Not a bad start. Mack had nullified Hall of Famer Nap Lajoie's contract and replaced him at second base with Murphy. Pretty big shoes to fill. Ironically, in 1908, the 31-year-old Murphy was moved from second to outfield to make room for another Hall of Famer, the young Eddie Collins.

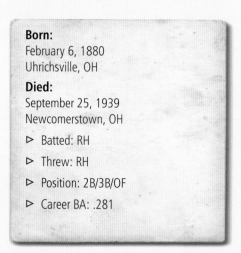

Born:
February 6, 1880
Uhrichsville, OH

Died:
September 25, 1939
Newcomerstown, OH

▷ Batted: RH

▷ Threw: RH

▷ Position: 2B/3B/OF

▷ Career BA: .281

Daniel Francis Murphy

Murphy was named captain of the team, graciously accepted his move to the outfield, and mentored young Collins.

He developed into a skilled outfielder and his .977 and .974 fielding percentage in 1909 and 1910 were good for second in the league. Unfortunately in 1912 Murphy suffered a serious knee injury which hampered him defensively, although he continued to flourish with his bat. He finished his career in the Federal League and went on to manage and coach in both the majors and minors. Murphy played on two World Series Champion teams (1910, 1911) as well as two pennant winners (1902, 1905). Danny Murphy was one of those ballplayers who did his job every day with no fanfare and was a credit to the game.

Teams:

New York Giants NL (1900–1901)
Philadelphia Athletics AL (1902–1913)
Brooklyn Tip-Tops FL (1914–1915)

Born:
August 11, 1876
Philadelphia, PA

Died:
November 22, 1955
Jersey City, NJ

▷ Batted: RH

▷ Threw: RH

▷ Position: 2B/OF

▷ Career BA: .289

Bert Niehoff

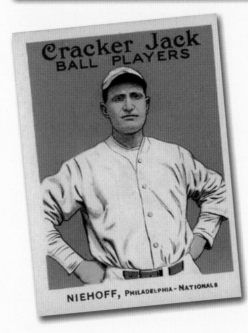

Cracker Jack BALL PLAYERS

NIEHOFF, Philadelphia - Nationals

Bert Niehoff had the classic good glove no bat. The contributions that he made to the game actually came after his playing days were over. Niehoff toiled in the minors for six seasons before finally making it to the Bigs at age 29. As a player he anchored second base for the Reds, Phillies, Cards and Giants. His most productive season was 1916, when he batted .243 and led the league in doubles. Niehoff was also the starting second baseman for the 1915 pennant-winning Phillies. A broken leg in 1918 forced his premature retirement after which he managed 24 seasons in the minors compiling a 1,824–1,713 record between 1922 and 1954. Fifteen of those seasons were spent in the Southern Association where he won two league championships.

Teams:

Cincinnati Reds NL (1913–1914)
Philadelphia Phillies NL (1915–1917)
St. Louis Cardinals NL (1918)
New York Giants NL (1918)

As manager of the Chattanooga Lookouts, Niehoff made a decision on April 1, 1931, that set off a firestorm in the press. An exhibition game was scheduled against the Yankees' juggernaut including Babe Ruth and Lou Gehrig. The Lookouts had signed a 17-year-old pitching phenom who happened to be a girl. Her name was Jackie Mitchell. Legend has it that Niehoff brought Mitchell into the game around the third or fourth inning and she proceeded to strike out both "The Bambino" as well as "Larrupin' Lou." Jackie threw a steady diet of curveballs to the two sluggers that they just were not able to hit. Word spread like wildfire and it was all the result of Bert Niehoff's decision to make the game interesting.

During the war, Niehoff managed the South Bend Blue Sox in the All-American Girls Professional Baseball League in 1943 and 1944 before returning to manage in the minors for six more seasons. He later coached for the Giants and was a Major League scout until 1969. Bert Niehoff passed away in 1974 at the age of 90.

John Albert Niehoff

Born:
May 13, 1884
Louisville, CO

Died:
December 8, 1974
Inglewood, CA

▷ Batted: RH

▷ Threw: RH

▷ Position: 2B/3B

▷ Career BA: .240

Del Pratt

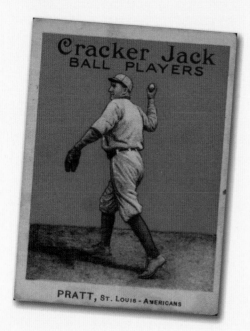

PRATT, ST. LOUIS - AMERICANS

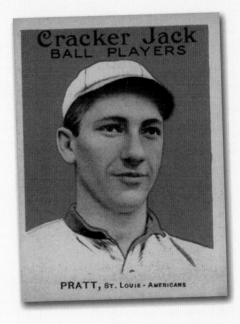

PRATT, ST. LOUIS - AMERICANS

In 13 big-league seasons, Del Pratt never got as much as a whiff of the postseason. He spent his first six years in that baseball purgatory known as the St. Louis Browns. Between 1912 and 1917, Pratt's Brownies were perennial losers. Even the legendary Branch Rickey couldn't help. Rickey managed the Browns from 1913 until 1915, but never climbed higher than fifth place.

Despite his team's woes, Pratt broke into baseball with a bang. He led the American League in games played four of his first five years, and approached or surpassed 170 hits and 30 doubles in that same time frame. He also played in 360 consecutive games between 1914 and 1917. Pratt was often a victim of bad timing. He joined the Yankees in 1918, just before their domination of baseball would begin. He moved to the Red Sox in 1921, just after their domination of baseball had ended. Pratt's final two teams may have been his best. The Tigers, managed by Ty Cobb, finished second and third, respectively, in 1923 and 1924. Pratt had a solid career batting average of .292 and led the American League in RBI with 103 in 1916.

Before turning to baseball, Pratt played football for the University of Alabama and was rumored to be a coaching candidate for the team on more than one occasion. His gridiron grit carried over to baseball in some notorious umpire brush ups, clubhouse arguments and manager battles. After his Major League career, Pratt managed in the Texas League for nine seasons. Del Pratt was elected into the Alabama Sports Hall of Fame in 1972 and was universally recognized as one of the top second sackers of his era.

Derrill Burnham Pratt

Born:
January 10, 1888
Walhalia, SC

Died:
September 30, 1977
Texas City, TX

▷ Batted: RH

▷ Threw: RH

▷ Position: 2B/1B

▷ Career BA: .292

Teams:
St. Louis Browns AL (1912–1917)
New York Yankees AL (1918–1920)
Boston Red Sox AL (1921–1922)
Detroit Tigers AL (1923–1924)

Rollie Zeider

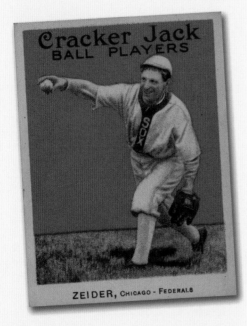

ZEIDER, CHICAGO - FEDERALS

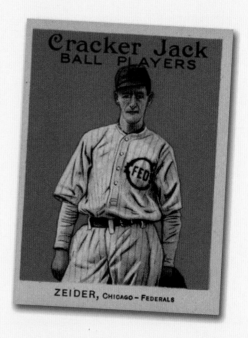

ZEIDER, CHICAGO - FEDERALS

Born in Auburn, Indiana, in 1883, Rollie Hubert Zeider packed a bunch of really cool baseball lore into a fair to middling nine-year career. In his rookie season of 1910, Zeider hit just .217 with no home runs, but the 5-foot, 10-inch, 162-pound White Sox second baseman put the wind in the Windy City. The cyclone-fast Zeider set the rookie record for stolen bases with 49 swipes. His Major League mark would stand until 1986 when it was shattered by John Cangelosi, another South Side speedster and White Sox outfielder. Cangelosi would steal 50 bases that year ending Zeider's small slice of immortality. Zeider finished in the top 10 in steals three different times in his career. He was also among the league leaders in errors on three occasions, but was widely recognized for his uncommon range in the field.

Zeider's most famous nickname is "Bunions," a moniker that essentially came from a disease. Legend has it that Zeider was on the receiving end of a patented Ty Cobb spiking that severed a bunion. The infection resulted in a case of blood poisoning, hence, a rather painful and somewhat disgusting nickname. Zeider also holds the distinction of playing for a Chicago franchise three different times in three different leagues: the White Sox in the American League, the Chi-Feds/Whales in the Federal League, and the Cubs in the National League. Zeider's overall career is hardly noteworthy, but some fun factoids make him one of our favorite players in the collection.

Rollie Hubert Zeider

Teams:
Chicago White Sox AL (1910–1913)
New York Yankees AL (1913)
Chicago Chi-Feds/Whales FL (1914–1915)
Chicago Cubs NL (1916–1918)

Born:
November 16, 1883
Auburn, IN
Died:
September 12, 1967
Garrett, IN

▷ Batted: RH

▷ Threw: RH

▷ Position: 2B/3B/SS

▷ Career BA: .240

5

INFIELD CAPTAINS

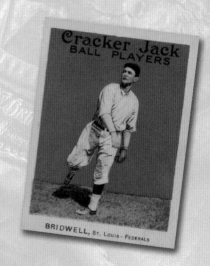

Typically the shortstop is the best athlete on the field. He usually has the strongest arm, the greatest range, and fields most of the grounders hit in a ball game. Although there have been some tremendous offensive shortstops throughout the annals of baseball history, some teams have sacrificed offensive output in return for good solid defense. Mark Belanger of the Baltimore Orioles and Ray Oyler of the Detroit Tigers, two outstanding shortstops during the 1960s and 1970s, come to mind. And of course, there is Mario Mendoza, a National League shortstop during the 1970s and 1980s, whose offensive ineptitude created the standard for determining just how bad a hitter a particular player is. The "Mendoza Line" is the threshold of a .200 batting average. When a player's average falls below .200, he is below the Mendoza Line. Mario batted both above and below his own line over his career. His .215 lifetime batting average barely keeps him from falling into the abyss. We have a mixed bag with this group in the Cracker Jack Collection. There are some great ones and some that hovered around the Mendoza Line. Of course, Honus Wagner has already been mentioned in the All-Star chapter. Putting him aside, we would like you to meet the infield captains of the Cracker Jack Collection.

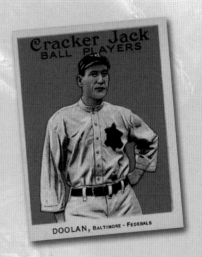

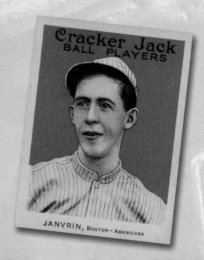

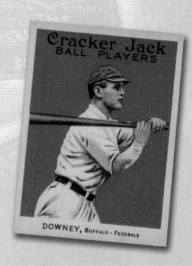

Jack Barry

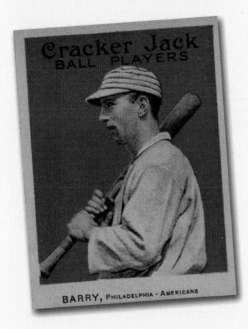

"Black Jack" Barry played on six pennant-winning teams as well as five World Series Champions. Not bad for a guy with a .243 lifetime batting average. As part of Connie Mack's $100,000 infield along with Eddie Collins, Stuffy McInnis and Home Run Baker, Barry was a dependable shortstop with great range and instincts.

Signed out of Holy Cross College, Barry never batted higher than .275 but was a valuable clutch hitter, with all of the tools to be a leader on the field and in the clubhouse. On September 20, 1909, in a heated pennant race with the Detroit Tigers, Barry was spiked by Ty Cobb, who was known to come into the bag with reckless abandon, not caring who he took out in the process. Needless to say, Barry was injured and lost to the team. Some say that was the reason why the Tigers won the pennant. Cobb evidently accomplished his mission.

Black Jack had some pretty good seasons thereafter, anchoring the A's in the leadership category. After the 1915 season, Barry was purchased by the Red Sox, and continued his winning ways playing on the 1915 and 1916 World Series Champs. He became player-manager of the 1917 team leading them to 90 wins. Barry left to serve in the military during WWI, missing the 1918 season, and retired early in 1919.

He went on to coach the Holy Cross Crusaders for the next 40 years with the highest winning percentage in collegiate history. Over a span of 39 seasons, he compiled a remarkable 616–150 record. His 1924 team went undefeated and the small college won the NCAA championship in 1952. Referred to as the "Knute Rockne" of college baseball, Jack Barry is a member of the American Baseball Coaches Association Hall of Fame.

John Joseph Barry

Born:
April 26, 1887
Meriden, CT

Died:
April 23, 1961
Shrewsbury, MA

▷ Batted: RH

▷ Threw: RH

▷ Position: SS/2B

▷ Career BA: .243

▷ Managerial Record: 90–62

Teams:
Philadelphia Athletics AL (1908–1915)
Boston Red Sox AL (1915–1916, 1919; player-manager: 1917)

Al Bridwell

A tough, hard-nosed shortstop, Al Bridwell was not afraid to mix it up once in a while. As a matter of fact, he once got into a pretty good scrap with his own manager, John McGraw. As the story goes, Bridwell punched McGraw in the nose, but was only suspended from play for a few games. In reality, McGraw actually respected Bridwell's tough style of play and wished he had more like him on the team. McGraw understood Bridwell's temperament and knew what buttons to push. Bridwell later acknowledged that McGraw was the best manager he ever had, because he knew how to handle the players to get the most out of them.

Bridwell was the catalyst for the famous "Merkle Boner" on September 23, 1908, stroking the single that started the controversial episode. Over a period of 11 years, he played for five different teams, and put together some fine seasons between 1908 and 1911 with good offensive numbers. In 1909 Bridwell batted .294 with 140 hits and a .386 on base percentage. Over his Major League career, he was involved in some pretty big trades. In 1907, Boston traded Bridwell,

Tom Needham and Fred Tenney to New York for Frank Bowerman, George Browne, Bill Dahlen, Cecil Ferguson and Dan McGann.

Defensively, Bridwell was adequate but certainly no Gold Glover. His true value could not be measured in batting average, OBP, or hits. Bridwell was one of the original "Dirt Dogs" in baseball history. He ended his Major League career playing for the St. Louis Terriers in the doomed Federal League. After the league folded, Bridwell, like many others, played and managed for a few seasons in the minors before hanging up the spikes. He went on to live a very long life and passed away at the ripe old age of 85.

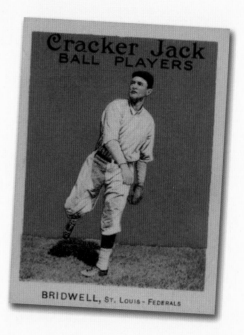

Albert Henry Bridwell

Teams:
Cincinnati Reds NL (1905)
Boston Beaneaters/Doves/Rustlers/Braves NL (1906–1907, 1911–1912)
New York Giants NL (1908–1911)
Chicago Cubs NL (1913)
St. Louis Terriers FL (1914–1915)

Born:
January 4, 1884
Friendship, OH

Died:
January 23, 1969
Portsmouth, OH

▷ Batted: LH

▷ Threw: RH

▷ Position: SS

▷ Career BA: .255

Donie Bush

Mickey Doolan

The epitome of a Major League ballplayer, Donie Bush was a very disciplined hitter with an amazing eye for the ball. Bush never hit for high averages, but was consistently involved in the offense. Whether it was a walk, sacrifice, or a key hit, Donie Bush always delivered. As a shortstop, few were better. Bush still holds the American League record for most putouts (425) and chances (969) in a season by a shortstop, and holds the Major League record for most triple plays with nine. He led the AL in assists five times. Bush was also a whiz on the base paths, snatching 406 stolen

bases over his great career. One of the most respected players in the game at the time, many a manager wished they had Bush to anchor their team.

After his playing days, he managed in the American Association and then moved up to manage the Pirates in the National League. Although loaded with talent, his 1927 Pirates were swept in the Series by the greatest team of all time, the "Murderers' Row" Yankees. That Pirates team featured the likes of Paul and Lloyd Waner, Kiki Cuyler, Pie Traynor and Joe Cronin, but they were still no match for the Yanks. Bush went on to manage the White Sox and the Reds, and later was both a manager and owner in the American Association.

While managing the 1938 Minneapolis Millers in the AA, Bush was very instrumental in mentoring a young player. That kid became known as "The Kid," Ted Williams, and became one of the greatest hitters of all time. Bush continued in baseball until his death in 1972 at 84 years old. Known as "Mr. Baseball" in his hometown, the city of Indianapolis renamed Victory Field to Bush Stadium in his honor. A truly remarkable player and executive, Donie Bush is one of the highlights of the Cracker Jack Collection.

As shortstops go during the Deadball Era, the slick-fielding Mickey "Doc" Doolan was right up there defensively with the best. Forget about his lifetime .230 batting average. Mickey was one of those players whose defense was his offense. As a matter of fact, his fielding was so good that he was in the running for MVP honors on a few occasions.

A student at Bucknell College and Villanova University, Doolan earned a degree in dentistry and actually had a dental practice in the offseason during his baseball career. His first love, however, was filling the hole at short. A league leader in several fielding categories, Doolan was, at one time or another, tops in putouts, fielding percentage, assists and double plays. His lifetime fielding percentage of .941 does not seem spectacular compared to some of the other shortstops of that era, but he made plays that few others could make, and was respected for his stellar defensive play.

There is really not much to discuss

Born:
October 8, 1887
Indianapolis, IN
Died:
March 28, 1972
Indianapolis, IN
▷ Batted: Switch
▷ Threw: RH
▷ Position: SS
▷ Career BA: .250
▷ Managerial Record: 497–539

Owen Joseph Bush

Teams:
Detroit Tigers AL (1908–1921)
Washington Senators AL (1921–1922; player-manager: 1923)
Pittsburgh Pirates NL (manager: 1927–1929)
Chicago White Sox AL (manager: 1930–1931)
Cincinnati Reds NL (manager: 1933)

Michael Joseph Doolan

Born: Michael Joseph Doolittle

about his hitting although he managed to bat .263 for Philadelphia in 1910. Doolan was team captain with the Phillies from 1909 to 1913 and was vice president of the Fraternity of Professional Baseball Players of America, the Major League players' union of the day. After making a quick stop to the Federal League, Doolan returned to the National League through 1918 and then played for Jack Dunn's Baltimore Orioles in the International League in 1919. After retiring as a player, Doolan coached for the Cubs and the Reds for several years before leaving the game in 1932. He then went into dentistry full time for 15 years and retired from that profession in 1947.

Teams:

Philadelphia Phillies NL (1905–1913)
Baltimore Terrapins FL (1914–1915)
Chicago Whales FL (1915)
Chicago Cubs NL (1916)
New York Giants NL (1916)
Brooklyn Robins NL (1918)

Born:
May 7, 1880
Ashland, PA

Died:
November 1, 1951
Orlando, FL

▷ Batted: RH

▷ Threw: RH

▷ Position: SS

▷ Career BA: .230

Tom Downey

Thomas Edward Downey

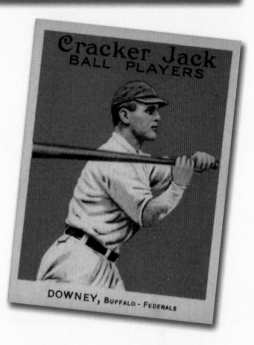

Although Tom Downey played several different infield positions, he is included with the shortstops because he had the most defensive chances at that position. Downey was an average to below-average fielder with mediocre range and a middling arm. The beginning of his career found him banging around the Connecticut State League from 1902 through 1905 playing for Meriden, New London and Bridgeport. Downey then moved up the Minor League ladder to the New York State League, the Tri-State League, and the Southern Association. There, while playing for Birmingham, Downey made a name for himself as a fleet-footed stolen base expert.

He finally made it to the big show with the Reds when he was 25 years old. Manager Clark Griffith put him in the lineup as starting shortstop, a position he held for most of his time with the Reds. As a hitter, he was average at best but did manage to bat .270 in 1910. His value to the teams he played for was his ability to fill in at any infield spot. Downey actually played quite a bit at both second and third base, and even had one chance at first base in his career.

After bouncing around with the A's as well as the Cubs, he went back to the minors to play for three teams in two different leagues during the 1913 season. Downey made the jump to the new Federal League in 1914 where he played two seasons for Buffalo. He had his best season defensively in 1914, leading the league with .962 fielding percentage, and stealing a career-high 35 bases. That year he also placed second in outs made, and fourth in assists. Downey played in the minors through 1919 and later scouted for the Dodgers in the 1940s and the Red Sox in the 1950s.

Born:
January 1, 1884
Lewiston, ME

Died:
August 3, 1961
Passaic, NJ

▷ Batted: RH

▷ Threw: RH

▷ Position: SS/2B/3B

▷ Career BA: .240

Teams:

Cincinnati Reds NL (1909–1911)
Philadelphia Phillies NL (1912)
Chicago Cubs NL (1912)
Buffalo Buffeds/Blues FL (1914–1915)

Hal Janvrin

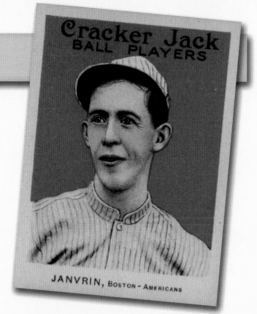

JANVRIN, BOSTON – AMERICANS

One of the most prolific athletes to come out the Boston school system, Hal Janvrin, never quite lived up to his expectations. Although he had value defensively at various infield positions, he was essentially a part-time player, often appearing late in a game for defensive purposes.

Sometimes referred to as the greatest schoolboy athlete in Massachusetts history, Janvrin excelled at baseball, football, track and hockey at Boston English High School, attracting large crowds to his games. The Red Sox brought Janvrin up right out of high school, which earned him the nickname of "Childe Harold." Unfortunately, fans expect big things of a local hero playing for the local pro team. Right out of the gate, Janvrin got off to a slow start and the fans got on him. After about 15 games, the Sox sent him down to the minors for some seasoning. Janvrin rejoined the team in 1913, and was lucky enough to play on the great Red Sox World Series Champs teams of 1915 and 1916.

We have him listed as a shortstop, although he could certainly be listed as a second baseman. One particular point of interest is that he had eight assists in one World Series game and set a record for

most at-bats (23) in a five-game Series. Offensively his most productive year was in 1914 when he batted .238 with 117 hits. Janvrin served as second lieutenant in the Army during WWI and was traded to the Senators upon his return. He bounced around the majors for a few years and played in the minors through 1924.

Janvrin then played and managed in Boston's Twilight League, coached for Harvard in the 1930s and scouted for the Indians in the 1950s. He owned a bowling alley, worked for the department of Civil Defense during WWII, and later worked for the Internal Revenue Service. Still a well-rounded athlete, Janvrin played semi-pro hockey in Boston after his baseball days. He was the grandfather of Dave Silk, who played on the 1980 United States gold medal hockey team and later played in the NHL.

Born:
August 27, 1892
Haverhill, MA
Died:
March 1, 1962
Boston, MA
▷ Batted: RH
▷ Threw: RH
▷ Position: SS/2B/1B
▷ Career BA: .232

Harold Chandler Janvrin

Teams:
Boston Red Sox AL (1911, 1913–1917)
Washington Senators AL (1919)
St. Louis Cardinals NL (1919–1921)
Brooklyn Robins NL (1921–1922)

Rabbit Maranville

The Hall of Fame career of Walter James Vincent "Rabbit" Maranville is not merely about statistics. His career batting average was an ordinary .258 and he slugged just .340. He slammed a scant 28 career home runs and hit over .300 just once. What Maranville did do, at a tireless pace, was show up to the ballpark every day and drive opponents crazy. He consistently approached or surpassed 150 games and led the league in plate appearances (746) and at-bats (672) with the Pirates in 1922. In two World Series, 1914 with the victorious Braves and 1928 with the losing Cardinals, Maranville batted .308.

Born:
November 11, 1891
Springfield, MA
Died:
January 5, 1954
New York, NY
▷ Batted: RH
▷ Threw: RH
▷ Position: SS/2B
▷ Career BA: .258
▷ Managerial Record: 23–30

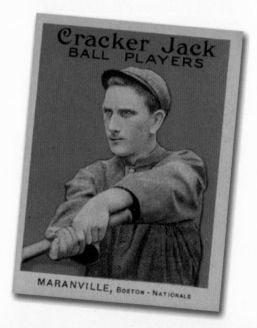

MARANVILLE, BOSTON – NATIONALS

Walter James Vincent Maranville

Now, about that nickname. If you check out any photo of Maranville, you would probably jump, or in this case, hop to the conclusion that the name Rabbit came from his rather large ears. Maranville related that the moniker actually came from a family friend describing his penchant for bounding and jumping about. With 2,605 career hits, Maranville was more than a diamond version of Peter Cottontail. In 1913, in his first game as the starting shortstop for the Braves, Maranville had three hits against Giants legend Christy Mathewson. Clutch hits were his specialty in leading Boston to a world title in 1914. For part of 1925, Maranville served as player-manager for the Cubs, posting a record of 23–30. In 1929, he returned to the Braves after an eight-year absence and, in 1929 and 1930, posted two of his best career batting averages, .284 and .281. He also continued to show up and drive opponents crazy, playing in over 140 games and registering close to or more than 600 plate appearances between 1929 and 1933.

Known for his battling style with umpires and opponents alike, Maranville retired after the 1935 season and managed in the minors through 1941. He taught the game to youngsters as director of baseball clinics sponsored by the *New York Journal-American* newspaper. Maranville died at the age of 62 in 1954, and was inducted into the Hall of Fame later that year. This Rabbit surely enjoyed a 24-"carrot" gold career.

Teams:
Boston Braves NL (1912–1920, 1929–1933, 1935)
Pittsburgh Pirates NL (1921–1924)
Chicago Cubs NL (player-manager: 1925)
Brooklyn Robins NL (1926)
St. Louis Cardinals NL (1927–1928)

Roger Peckinpaugh

Roger Thorpe Peckinpaugh

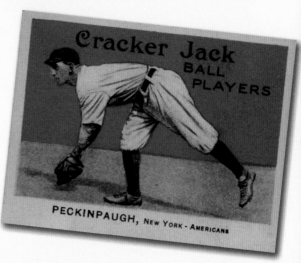

Considering that his career overlapped with Honus Wagner's for eight years, it would be a stretch to call Roger Peckinpaugh the best defensive shortstop of his generation. Still, his howitzer arm was widely deemed the best of the Deadball Era. Peckinpaugh played 17 seasons and had a respectable .259 career batting average. He was also an excellent baserunner with terrific speed. Of his 1,876 career hits, 331 were either doubles or triples. Peckinpaugh used his speed afield as well, leading the American League in assists as a shortstop four times.

As the ball came alive in baseball, so did Peckinpaugh's production. After 1920, he experienced a marked increase in home runs, RBI, and batting average. In 1925 at age 34, he won the American League MVP Award playing for Washington. That season, Peckinpaugh had 124 hits and batted .294 with 64 RBI and an OBP of .367. Ever the team player, Peckinpaugh was perennially among the league leaders in sacrifice bunts as well. In 1914, Yankee manager Frank Chance was so enamored with the 23-year-old Peckinpaugh's character that he named him team captain, and he became player-manager for the last 20 games of the season after Chance resigned.

Peckinpaugh spent nine seasons in New York. His last, 1921, saw the Yanks lose to the Giants in the World Series. Peckinpaugh would gain revenge over the Giants in 1924 as a member of the Senators. He hit .417 in the Series as Washington won the title in seven games.

Peckinpaugh was born in Wooster, Ohio, and attended East Tech High School in Cleveland. He broke into the Bigs in 1910 with the Cleveland Naps. Fittingly, when his playing career ended, Peckinpaugh returned to Cleveland as a manager and executive with the Indians. Peckinpaugh was a true Buckeye with one heck of an eye for the baseball.

Teams:
Cleveland Naps/Indians AL (1910, 1912–1913, manager: 1928–1933, 1941)
New York Yankees AL (1913–1921, player-manager: 1914)
Washington Senators AL (1922–1926)
Chicago White Sox AL (1927)

Born:
February 5, 1891
Wooster, OH

Died:
November 17, 1977
Cleveland, OH

▷ Batted: RH
▷ Threw: RH
▷ Position: SS
▷ Career BA: .259
▷ Managerial Record: 500–491

Joe Tinker

As part of the greatest double play combo of all time Joe Tinker, along with Johnny Evers and Frank Chance, led the Cubs to four World Series. A slightly above average hitter, Tinker made up for his offensive deficiencies with his slick-fielding play at shortstop. Considered one of the best, as shortstop Tinker led the league in assists three times, putouts two times, fielding percentage five times, and range factor four times. Interestingly enough, Tinker had an ongoing feud with his partner at second base, Johnny Evers, and as a result they did not speak to each other for 30 years.

Although he compiled a lifetime batting average of .262, Tinker was very skilled at bunting, delivering hit-and-run plays, and strategically placing hits. He was the catalyst in the one-game playoff against the Giants after the famous "Merkle" game in 1908. As a matter of fact, he was the one responsible for the lone run in the infamous game itself, hitting a home run off Christy Mathewson. Once that game was declared a tie, Tinker helped the Cubs take the subsequent playoff game when he hit a triple off Mathewson that triggered a four-run inning.

After the 1912 season, Johnny Evers was named manager of the Cubs and Tinker understandably wanted out. He was traded to the Reds where he played and managed for one season. Tinker then jumped to the new Federal League as player-manager of the Chicago Chi-Feds (later known as the Whales) and led his 1915 Whales to the Federal League pennant. After the league folded, the Cubs took him back as manager for the 1916 season. Tinker then owned

and managed teams in the American Association and the Florida State League. His business ventures included real estate development in Orlando, Florida, where the historic ballpark Tinker Field was named in his honor. He later scouted for the Cubs. Joe Tinker was elected to the Hall of Fame in 1946.

Born:
July 27, 1880
Muscotah, KS
Died:
July 27, 1948
Orlando, FL
▷ Batted: RH
▷ Threw: RH
▷ Position: SS
▷ Career BA: .262
▷ Managerial Record: 304–308

Joseph Bert Tinker

Teams:
Chicago Orphans/Cubs NL (1902–1912; player-manager: 1916)
Cincinnati Reds NL (player-manager: 1913)
Chicago Chi-Feds/Whales FL (player-manager: 1914–1915)

Baseball's Sad Lexicon
by Franklin Pierce Adams

These are the saddest of possible words:
"Tinker to Evers to Chance."
Trio of bear cubs, and fleeter than birds,
Tinker and Evers and Chance.
Ruthlessly pricking our gonfalon bubble,
Making a Giant hit into a double—
Words that are heavy with nothing but trouble:
"Tinker to Evers to Chance."

—Published July 10, 1910, in the *New York Evening Mail* newspaper.

Heinie Wagner

Although Heinie Wagner was not nearly as good as Honus Wagner at the shortstop position, he was a very steady performer on the baseball diamond. Playing for the Red Sox over the bulk of his career, Heinie Wagner anchored some exceptional teams. He was named captain of the 1912 World Series Championship team more for his leadership qualities than his playing abilities. Actually, it was Wagner's job to mentor the young Babe Ruth, and it is said he talked Ruth into staying on the team after he walked out in early July of 1918. Wagner also played on the 1915, 1916 and 1918 World Champs teams.

A steady influence at short, Wagner had a decent bat but his base stealing abilities were outstanding. His 141 steals place him fifth on the all-time stolen bases list for the Red Sox. Originally signed out of the New York State League by John McGraw's Giants, Wagner was released after only 17 games and played in the Eastern League until the Red Sox came

calling. Offensively his best year was in 1910 when he batted .273 and banged out 134 hits.

After his MLB days as a player, Wagner went on to manage in both the New England League and the Virginia League until he returned to coach on Bill Carrigan's Red Sox teams during the late 1920s. After they finished in last place for three seasons, Wagner took over the helm in 1930 and skippered the Red Sox to yet another last place finish, after which he retired. Heinie went into the lumber business, but stayed in the game by coaching club teams at the local level. The other Wagner left his mark as one of the greatest players of all time. Heinie Wagner left his mark as a great friend, teammate and leader to many.

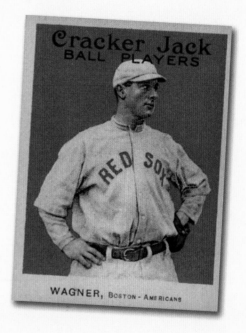

Charles F. Wagner

Teams:
New York Giants NL (1902)
Boston Americans/Red Sox AL (1906–1913, 1915–1916, 1918; manager: 1930)

Born:
September 23, 1880
New York, NY

Died:
March 20, 1943
New Rochelle, NY

▷ Batted: RH

▷ Threw: RH

▷ Position: SS/2B

▷ Career BA: .250

▷ Managerial Record: 52–102

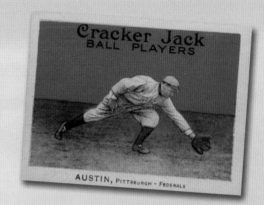

AUSTIN, PITTSBURGH - FEDERALS

6

THE HOT CORNER

A gun for an arm, great hand-eye coordination, and the ability to catch a line drive traveling at 130 mph are only a few of the talents required of a good third baseman. With this group of Cracker Jack players we have a mixed bag, with talent levels varying from great to mediocre. Unlike today, the third baseman of the Deadball Era was considered mostly a defensive player and was not required to have much power. A few from this group were outstanding both offensively and defensively. One was just plain offensive. The personalities of this group are fascinating. They range from unselfish team players who always put their team ahead of themselves, to one particularly selfish individual who cared only about the money he made. Several of these players were so dedicated to the game that they continued in baseball for their entire lives as managers, coaches, scouts or umpires. Meet the Cracker Jack third basemen guarding the Hot Corner.

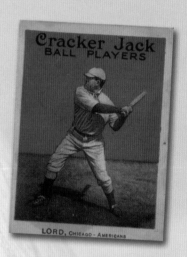

LORD, CHICAGO - AMERICANS

PERRING, KANSAS CITY - FEDERALS

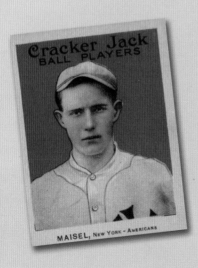

MAISEL, NEW YORK - AMERICANS

GROH, CINCINNATI NATIONALS

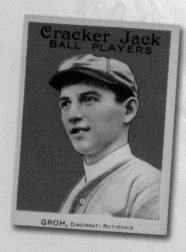

LOBERT, NEW YORK - NATIONALS

Jimmy Austin

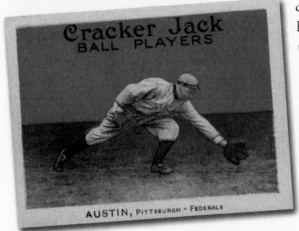

Born:
December 8, 1879
Swansea, Wales
Died:
March 6, 1965
Laguna Beach, CA

▷ Batted: Switch

▷ Threw: RH

▷ Position: 3B/SS

▷ Career BA: .246

▷ Managerial Record: 31–44

Teams:
New York Highlanders AL (1909–1910)
St. Louis Browns AL (1911–1923, 1925–1926, 1929; player-manager: 1913, 1918, 1923)

James Philip Austin

Born in Wales, the sport of rugby and a job as a machinist delayed Jimmy Austin's Major League baseball career until the age of 29, but he made up for lost time with a dogged determination that won the hearts of fans, teammates, and coaches alike. Austin played 18 seasons, the last 16 for the lowly St. Louis Browns. His statistics were hardly remarkable, but he played ball like every game was his last. Maybe it was his way of compensating for his late arrival to the big leagues. Austin played until the age of 49, although he only played in 46 games after the age of 40.

A third baseman with effective speed, Austin was a double-edged sword for his clubs. In 1911, he led the American League in both strikeouts and sacrifice bunts. Austin's Jekyll-and-Hyde nature carried over to the field where he led the league in errors three times, but also in assists and putouts two times each. Good or bad, you could never question Austin's effort. George Stallings, his manager with the New York Highlanders, gave Austin the nickname "Pepper" due to his non-stop nature. Constant movement and a bouncy, child-like demeanor characterized Jimmy Austin, who served as player-manager for the Browns for parts of 1913, 1918 and 1923.

He remained with the Browns as a coach through 1932 but did play one game only in 1925, 1926 and 1929 before retiring as a player at age 49. He then coached for the Chicago White Sox until 1940. In retirement, Austin took his leadership skills to another level, becoming mayor of Laguna Beach, California, making him one of the few Major Leaguers to make an improbable yet seamless move from the hot corner to the corner office.

Heinie Groh

One of the best third baseman of the Deadball Era, Heinie Groh was certainly given consideration for our Cracker Jack All-Stars Team. With a solid .292 lifetime batting average and very good defensive numbers, Groh led the National League in various categories over his 16-year big-league career. At one time or another, he was league leader in on-base percentage, runs, doubles, hits, and walks; and he was near the top in batting average on a couple occasions.

The diminutive 5-foot, 6-inch Groh had such small hands that he needed custom made bats to accommodate his small grip. The "bottle bat," featuring a thicker barrel and thinner handle than normal, was designed for Groh and he became a holy terror with the bat. Groh's best years were with the Reds where in 1918 he batted a lofty .320 and took over as manager at the end of the season when Christy Mathewson left to join Uncle Sam. He starred in the 1919 World Series against the infamous Black Sox, and in 1922 he had an outstanding Series against the Yanks, batting .474 in the five-game set. Groh also played on three other pennant-winning teams: the 1923 and 1924 Giants, and the 1927 Pirates.

There are not many third basemen in the history of the game that surpass Groh as a fielder, especially if you take into consideration the equipment and playing surfaces of his day. As a third baseman, Groh led the league in putouts three times and fielding percentage five times. After a knee injury in 1924, Groh essentially became a part-time player during his last three Major League seasons. He went on to manage in the minors and scouted for the Giants, Dodgers and the Phillies until 1953. The little guy with the big stick, Heinie Groh deserves another look by the Hall of Fame.

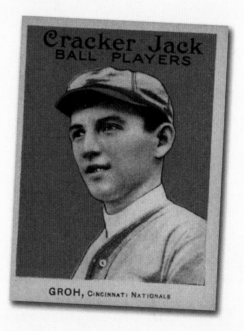

GROH, Cincinnati Nationals

Henry Knight Groh

Teams:

New York Giants NL (1912–1913, 1922–1926)

Cincinnati Reds NL (1913–1921, player-manager: 1918)

Pittsburgh Pirates NL (1927)

Born:
September 18, 1889
Rochester, NY

Died:
August 22, 1968
Cincinnati, OH

▷ Batted: RH

▷ Threw: RH

▷ Position: 3B/2B

▷ Career BA: .292

▷ Managerial Record: 7–3

Hans Lobert

Harry Lord   (1914)

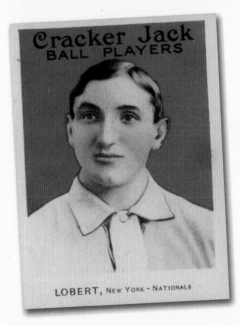

LOBERT, New York - Nationals

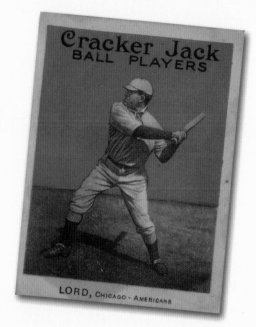

LORD, Chicago - Americans

Known for his offensive prowess as well as his blazing speed. Hans Lobert was considered one of the fastest players of the Deadball Era. Over his 14-year career he batted over .300 on four occasions, and stole 316 bases. Defensively, he was very good with a tremendous arm. As a third baseman, he led the league in putouts in 1911 and 1913; and in fielding percentage when he posted .974 in 1913.

Purely from the speed perspective,

legend has it that Lobert actually raced a thoroughbred before a game and also beat the legendary Jim Thorpe in a 100 yard dash. Dubbed "Hans Number 2" during his rookie year with the Pirates by teammate Honus Wagner ("Hans Number 1"), Lobert did not last long with the Pirates, but the nickname stayed with him for life. His best days were with the A's, although he did have some successful campaigns with the Reds. By the time he reached the Giants his better playing days were behind him. Plagued by a knee injury, his last two years as a player were not productive.

After he retired, Lobert had eight good seasons at the U.S. Military Academy at West Point as baseball coach, followed by management stints in the Eastern League and the International League. He returned to the Bigs to manage the Phillies for two games in 1938 going 0–2, and had one full, but dismal, season managing them in 1942, posting a 42–109 record. Lobert went on to spend many years in professional baseball serving as a scout for the Giants right up until his death at the age of 86.

At age 25, Bates College graduate Harry Lord was brought up from the minors by the Boston Americans to replace the great Jimmy Collins at third base. With big shoes to fill, Lord proved himself to be fiercely competitive and practically immovable at third, never giving way on the basepaths, not even to the spikes-high approach of Ty Cobb. After four good years with the Red Sox, where he batted .315 in 1909 and stole 36 bases, Lord was traded to the Chicago White Sox where his leadership skills earned him the title of team captain. Known for his hustle, Lord was timed in 1910 covering the distance from home to first in just 3.4 seconds. While with Chicago in 1911, he batted .321 and stole 43 bases.

Although a strong contributor, Lord was released by the White Sox in 1914 due to a salary dispute with their notoriously stingy owner, Charles Comiskey. He jumped to the Buffalo Blues in the new Federal League and was named player-manager within his

---

Born:
October 18, 1881
Wilmington, DE

Died:
September 14, 1968
Philadelphia, PA

▷ Batted: RH

▷ Threw: RH

▷ Position: 3B/SS

▷ Career BA: .274

▷ Managerial Record: 42–111

John Bernard Lobert

Teams:

Pittsburgh Pirates NL (1903)

Chicago Cubs NL (1905)

Cincinnati Reds NL (1906–1910)

Philadelphia Phillies NL (1911–1914; manager: 1938, 1942)

New York Giants NL (1915–1917)

Harry Donald Lord

first few weeks with the team. After the league folded, Lord played and managed in the minors for two years, and coached at Bates College. He was later involved in business ventures in Portland, Maine, including a grocery business and a coal company, but stayed active in baseball as player-manager at the semi-pro level. Lord always regretted leaving the White Sox as he believed he could have squashed the 1919 Black Sox scandal before it happened with his leadership and tenacity.

Teams:

Boston Americans/Red Sox AL (1907–1910)
Chicago White Sox AL (1910–1914)
Buffalo Blues FL (player-manager: 1915)

Born:
March 8, 1882
Porter, ME

Died:
August 9, 1948
Westbrook, ME

▷ Batted: LH

▷ Threw: RH

▷ Position: 3B

▷ Career BA: .278

▷ Managerial Record: 60–49

Fritz Maisel

Frederick Charles Maisel

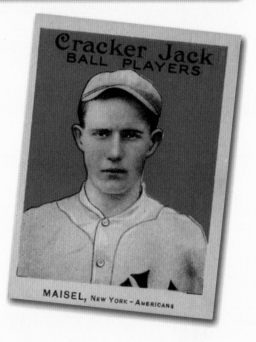

MAISEL, New York - Americans

To say that baseball was a family affair for the Maisel clan would be an understatement. In addition to Fritz, who played six seasons in the majors with the Yankees and Browns, the family also featured big leaguers George Maisel (Fritz's younger brother) and Charlie Maisel (Fritz's cousin). Unfortunately, short-lived Major League careers were prevalent in the Maisel family. George played just four seasons and had a career average of .282. Cousin Charlie played just one game with the Baltimore Terrapins of the Federal League. He had four at-bats with no hits. You could say that Fritz was the family jewel. While his career batting average was some 40 points lower than brother George, Maisel did lead the American League with 74 steals in 1914. He also scored 78 runs and had 23 doubles that season. On the flip side, he led the league in errors at third base. Maisel's 74 steals stood as the Yankees' team record until Rickey Henderson smashed the mark with 80 steals in 1985.

Nicknamed "Flash," Fritz Maisel made his living with his legs, stealing home 14 times during his career. In 1915, he stole 51 bases and scored 77 runs with a career high .281 batting average. A versatile player who also spent time at second base and the outfield, Maisel broke his collarbone in 1916 and never

truly recovered. He was traded to St. Louis in January of 1918 and played his final MLB season with the Browns. However, the story does not end there. Maisel returned to the Baltimore Orioles of the International League as a player through 1928, batting .310 over his 12 total seasons with them. He managed the International League Orioles from 1929 through 1932, and later scouted for the American League Orioles from 1954 until his death in 1967. Maisel was elected to the International League Hall of Fame in 1959.

Born:
December 23, 1889
Catonsville, MD

Died:
April 22, 1967
Baltimore, MD

▷ Batted: RH

▷ Threw: RH

▷ Position: 3B/2B/OF

▷ Career BA: .242

Teams:

New York Yankees AL (1913–1917)
St. Louis Browns AL (1918)

George Moriarty

George Perring

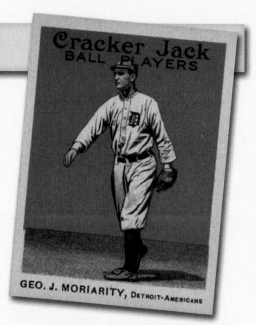

GEO. J. MORIARITY, DETROIT-AMERICANS

One of the most colorful characters in the annals of baseball history, George "The Man Who Won't Die on Third" Moriarty did it all. A solid ballplayer, manager, respected umpire, newspaper columnist, poet and songwriter, Moriarty was a popular individual over his four decades in baseball. As a player, he was a demon on the basepaths, swiping 251 bases over his career, and stealing home 11 times. Used as a utility player early on, he excelled as a third baseman due to his strong arm and accuracy. As captain of the Tigers from 1911 through 1915, Moriarty was acting manager for Hughie Jennings on several occasions.

After his playing days, he went on to umpire in the big leagues for 22 years, participating in five World Series as well as the 1934 All-Star Game. A respected no-nonsense umpire, Moriarty stood his ground with players and managers. Known as a brawler as a player, he continued the brawling as umpire. In 1932, at age 47, Moriarty fought four White Sox players at the same time for taking exception to his calls. He is famous for ejecting three Cubs players from Game 3 of the 1935 World Series for heckling

Detroit star Hank Greenberg with anti-Semitic remarks. Moriarty took a two-year break in umpiring to manage the Tigers in 1927 and 1928, and later scouted for the Tigers in the 1940s and 1950s.

Known for his hot temper and brawling, Moriarty had a softer side off the field. He wrote poetry and columns for several newspapers and actually penned the lyrics to three popular songs written by famous songwriter Richard Whiting. Not bad considering he never finished grammar school. Considered one of the best umpires of the era, George Moriarty was truly loved and respected until his death in 1964. Interestingly enough, his grandson, actor Michael Moriarty, starred in the 1973 baseball movie "Bang the Drum Slowly."

George Joseph Moriarty

Teams:

Chicago Cubs NL (1903–1904)
New York Highlanders AL (1906–1908)
Detroit Tigers AL (1909–1915; manager: 1927–1928)
Chicago White Sox AL (1916)

Born:
July 7, 1885
Chicago, IL
Died:
April 8, 1964
Miami, FL
▷ Batted: RH
▷ Threw: RH
▷ Position: 3B/1B/OF
▷ Career BA: .251
▷ Managerial Record: 150–157

Born:
August 13, 1884
Sharon, WI
Died:
August 20, 1960
Beloit, WI
▷ Batted: RH
▷ Threw: RH
▷ Position: 3B/1B/SS
▷ Career BA: .248

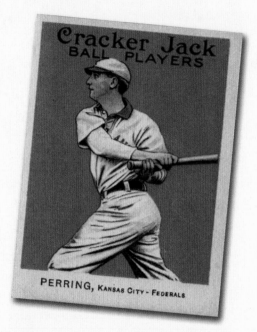

PERRING, KANSAS CITY - FEDERALS

The pride of the Beloit College Buccaneers, George Perring didn't do a heck of a lot in the majors. As the story goes, Perring honed his hurling ability by throwing crabapples at a hole in the barn door when he was a kid. Unfortunately he was weak offensively and as a part-time player for the Cleveland Naps batted only .220 over a span of three seasons. After an unproductive 1910 season, Perring was sent back to the minors where played for

George Wilson Perring

the Columbus Senators in the American Association through the 1913 season. He resurfaced in 1914 playing for the Kansas City Packers of the new Federal League. Perring actually became the starting third baseman for the Packers, which is a good indication of the talent level that existed in the newly formed league. He also played some first base and shortstop, which added to his value in the majors.

The Federal League years were the apex of Perring's career. Over two seasons he hit .268 with nine home runs and a .375 slugging percentage. In 1915 he was second in the league in assists with 226 and his .958 fielding percentage was good for third in the league. After the demise of the Federal League, Perring went back to the minors for a couple of seasons until he finally hung up his spikes in 1919. He returned to Beloit, where he played and managed at the semi-pro level, and made a name for himself by winning the Wisconsin State Senior Golf Championship four times. A respected civic leader and insurance underwriter, Perring was inducted into the Beloit College Hall of Fame in 1960.

Teams:

Cleveland Naps AL (1908–1910)
Kansas City Packers FL (1914–1915)

Heinie Zimmerman

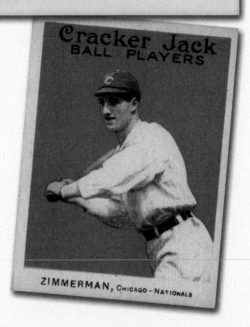

Heinie Zimmerman could have gone down in baseball annals as one of the great third baseman, one that certainly could have been considered for entrance into the Hall of Fame. Instead, he represents everything that a player should not be. "The Great Zim," as he was known during his days as an impact player, eventually wasted what could have been a truly great career.

In 1912, Zimmerman took over as starting third baseman for the Cubs after the sudden death of Jimmy Doyle from appendicitis. That proved to be a watershed year for Zim as he led the league with his .372 batting average, 207 hits, .571 slugging percentage, 14 home runs, and in several other categories. Although he had a total of three .300 seasons, and played on the 1907 and 1908 World Series Championship teams, Zimmerman was always surrounded by controversy. The suspicion that he threw games and took bribes saddled him for his entire career, until he was finally banned for life in 1921 by the Commissioner of Baseball, Judge Kenesaw Mountain Landis.

There are many examples of indiscretion on the part of Zimmerman, including purposely muffing a rundown in the decisive game of the 1917 World Series, although some take issue with that allegation. Then, there is the fact that he batted .120 in that same Series. Zimmerman was also indirectly implicated in the 1919 Black Sox Scandal. The fatal flaw that contributed to his final demise was that Zimmerman had a problem holding onto money. He was always broke because of his penchant for spending money on extravagant things. His association with the likes of

Henry Zimmerman

Hal Chase during his playing days and notorious gangster Dutch Schultz outside of the lines did not help his reputation either. All in all "The Great Zim" turned out to be a major black eye for the game. He later operated a mob-connected speakeasy, and worked as a plumber and steamfitter.

Teams:

Chicago Cubs NL (1907–1916)
New York Giants NL (1916–1919)

Born:
February 9, 1887
New York, NY

Died:
March 14, 1969
New York, NY

▷ Batted: RH
▷ Threw: RH
▷ Position: 3B/2B/SS
▷ Career BA: .295

BECKER, Philadelphia - Nationals

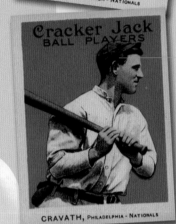

CAREY, Pittsburgh - Nationals

7

PATROLLING THE OUTFIELD

This is a very interesting and diverse group of ballplayers. The talent level of the Cracker Jack outfielders goes from mediocre to great, and the personalities go from congenial to downright nasty. Including two of the three players chosen for our all star team (Cobb and Speaker) there are a total of seven Hall of Famers in this group, and another few that should certainly be considered. We also have a Circus, a Wildfire and a Deerfoot along with a Doc. There are power hitters and singles hitters. We have very good glove men and others who had rifles for arms. In any event, these are the Cracker Jack players who spent their time patrolling the outfield.

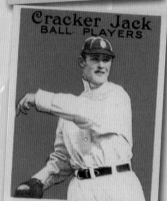

CRAVATH, Philadelphia - Nationals

CRAWFORD, Detroit - Americans

WHITTED, Philadelphia - Nationals

WHEAT, Brooklyn - Nationals

VEACH, Detroit - Americans

ROUSCH, Indianapolis - Federals

ARTIE HOFFMAN, Brooklyn - Federals

Beals Becker

Bob Bescher

Considered a power hitter during the Deadball Era, southpaw Beals Becker broke into the majors at age 21 after five seasons in the minors. A three-sport star in school, Becker excelled in football, basketball and certainly baseball. He was honored for his achievements in 1903 with the Wentworth Champion Athlete Award.

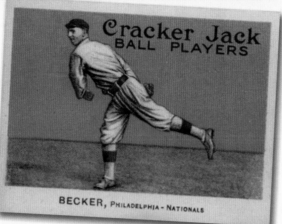

BECKER, PHILADELPHIA - NATIONALS

As a Major Leaguer, Becker played for five different teams over his eight-year career, mostly as a part-time player getting platooned against lefties. From an offensive standpoint, his best year was in 1914, when he batted a robust .325, led the league in singles, and went yard nine times. As a matter of fact, on June 9, 1913 Becker hit two inside–the–park homers against his former team, the Cincinnati Reds, just four days after being traded to the Phillies. He was in the top 10 in home runs on four different occasions, and played in three World Series: 1911 and 1912 for the Giants, and 1915 for the Phillies. An average fielder, Becker had a fairly good arm and was always a positive presence in the clubhouse. He was known to play better on the road than under the close scrutiny of the fans at home. Beals Becker was one of those players who added value to a team coming off the bench because he could do a little of everything.

Both as a schoolboy star at Wentworth Military Academy and as a pro, Becker always set the example as a consummate team player. After his Major League days Becker, like many others, went back to the Minor Leagues where he played for Kansas City in the American Association for seven seasons. He then spent 1924 and 1925 between three teams in the Pacific Coast League before retiring from the game. The only graduate to play in the Major Leagues, Becker was inducted into the Wentworth Military Academy Athletic Hall of Fame in 2000.

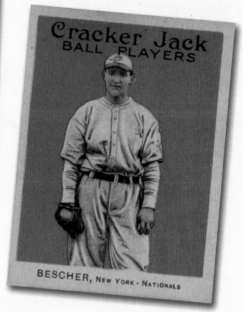

BESCHER, NEW YORK - NATIONALS

As a big-league base stealer, Bob Bescher was simply the best for several years. Known as the "Master of the Hook Slide" by some and "The London Flash" by others, Bescher led the National League in swipes four years in a row from 1909 through 1912. His 81 steals in 1911 stood as the National League record until 1962 and is still the single-season record for the Cincinnati Reds.

By way of the University of Notre Dame and Wittenberg College, Bescher developed his tremendous athletic skills more as a football player than as a baseball player. Actually, as a football player, Bescher was considered one of the greatest to ever come out of Wittenberg. He was so good that, during the baseball offseason, he played halfback under an assumed name for the professional football Dayton Oakwoods. As a baseball player, he maneuvered through the minors fairly quickly to make his debut with the Cincinnati Reds in 1908. Offensively, Bescher's best year was in 1912 when he

---

Born:
July 5, 1886
El Dorado, KS
Died:
August 19, 1943
Huntington Park, CA
▷ Batted: LH
▷ Threw: LH
▷ Position: OF
▷ Career BA: .276

David Beals Becker

Teams:
Pittsburgh Pirates NL (1908)
Boston Doves NL (1908–1909)
New York Giants NL (1910–1912)
Cincinnati Reds NL (1913)
Philadelphia Phillies NL (1913–1915)

Robert Henry Bescher

batted .281 and had a league-leading 120 runs scored. With a keen eye for the ball, Bescher also led the league in walks in 1913. As an outfielder, Bob Bescher could effortlessly track down fly balls and had a strong arm.

Once referred to as the "King of the Base Stealers" by *Baseball Magazine*, Bescher was traded down to the minors as his career declined, but he came back up to finish his Major League career in 1918 with Cleveland. He then competed in the minors for seven more years until he was well into his forties. After retirement, Bescher worked as an oil inspector, but also gained the reputation as a proficient brewmaster during prohibition. Tragically "The London Flash" lost his life in a flash when his car was hit head-on by an oncoming train in 1942.

Teams:
Cincinnati Reds NL (1908–1913)
New York Giants NL (1914)
St. Louis Cardinals NL (1915–1917)
Cleveland Indians AL (1918)

Born:
February 25, 1884
London, OH

Died:
November 29, 1942
London, OH

▷ Batted: Switch

▷ Threw: LH

▷ Position: OF

▷ Career BA: .258

Joe Birmingham

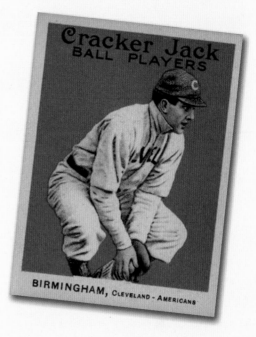

Joseph Leo Birmingham

We had a bit of a dilemma when it came to categorizing Joe "Dode" Birmingham in this book. Should we list him as an outfielder or a manager? His playing career ended in 1914 yet he managed in 1915. Should he be listed with the front-office decision makers as he was in fact a player-manager beginning in 1912? We decided to break our own rules and list him as an outfielder because he only managed for 28 games in 1915, and quite frankly he was a much better baseball player than manager. It would not have been fair to list Dode in with the decision makers, because he was not a very good one.

However, as a player Joe Birmingham wasn't half bad. A decent situational hitter with a rocket for an arm, he played his entire career with the Naps and batted .304 in 1911. He was second in the league in assists in 1907 and 1908, but was also second in the league in errors in 1907. Birmingham had the good fortune at one time or another to share outfield duties with Joe Jackson and future Hall of Famer Elmer Flick. At the young age of 27, he was named player-manager of the Naps and promptly proceeded down the path of mediocrity as a skipper.

Birmingham was finally put out of his managerial misery in May of 1915 after getting off to a 12–16 start. He then played and managed in the minors from 1916 until he retired from baseball in 1921 when he was 36 years old. He eventually wound up in Mexico and lived out his days there. Outfielder or manager? The bottom line is that Joe Birmingham got to play Major League baseball for nine years and not many people can say that.

Team:
Cleveland Naps AL (1906–1911; player-manager: 1912–1914; manager: 1915)

Born:
December 3, 1884
Elmira, NY

Died:
April 24, 1946
Tampico, Mexico

▷ Batted: RH

▷ Threw: RH

▷ Position: OF

▷ Career BA: .253

▷ Managerial Record: 170–191

Ping Bodie

His real name was Francesco Stephano Pezzolo, or was it Franceto Sanguenitta Pizzola? While historians have argued about Ping Bodie's name, no one can debate his consistency. During his nine-year career as an outfielder with the White Sox, Athletics, and Yankees, you could most often pencil Bodie in for 60 to 80 RBI, 5 to 10 home runs, 20 to 30 doubles, and a .270 to .290 batting average. One of the first Italian-Americans to make the big leagues, Bodie got the nickname Ping from the sound the ball made careening from his 52-ounce bat. That sound was made most often in 1917 when he had 162 hits, 74 RBI and a .291 batting average.

Legend has it that he took the name Bodie from a California town where he lived as a boy. As a star in the Pacific Coast League, he hit 30 home runs in 1910 for the San Francisco Seals, and batted .308 over his 15 seasons in the minors. In the Major Leagues, Bodie had a couple of nice seasons, but his numbers never quite lived up to his own braggadocio. Yes, old Francesco was never shy about trumpeting his own accomplishments and abilities. He was

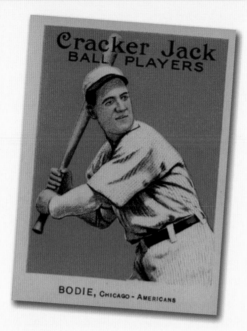

BODIE, Chicago - Americans

a fitting roommate for the equally brash Babe Ruth when the two were Yankees teammates in 1920 and 1921.

Bodie never got to see the Yanks win it all, as his career ended after the team's 1921 World Series loss to the Giants, but he certainly left his mark in the Yankees' clubhouse. One of the game's true characters, he was known for pranks such as putting live ducks in the team photographer's hotel room and engaging in a pasta-eating contest with an ostrich. Bodie did eventually find his way to show business, working as an electrician and bit actor at Universal Studios in Hollywood.

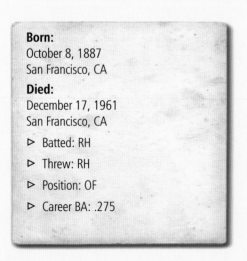

Born:
October 8, 1887
San Francisco, CA

Died:
December 17, 1961
San Francisco, CA

▷ Batted: RH
▷ Threw: RH
▷ Position: OF
▷ Career BA: .275

Frank Stephen Bodie

Born: Francesco Stephano Pezzolo

Teams:
Chicago White Sox AL (1911–1914)
Philadelphia Athletics AL (1917)
New York Yankees AL (1918–1921)

Vin Campbell

The career of Vin Campbell is a bit of a head scratcher. Here's a guy that had only a short-lived career, even though he put up very good numbers on the field. The son of a prominent St. Louis family, Campbell was a graduate of Vanderbilt University. He came up to the majors for a brief stint with the Cubs in 1908. Awkward and green, Campbell blew his one at-bat, and ended up in the minors where he had a very good 1909 season playing outfield for Aberdeen of the Northwestern League.

Born:
January 30, 1888
St. Louis, MO

Died:
November 16, 1969
Towson, MD

▷ Batted: LH
▷ Threw: RH
▷ Position: OF
▷ Career BA: .310

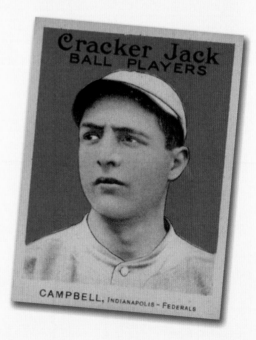

CAMPBELL, Indianapolis - Federals

Arthur Vincent Campbell

Pittsburgh manager Fred Clarke saw potential in Campbell with his ability to hit over .300 and his speed both on the basepaths and in the field. When he came up to the Pirates for the 1910 season, Campbell batted .326, which was a good indicator of his offensive skill given the fact that he had 282 at-bats that season. In 1911, coming off the bench, Campbell batted .312 as a part-time player. The following year, the Braves acquired Campbell for his bat, trading an aging "Turkey" Mike Donlin for him. Campbell proceeded to bat .296, led the league in at-bats with 624, and banged out 185 hits. Not bad for a 24-year-old kid beginning his career. He also led the team in runs scored and doubles.

Unfortunately, the Braves finished in last place that year, and Campbell was released. As a free agent, he signed with the Indianapolis Hoosiers of the newly formed Federal League in 1914, and had another great season batting .318, leading the team to the pennant. The Hoosiers relocated to New Jersey and became the Newark Pepper, and in 1915 Campbell batted .310 for yet another very good season. After the Federal League folded that year, Campbell sued for his wages and won his suit but never got the opportunity to play in the majors again.

Teams:

Chicago Cubs NL (1908)
Pittsburgh Pirates NL (1910–1911)
Boston Braves NL (1912)
Indianapolis Hoosiers FL (1914)
Newark Pepper FL (1915)

Max Carey

In his twenty Major League seasons, Max Carey hit above .300 eight times. He is ninth all-time in steals with 738, and is one of baseball's greatest triples hitters with 159. The quintessential five-tool player, Carey could catch, throw, hit for average, run, and hit for power. That last tool could be debated given Carey's career total of just 70 home runs, but he played in an age when the home run was not valued as an offensive weapon.

Elected to the Hall of Fame in 1961, Carey led the National League in stolen bases 10 times, and is still the league leader in steals of home. At various times he led the league in games, at-bats, walks and triples. Carey played 17 seasons for the Pirates, and although he hit .343 in 1925, his best year, arguably, was in 1922. That season, he batted .329, had career highs in home runs (10) and RBI (70), and led the league with his 80 walks and 51 steals.

Born and bred in Indiana, Carey had a strict upbringing and attended divinity school for a short time. His given surname of Carnarius was changed early on so Carey could play in Indiana's Central League without losing his amateur status. As a Pirates rookie in 1910, Carey was reportedly being groomed to replace Honus Wagner at shortstop, but he soon staked his claim in the Pittsburgh outfield. Carey's wife credited her husband with being the first player to use flip-down sunglasses in the field. He managed in Brooklyn for a short stint, but was

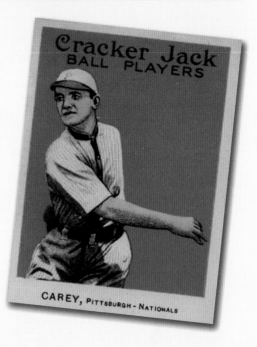

Max George Carey

Born: Maxmillian George Carnarius

replaced in 1934 by a young pup in his first managerial gig named Stengel. Carey stayed in the game until 1950 as a Minor League manager and league president of the All-American Girls Professional Baseball League. He later authored a book on baseball strategy.

Born:
January 11, 1890
Terra Haute, IN

Died:
May 30, 1976
Miami, FL

▷ Batted: Switch

▷ Threw: RH

▷ Position: OF

▷ Career BA: .285

▷ Managerial Record: 146–161

Team:

Pittsburgh Pirates NL (1910–1926)
Brooklyn Robins/Dodgers NL (1926–1929; manager: 1932–1933)

Ted Cather

Fred Clarke

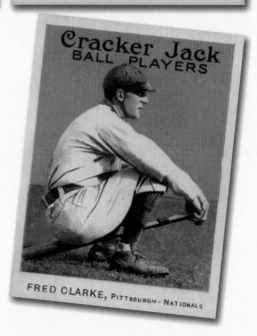

Ted Cather's career was a case of good news/bad news. He broke into the majors with the Cardinals in 1912, but suffered through a sixth-place season. Cather showed promise with eight hits in 19 at-bats for a .421 average, but the Cards' lineup was weak, and the pitching was even worse. The team's top two starters, Slim Sallee and Bob Harmon, were a combined 34–35. Cather was a real prospect, but in 1913 his batting average dipped to a disappointing .213 as the Cards finished eighth. In 1914, St. Louis was on the rise, but Cather, in the midst of his best season to date, was traded to the last place Boston Braves. It seemed like more bad news, but the "Miracle Braves" staged a torrid rush over the latter part of the season to clinch the National League flag.

Cather's fortunes had changed, and he would have a chance to compete in the World Series against the Philadelphia Athletics, but fittingly, it would be bittersweet. The Braves upset the favored A's in a 4–0 sweep. Cather, however, had

Theodore Physick Cather

Born:
May 20, 1889
Chester, PA
Died:
April 9, 1945
Elkton, MD
▷ Batted: RH
▷ Threw: RH
▷ Position: OF
▷ Career BA: .252

no hits in five World Series at-bats. His performance dampened an otherwise excellent second half run for Cather. He hit .297 as a Brave with 43 hits and 27 RBI. Just when it seemed Cather was ready to crack the Braves starting lineup, his average dipped to .206 in 1915, his final season. Like a baseball bounding towards him in the outfield, Ted Cather saw, first hand, the ups and downs of life in the big leagues.

Teams:

St. Louis Cardinals NL (1912–1914)
Boston Braves NL (1914–1915)

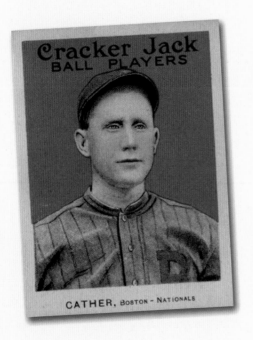

Hall of Famer Fred Clarke was a successful player-manager from 1897 to 1915. His playing career began with a bang in 1894 as Clarke went 5-for-5 playing for the Louisville Colonels. The following season, he proved to be no fluke with 191 hits, 82 RBI, and a .347 batting average. Clarke's numbers dipped slightly in 1896, but he still batted .325 with 79 RBI. Sadly, the Colonels were perennial losers, finishing no higher than ninth in Clarke's six seasons.

In 1900, Clarke jumped from the sinking Louisville barge to a Pittsburgh Pirate ship as player-manager. The move would forever cement his baseball legacy. After a second place finish in 1900, Clarke's Bucs won three straight National League pennants, and Clarke hit .324, .316, and .351 respectively. In 1903, he led the league in doubles, slugging, and OPS. Ever the patient hitter, Clarke frequently recorded twice as many walks as strikeouts. In 1899, he had just 17 Ks in 606 at-bats. Clarke would spend 15 seasons in Pittsburgh, but undoubtedly, his favorite year was 1909. That season, the Pirates won 110 games and Clarke, at age

Fred Clifford Clarke

36, was still impressive at the plate with 68 RBI, a .287 batting average, and a league-leading 80 walks. With a lineup that featured Honus Wagner, and a mound staff with two 20-game winners, Vic Willis and Howie Camnitz, Pittsburgh won the NL pennant and played Ty Cobb's Detroit Tigers in the World Series. Clarke hit just .211 in the Series, but the Pirates prevailed in seven games.

Known for his carousing at an early age, Clarke matured into a fearless skipper whose managerial strategy was unmatched. He was also a shrewd entrepreneur, earning millions in various business ventures. After retiring in 1915, Clarke returned to the Pirates in 1925 as an executive and assistant to the manager. He helped Pittsburgh win another world championship that season, but his presence undermined manager Bill McKechnie's power and he retired for good in 1926. Fred Clarke was truly one of the game's great leaders, on the diamond, at the helm, and in life.

Teams:

Louisville Colonels NL (1894–1896; player-manager: 1897–1899)

Pittsburgh Pirates NL (player-manager: 1900–1911, 1913–1915; manager: 1912)

Born:
October 3, 1872
Winterset, IA

Died:
August 14, 1960
Winfield, KS

▷ Batted: LH

▷ Threw: RH

▷ Position: OF

▷ Career BA: .312

▷ Managerial Record: 1,602–1,181

Joe Connolly

Joseph Francis Connolly

Had his career not been curtailed by a serious ankle injury, Joe Connolly probably would have been very successful as a ballplayer. Sometimes life takes a strange turn but things still work out pretty well. Coming up through the Minor League ranks, Connolly started out as a pitcher, but quickly realized that he was a much better hitter. As a .300 hitter in the minors, Connolly finally got his shot in 1913 with the Braves.

Growing up in North Smithfield, Rhode Island, he was thrilled to be playing for the "home" team. As a 29-year-old rookie, Joe batted a very respectable .281, but a broken ankle curtailed his season. Although he lost a step in his play, Connolly came back in the 1914 season to bat .306 and helped the "Miracle Braves" on their famous run from last place in July to winning the pennant and beating Connie Macks' Athletics juggernaut in four games. Over the next two years, Connolly's ankle became very bothersome and his production began to wane. He was sent down to the minors but he soon retired to farming and playing semi-pro ball.

The story does not quite end there. Joe Connolly went on to become one of the favorite sons of the state of Rhode Island. He spent many hours working with youth groups throughout the state,

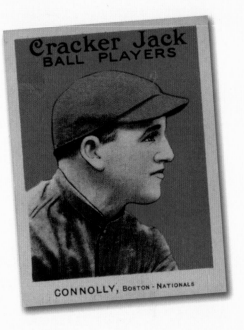

became a town council member in North Smithfield, proceeded into the state legislature and went on to become a state senator. Joe Connolly did not necessarily leave his mark on baseball, but certainly left it on his beloved "Rhody."

Born:
February 1, 1884
North Smithfield, RI

Died:
September 1, 1943
North Smithfield, RI

▷ Batted: LH

▷ Threw: RH

▷ Position: OF

▷ Career BA: .288

Team:

Boston Braves NL (1913–1916)

Gavvy Cravath

The first player from the San Diego area to make the Major Leagues, Clifford Carlton "Gavvy" Cravath was called "Cactus" by teammates because of his western roots. The origin of the name Gavvy is even more interesting. While playing in the Pacific Coast League, Cravath reportedly crunched a ball with such power that it struck and killed a seagull. Fans in attendance began screaming, "Gaviota," the Spanish word for seagull, and Carlton soon became known as Gavvy.

The son of the first mayor of Escondido, CA, Gavvy would also blaze a unique trail. During baseball's Deadball Era, Cravath stood alone as the top power hitter in the National League between 1912 and 1919. He led the NL in home runs six times during that period and frequently approached or surpassed .500 in slugging. In 1915, as a member of the Phillies, Cravath slammed 24 dingers, a new 20th-century single-season home run record. He also led the league in runs, RBI, walks, OBP, slugging, and OPS. The Phillies won their first pennant in 1915 led by Cravath and 31-game winner Pete Alexander.

Also an excellent outfielder, Cravath registered 161 assists between 1912 and 1918. His last great season, 1919, saw Cravath bash a league-leading 12 homers and slug .640 at the age of 38. He was an on-base machine that year with a .341 average, .438 OBP and 1.078 OPS. As Cravath was putting the finishing touches on a great season, Babe Ruth was doing the same to Cravath's single-season home run record set in 1915. The 24-year-old Red Sox phenom swatted 29 big flies, essentially signaling the arrival of the home run as the game's biggest attraction. Before pursuing baseball, Cravath held jobs as a fumigator and telegraph operator. He upgraded his post-baseball profession, becoming a judge in Laguna Beach, CA. Cravath's Major League career home run record of 119 was obliterated by Ruth in 1921, but Cactus is still recognized as the best power hitter of his time. Just ask that seagull.

Teams:

Boston Red Sox AL (1908)

Chicago White Sox AL (1909)

Washington Senators AL (1909)

Philadelphia Phillies NL (1912–1918; player-manager: 1919–1920)

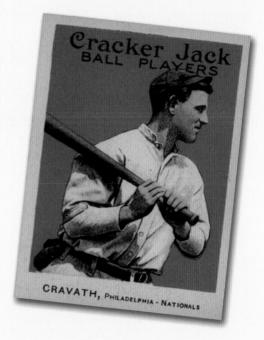

Clifford Carlton Cravath

Born:
March 23, 1881
Escondido, CA

Died:
May 23, 1963
Laguna Beach, CA

▷ Batted: RH

▷ Threw: RH

▷ Position: OF

▷ Career BA: .287

▷ Managerial Record: 91–137

Sam Crawford

One of the founding fathers of our National Pastime, Sam "Wahoo" Crawford was a major contributor as a player and coach, and was instrumental in developing baseball at the collegiate level. Crawford still holds the MLB record for triples in a career with 309, and was considered a major power hitter during the Deadball Era. He hit 16 round trippers in 1901, which was a major feat at the time, and was the first player to lead the American League and National League in home runs.

While with the Tigers, Crawford hit .300 or better eight times, and was highly regarded for his skillful play. An excellent outfielder, Crawford was always among the league leaders in most offensive categories. An unschooled, natural hitter, Crawford enjoyed the limelight as the Tigers best player until a rookie named Cobb started to produce in 1906. Crawford was a big part of the hazing Cobb endured as a rookie, and unfortunately this colored their relationship both on and off the field for years. Some say that once the young Cobb began to upstage the veteran Crawford, things got a bit dicey. In any event, they respected each other on the field and, in later years, Cobb lobbied hard for Crawford to get into the Hall, which did come to fruition in 1957.

After his days with the Tigers, Crawford played for Los Angeles in the Pacific Coast League, leading them to two league championships. He coached at USC, helping them to develop into a first-rate college program, and later was an umpire in the Pacific Coast League. Crawford retired to his walnut farm in California, and was immortalized by Lawrence Ritter in *The Glory of Their Times*.

Samuel Earl Crawford

Born:
April 18, 1880
Wahoo, NE

Died:
June 15, 1968
Hollywood, CA

▷ Batted: LH

▷ Threw: LH

▷ Position: OF

▷ Career BA: .309

Teams:
Cincinnati Reds NL (1899–1902)
Detroit Tigers AL (1903–1917)

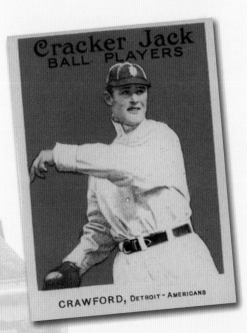

Josh Devore

Steve Evans

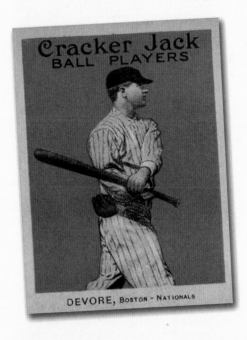

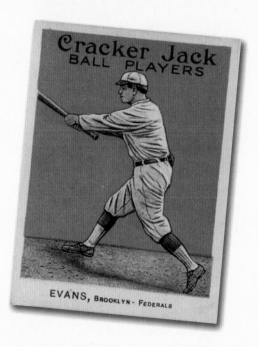

For Josh Devore, the third time was definitely the charm. A native of Murray City, Ohio, Devore broke into the Bigs with the New York Giants in 1908. Pennant bridesmaids in Devore's first three seasons, New York finally made it to the World Series in 1911, only to lose in six games to the Philadelphia Athletics. Devore and the Giants returned to the Fall Classic in 1912, but again were vanquished, this time by the Red Sox in seven games. The year 1913 was a whirlwind for Devore. He played for the Giants, Reds, and Phillies before landing with the Boston Braves just in time for another trip to the World Series. In his third chance at glory, Devore's team came through as the "Miracle Braves" beat the A's in a four-game sweep. Devore was no Mr. October, batting just .204 in 14 career World Series games, but he was a steady contributor to all of his clubs.

A fantastic leadoff man, Devore was adept at the arts of bunting and stealing. He once swiped four bases in a single inning. He also made many a game-saving play in the outfield, including a memorable snag in Game 3 of the 1912 World Series. Some 36 years before Jackie Robinson broke the color barrier, Devore and the Giants played in the Cuban-American Major League Club Series versus two Cuban clubs, Almendares Park and Havana Park. Devore hit over .300 just one time, in his first full season with the Giants, but he finished with a respectable career batting average of .277. With speed and savvy to spare, we'd take Josh Devore in our outfield any day.

Joshua M. Devore

Teams:

New York Giants NL (1908–1913)
Cincinnati Reds NL (1913)
Philadelphia Phillies NL (1913–1914)
Boston Braves NL (1914)

Born:
November 13, 1887
Murray City, OH

Died:
October 6, 1954
Chillicothe, OH

▷ Batted: LH

▷ Threw: RH

▷ Position: OF

▷ Career BA: .277

One of baseball's original flakes, Steve Evans crafted a career that was as much about personality as performance. In 1908, he played two games for the Giants before joining the Cardinals for a five-year run. His best season overall was 1911 when he hit .294 with five home runs and 71 RBI. Evans had 161 hits that year with an impressive .369 OBP. Many viewed Evans' career as a study in unfulfilled potential, but it was really about the level of competition.

When he moved to the Federal League in 1914, Evans hit .348 with a league-leading 15 triples and a .556 slugging percentage for the Brooklyn Tip-Tops. Shipped to the Baltimore Terrapins midway through the next year, he hit .308 and smacked a league-high 34 doubles. In the outfield, Evans was a reliable assist man, but was also among the league leaders in errors. On four different occasions, Evans led his league in getting hit by pitches. In 1910 alone, he was plunked 31 times. That set a 20th century

Louis Richard Evans

record which stood until 1971 when Ron Hunt of the Expos was hit 50 times.

An insufferable clubhouse prankster, Evans never passed up an opportunity to get a laugh. On a tour of Egypt, he once stood on one side of the Sphinx and caught a ball tossed by Giants' catcher Ivey Wingo from the other side. Whether it was his .287 career batting average, his penchant for bean balls, or his showmanship, I guess you could say that Steve Evans was always a big hit.

Teams:

New York Giants NL (1908)
St. Louis Cardinals NL (1909–1913)
Brooklyn Tip-Tops FL (1914–1915)
Baltimore Terrapins FL (1915)

Born:
February 17, 1885
Cleveland, OH

Died:
December 28, 1943
Cleveland, OH

▷ Batted: LH
▷ Threw: LH
▷ Position: OF/1B
▷ Career BA: .287

Doc Gessler

Henry Homer Gessler

Henry "Doc" Gessler was probably a better physician than he was a ballplayer. A graduate of Baltimore Medical College, Gessler chose baseball over practicing medicine, and ended up playing for five different teams over a period of eight seasons. For Red Sox historians, in 1908 Gessler became the first Boston Red Sox player to hit a home run in a regular-season game. That year he batted .308 and his .394 on-base percentage was good enough to lead the American League. As an outfielder, Gessler was average with a .945 fielding percentage.

When Fred Lake took over the helm as manager of the Red Sox late in the 1908 season, he was so impressed with Gessler that he named him team captain. A popular player, he was even invited to the inauguration of President William Howard Taft in March 1909. Although he only hit 14 home runs in his career, Gessler did have another home run first. In August 1911, he hit the first home run over the fence of the Senators' brand new Griffith Stadium.

A very interesting character, Gessler spent much of his offseason time in various business ventures, one of which was drilling for oil. Doc Gessler retired after the 1911 season to pursue his medical career. He refreshed his skills with course work at John Hopkins University before going into practice. He had one last fling with baseball in 1914 as manager of Pittsburgh in the Federal League but was replaced after only 11 games. Unfortunately, Doc Gessler did not have a very lengthy medical career either. He became ill in 1924 and died at the young age of 44.

Teams:

Detroit Tigers AL (1903)
Brooklyn Superbas NL (1903–1906)
Chicago Cubs NL (1906)
Boston Red Sox AL (1908–1909)
Washington Senators AL (1909–1911)
Pittsburgh Rebels FL (manager: 1914)

Born:
December 23, 1880
Greensburg, PA

Died:
December 24, 1924
Greensburg, PA

▷ Batted: LH
▷ Threw: LH
▷ Position: OF/1B
▷ Career BA: .280
▷ Managerial Record: 3–8

Solly Hofman

Considered by many to be the first great utility man in baseball history, "Circus Solly" Hofman played just about every position at some point in his career. Known for his timely hitting, good defense and colorful character, Hofman was popular with the fans and teammates alike. He also had a reputation for speed on the basepaths and was an expert sign stealer. Some say Hofman got his nickname because of the spectacular "circus catches" that he made, but others say that the moniker was from a popular comic strip.

With the Cubs for most of his career, Hofman was utility man during the Cubs three straight National League pennant years from 1906 through 1908. The Cubs were Series Champs in 1907 and 1908, and Hofman was a contributor in the post season, batting .298 in three World Series. As a matter of fact, he is credited with calling attention to Fred Merkle's 1908 base-running error, the famous "Merkle Boner." According to Hofman, Merkle did not touch second base. This eventually led to a one-game playoff with the Giants and the victorious Cubs won the pennant and the Series.

Hofman finally became a regular in the centerfield during the 1909 season and

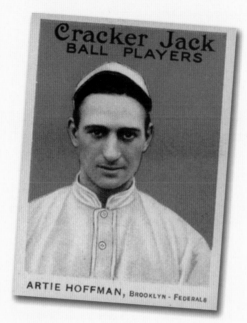

ARTIE HOFFMAN, BROOKLYN - FEDERALS

maintained that slot for the next few years. He had some solid offensive years with his best being in 1910 when he batted .325 with 155 hits. Although popular with teammates, Hofman did butt heads a few times with manager Lee Magee in the Federal League. Magee fined Hofman for smoking, which was against team rules. This led to a confrontation after which Hofman was immediately shipped out to Buffalo. After the demise of the Federal League, he played a few games for both the Yankees and the Cubs before retiring for good. All in all, between his hitting, fielding and base stealing "Circus Solly" Hofman was no clown.

Arthur Frederick Hofman

Teams:
Pittsburgh Pirates NL (1903, 1912–1913)
Chicago Cubs NL (1904–1912, 1916)
Brooklyn Tip-Tops FL (1914)
Buffalo Blues FL (1915)
New York Yankees AL (1916)

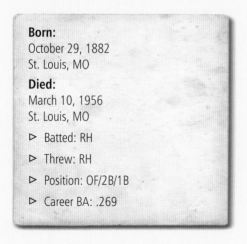

Born:
October 29, 1882
St. Louis, MO
Died:
March 10, 1956
St. Louis, MO
▷ Batted: RH
▷ Threw: RH
▷ Position: OF/2B/1B
▷ Career BA: .269

Harry Hooper

An outstanding defensive player, Harry Hooper had the luck to team up with Tris Speaker and Duffy Lewis early in his career, and from 1910 to 1915 they were considered one of the greatest outfields in baseball history. As solid a ballplayer as they come, he also was a good batsman who banged out almost 2,500 hits during his career. Hooper first played baseball at Saint Mary's College in California, where he graduated with a degree in civil engineering. He worked as a surveyor for a couple of years while playing Minor

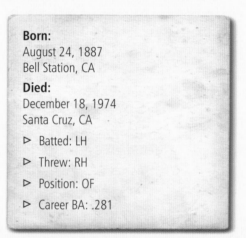

Born:
August 24, 1887
Bell Station, CA
Died:
December 18, 1974
Santa Cruz, CA
▷ Batted: LH
▷ Threw: RH
▷ Position: OF
▷ Career BA: .281

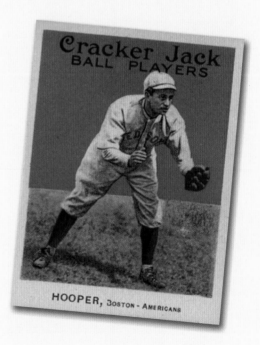

HOOPER, BOSTON - AMERICANS

Harry Bartholomew Hooper

League ball before the Red Sox came calling. Hooper played on four Red Sox World Series Champion teams (1912, 1915, 1916, 1918), but his best offensive year was with the White Sox when he batted .328 with 10 round trippers in 1924.

A stellar leadoff hitter, Hooper was the first person to hit leadoff home runs in both games of a doubleheader, a feat he accomplished in 1913 that stood for 80 years until Rickey Henderson matched it. He still holds the Red Sox record for most triples (130) and stolen bases (300). October 13, 1915 saw another first for Hooper when he hit two home runs in a single World Series game, becoming the first player to do so. Over the course of his illustrious 17-year career, Hooper led the league in outs made, putouts, assists, fielding percentage and several other categories.

Considered one of the best in the game, Hooper later managed in the Pacific Coast League and coached at Princeton University in the early 1930s before leaving baseball to become postmaster at Capitola, California, a position he held for 24 years. In his 1971 induction speech at the Hall of Fame, Hooper said that as a young kid he developed his arm by throwing rocks, and claimed to have used that method to kill rattlesnakes and even a coyote. As an engineer, Hooper constructed a very good career for himself, and certainly left his stamp on the game.

Teams:
Boston Red Sox AL (1909–1920)
Chicago White Sox AL (1921–1925)

Benny Kauff

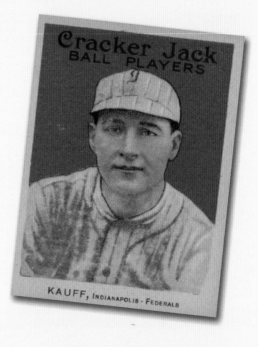

Periodically, a player comes up through the ranks that fans attach to because of their antics as well as their talent. Piersall, Belinsky, Fidrych; the list of good players with a side show is endless. Benny Kauff certainly fits the bill. A trash-talking, brash self-promoter, Kauff was as colorful as he was talented.

Nicknamed the "Ty Cobb of the Federal League," Kauff tore up the short-lived Federal League for two years, batting a whopping .370 in 1914 followed by .342 in 1915. Once the Federal League folded and Kauff was signed by the Giants, he had some productive offensive years in the National League, but never lived up to his self-promotion. Not known for being humble, Kauff often bragged about what a good player he was. His best year in the NL was 1917 when he batted .308 for the Giants. As a kid he developed unusual strength from working in the mines. Known for his combination of power and speed, Kauff was actually a very good player...with a big mouth, and fans found him to be entertaining both on and off the field.

Kauff enjoyed the high life, wearing expensive suits, drinking expensive liquor and smoking expensive cigars. Unfortunately Kauff was caught in the

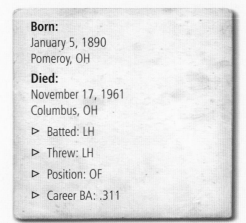

Born:
January 5, 1890
Pomeroy, OH
Died:
November 17, 1961
Columbus, OH
▷ Batted: LH
▷ Threw: LH
▷ Position: OF
▷ Career BA: .311

Benjamin Michael Kauff

swirl of allegations of the 1919 World Series fix, although there was no proof of his involvement. His run in the Bigs ended abruptly when he was indicted as part of a stolen car operation. Even though he was acquitted, Commissioner Kenesaw Mountain Landis banned Kauff for life because he did not believe he was innocent. Although banned from playing the game, Kauff worked as a scout for 22 years before retiring to work as a salesman at a high-end men's clothier. Add Kauff to the list of Piersall, Belinsky and the rest. There is always a place for guys like him who make the game more entertaining.

Teams:
New York Highlanders AL (1912)
Indianapolis Hoosiers FL (1914)
Brooklyn Tip-Tops FL (1915)
New York Giants NL (1916–1920)

Tommy Leach

Lee Magee

Who had the very first hit in the very first World Series? It was none other than "Wee" Tommy Leach. At 5-foot, 6-inches and 135 pounds, the tiny Leach packed a lot of power. With 63 career home runs in the Deadball Era, "Wee" Tommy was considered one of the premier power hitters of the day. Leach could have been included in our Hot Corner chapter because he played nearly as many games at third as he did in the outfield. It really does not matter as he excelled at both positions.

A very durable player, Leach played for 19 years. His best offensive year was 1907 when he batted .303 and banged out 166 hits, but in that first World Series in 1903, Leach set a record that still stands by smacking four triples. In 1904 he was named acting manager of the Pirates when manager Fred Clarke had surgery on a nasty spike wound. Over his historic career, Leach played alongside the likes of Honus Wagner, Rube Waddell, Max Carey and Casey Stengel. He led the

Thomas William Leach

Born:
November 4, 1877
French Creek, NY

Died:
September 29, 1969
Haines City, FL

▷ Batted: RH

▷ Threw: RH

▷ Position: OF/3B

▷ Career BA: .269

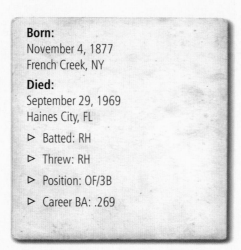

National League in runs scored, triples, fielding percentage, putouts, assists and several other categories. Leach played on one World Series Champion, three National League pennant winners, and was the NL Home Run Champ in 1902.

After his playing days, Leach managed in the minors and scouted for the Boston Braves before he went into the citrus business in Florida. The little guy with the big bat lived to the ripe old age of 92 and was the last surviving Pirate from the first World Series when he died in 1969.

Teams:
Louisville Colonels NL (1898–1899)
Pittsburgh Pirates NL (1900–1912, 1918)
Chicago Cubs NL (1912–1914)
Cincinnati Reds NL (1915)

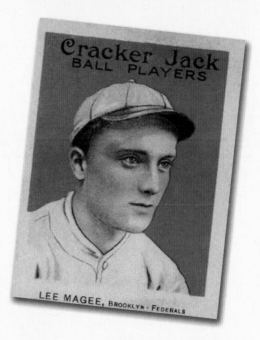

Another player on the Deadball Era's disturbing list of unsavory characters, Lee Magee was linked to gambling and throwing games. His first mistake was to hang around with Hal Chase, the most notorious of the lot. A decent offensive player, Magee started in the minors in 1906 and got his shot in the majors with the St. Louis Cardinals in 1911. In 1915 he jumped to the Federal League as player-manager of the Brooklyn Tip-Tops, and batted a career high .323 in the new league. After the FL folded, he was purchased by the Yankees, traded to the Browns and quickly traded again to the Cincinnati Reds. His offensive numbers were adequate, but he was considered a poor base runner and was below average defensively.

While he was with the Reds, Magee took a detour down the path of professional suicide with the help of his friend and teammate, Hal Chase. Evidently, in June of 1918, both players agreed to throw a ballgame against the Boston Braves and each wagered $500

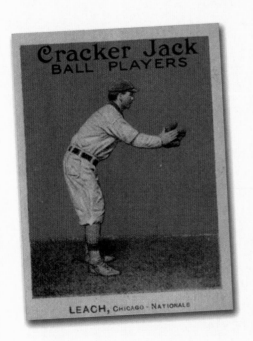

Leo Christopher Magee

Born: Leopold Christopher Hoernschemeyer

in the form of a check. The Reds ended up winning the game because Chase double-crossed Magee. As a result, Magee sang like a bird and blew the whistle. He was immediately shipped off to the Brooklyn Robins and then to the Chicago Cubs. In the meantime, the gambler that handled the wagers sued Magee because the ever-bright Magee stopped payment on his check since the Reds had won. After all of this came to light, the Cubs tossed him. Magee sued the Cubs for back wages but lost in court. More importantly, this entire scenario brought Hal Chase's dishonesty out in the open and Chase was eventually blacklisted forever. Lee Magee and Hal Chase deserved each other. Both players were an embarrassment to the game.

Teams:

St. Louis Cardinals NL (1911–1914)
Brooklyn Tip-Tops FL (1915)
New York Yankees AL (1916–1917)
St. Louis Browns AL (1917)
Cincinnati Reds NL (1918)
Brooklyn Robins NL (1919)
Chicago Cubs NL (1919)

Born:
June 4, 1889
Cincinnati, OH

Died:
March 14, 1966
Columbus, OH

▷ Batted: Switch

▷ Threw: RH

▷ Position: OF/2B/1B

▷ Career BA: .276

Sherry Magee

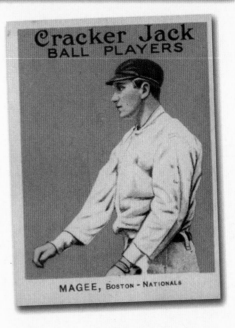

MAGEE, BOSTON - NATIONALS

Sherwood Robert Magee

Why isn't Sherry Magee in the Hall of Fame? Taking a hard look at his stats, Magee measures up against many who are in Cooperstown's hallowed Hall. The prototypical five-tool player, Sherry Magee was one of the true stars of the Deadball Era. An outstanding offensive and defensive player, Magee scored 100-plus runs twice, was the NL RBI champ four times (1907, 1910, 1914, 1918), the NL batting champ in 1910, and played for the World Champion Reds in 1919. He knocked in 1,176 runs and had 2,169 hits over his brilliant 16-year career. Magee's best year was 1910 when he batted .331 and led the league with 110 runs and 123 RBI. That year he also had a sparkling .445 on base percentage, and let's not forget his .507 slugging percentage. Magee was also a whiz on the basepaths, swiping 441 bases.

Known for his hot temper and orneriness, he developed a reputation as a troublemaker. During a game in 1911, Magee punched out an umpire, sending him to the hospital with a broken nose, and ended up suspended for most of the season. Many fans enjoyed getting on Magee during games because they felt he always put himself ahead of his team. He eventually wore out his welcome wherever he played and found himself back in the minors as was very common in those days. Magee played for another seven seasons in the minors and had some outstanding offensive years.

It is ironic that after so many scraps with umpires over his career, he worked as an umpire in the New York-Penn League and the National League after his playing career ended. However, Magee's career as umpire was cut short when he contracted pneumonia in early March of 1929 and died two weeks later at the age of 44. A great hitter? Certainly. A great defensive player? Undoubtedly. A Hall of Famer? Unfortunately, Sherry Magee has not yet made the grade.

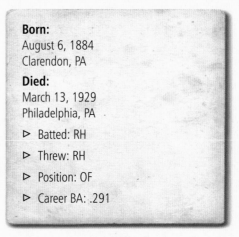

Born:
August 6, 1884
Clarendon, PA

Died:
March 13, 1929
Philadelphia, PA

▷ Batted: RH

▷ Threw: RH

▷ Position: OF

▷ Career BA: .291

Teams:
Philadelphia Phillies NL (1904–1914)
Boston Braves NL (1915–1917)
Cincinnati Reds NL (1917–1919)

Armando Marsans

One of the pioneers that helped open up the doors for the likes of Tony Oliva, José Cardenal and many others, Armando Marsans was the first really good player to come out of Cuba. As a result of several exhibition games between the Cincinnati Reds and Cuba's finest, Marsans was signed to a Minor League contract after his team took four out of five games from the Reds. After a few seasons, he was called up in 1911 and batted a respectable .261 in a reserve role. The next year Marsans batted a tidy .317 and swiped 35 bases to go along with his capable outfield play.

Known for his speed on the basepaths, Marsans was one of the National League's bright young stars for a few years. The son of a wealthy aristocrat, Marsans did not need the money from baseball, playing more for the enjoyment and fame. During the offseason he ran a cigar factory that he owned in Cuba. He also owned a successful cigar store in Cincinnati. After an argument with Red's manager, Buck Herzog, the egotistical and obstinate

Marsans took it upon himself to challenge the reserve clause and jump ship to the Federal League in 1914. The National League filed suit and Marsans was temporarily prohibited from playing. The injunction was finally reversed and he was allowed to play in 1915.

After the Federal League folded, Marsans hooked up with the Browns and the Yankees, but a broken leg ended his Major League career. Marsans played in the Cuban Winter League before, during and after his time in the minors and majors, playing for 21 seasons, 10 of them on pennant-winning teams. A noted player-manager in the Cuban League, Marsans continued to manage into the 1940s, and was one of the first inductees into the Cuban Baseball Hall of Fame in 1939.

MARSANS, St. Louis - Federals

Teams:

Cincinnati Reds NL (1911–1914)

St. Louis Terriers FL (1914–1915)

St. Louis Browns AL (1916–1917)

New York Yankees AL (1917–1918)

Armando Marsans

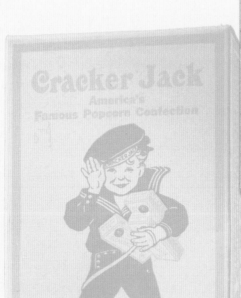

Born:
October 3, 1887
Matanzas, Cuba

Died:
September 3, 1960
La Habana, Cuba

▷ Batted: RH

▷ Threw: RH

▷ Position: OF

▷ Career BA: .269

Clyde Milan

Some referred to him as "Deerfoot," while others called him "Milan the Marvel." Call him what you want, Clyde Milan was a darn good baseball player. Over his 16 years with the Senators, Milan batted a tidy .285 with 2,100 hits, and perfected the fine art of base stealing. When you talk about the best robbers during that era, Milan was right up there with Ty Cobb and Eddie Collins. In 1912 he set a Major League record with 88 steals, which stood until Cobb broke it three years later.

Milan got his start beating the bushes in 1905 and 1906 with stops in Clarksville, Texas, and Shawnee, Oklahoma, before making it to Wichita, Kansas, in the Western Association. When the Senators called him up to the big leagues, Milan played sparingly for a few seasons. It all finally clicked in 1910 when he batted .279 followed by a 1911 season in which he batted a robust .315. From that point on, Clyde Milan established himself as a solid player who could hit, field and run. Perfecting the hook slide, "Deerfoot" went on to steal 495 bases over his career. That is not anywhere near Cobb's record, but very is good nonetheless.

Milan had some very good seasons over his long career. He averaged 30 stolen bases per year and was always productive offensively. In 1920, he batted .322 with 163 hits. Like many others at the time, Milan returned to the minors for several years before hanging them up. He went on to manage in the minors through 1937. Milan returned to the Senators to scout in 1937 and coached for them from 1938 until his death. One scorching day in 1953, Clyde Milan suffered a heart attack after hitting fungoes to his infielders. He passed away three weeks later. "Milan the Marvel" was robbed of life as quickly as he robbed those bases.

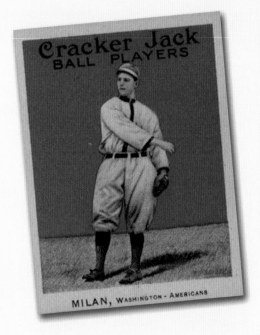

MILAN, WASHINGTON - AMERICANS

Born:
March 25, 1887
Linden, TN

Died:
March 3, 1953
Orlando, FL

▷ Batted: LH

▷ Threw: RH

▷ Position: OF

▷ Career BA: .285

▷ Managerial Record: 69–85

Jesse Clyde Milan

Team:
Washington Senators AL (1907–1921; player-manager: 1922)

Ward Miller

Herbie Moran

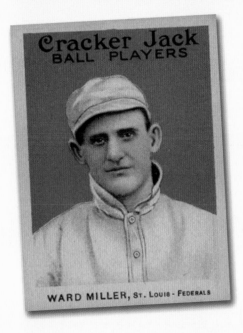

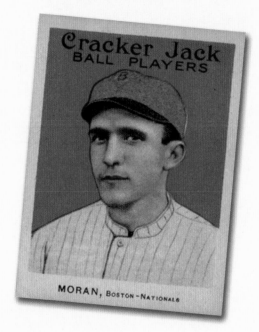

the 1911 season where he honed his skills batting .332 for Montreal in the Eastern League. Miller saw Major League action again when he hooked up with the Cubs for the 1912 and 1913 seasons and put up some decent numbers as a part-time player. He then jumped to the new Federal League where he played more regularly and had his best seasons. After the collapse of the Federal League, Miller moved on to the American League to play for the St. Louis Browns and batted a respectable .266 with 485 at-bats.

The story really begins after his playing days were over. Miller went back to Dixon, Illinois, and became one of its most prominent citizens. He was named the sheriff of Lee County, treasurer of Lee County and chief of police of Dixon State School. Miller worked with youth baseball teams and did whatever he could to help his hometown. A beautiful monument, dedicated in 2011, now stands in front of the Lee County Courthouse honoring one of their favorite sons, Ward Miller. Although his baseball career spanned just eight Major League seasons, Miller's legacy in Dixon, Illinois, has stood the test of time for 100 years.

W ard "Grump" Miller, a graduate of Northern Illinois University, had a fairly mediocre baseball career. Statistically his best year was in 1915 when he batted .306 for the St. Louis Terriers of the short-lived Federal League. As a 24-year-old rookie with Pittsburgh, Miller became ill soon after the season began. After he was diagnosed with tuberculosis, manager Fred Clarke traded him to Cincinnati at the end of May, ending Miller's shot at playing with the Pirates World Series Championship team.

Only a part-time player for the Reds, Miller was sent down to the minors for

H erbie Moran's career was like one giant vanilla ice-cream cone, very plain and simple. There is however a single cherry on top of the cone if you consider that he played on the 1914 "Miracle Braves" team that went from last place on July 18th to first place on August 25th, took the pennant, and swept the Series. Purchased by the Braves on August 23, 1914, the 30-year-old Moran got to Boston just in time to participate in the run up to the pennant. He did get the

---

Born:
July 5, 1884
Mount Carroll, IL

Died:
September 4, 1958
Dixon, IL

Batted: LH

Threw: RH

Position: OF

Career BA: .278

Ward Taylor Miller

Teams:
Pittsburgh Pirates NL (1909)
Cincinnati Reds NL (1909–1910)
Chicago Cubs NL (1912–1913)
St. Louis Terriers FL (1914–1915)
St. Louis Browns AL (1916–1917)

Born:
February 16, 1884
Costello, PA

Died:
September 21, 1954
Clarkson, NY

▷ Batted: LH

▷ Threw: RH

▷ Position: OF

▷ Career BA: .242

John Herbert Moran

opportunity to play in the World Series but did not fare well, batting a paltry .077 in three games and 13 at-bats.

Before, during and after his seven-year Major League career spent with four different teams, Moran played for the likes of the Coudersport Giants, DuBois Miners, Trenton Tigers, Providence Grays, Kansas City Blues, Rochester Bronchos, Montreal Royals and Little Rock Travelers. Moran's best Major League years were with Brooklyn when he batted .276 and .266 in 1912 and 1913, respectively. He also had a career-high 28 stolen bases in 1912, followed by 21 in 1913, and had 26 swipes with Cincinnati in 1914. After the 1915 season, he went on to play for Montreal in the International League and ended his playing days in 1918 with Little Rock in the Southern Association.

Moran resurfaced in the 1930s to manage the Williamsport Grays in the New York–Pennsylvania League and the New Waterford Dodgers in the Cape Breton Colliery League for a brief period before fading into the sunset. Four Major League teams in seven years, a .242 lifetime batting average with a total of 135 RBI neatly sums up Moran's very vanilla career.

Teams:
Philadelphia Athletics AL (1908)
Boston Doves/Braves NL (1908–1910, 1914–1915)
Brooklyn Dodgers/Superbas NL (1912–1913)
Cincinnati Reds NL (1914)

Eddie Murphy

John Edward Murphy

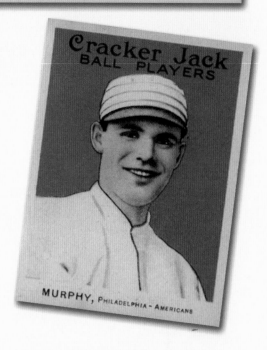

When you think of the 1919 Chicago White Sox, words like deceitful, embarrassing and dishonest come to mind. It becomes a bit unfair to the majority of players on that team who did not participate in the shenanigans that took place during that infamous World Series. One such player even earned his nickname because he had absolutely nothing to do with the scandal. Because of his non-participation, Eddie Murphy was given the nickname "Honest Eddie."

As a young man, Murphy attended Villanova University and played for several local Minor League teams in Pennsylvania. With a good bat and decent speed, he was signed by Connie Macks' Athletics and quickly established himself in the outfield. Murphy played in the World Series in 1913 and 1914 and had two good seasons batting .295 and .272 respectively. World Series Champs in 1913, the A's were swept by the Braves in 1914. After Mack dismantled the team in 1915, Murphy was dealt to the White Sox where he played a utility role for the next seven years. In 1919, he got one more chance to play in a World Series, but of course it happened to be the most famous (or infamous) Series in baseball history.

"Honest Eddie" finished out his career with the Pirates in 1926 after a five-year run with the Columbus Senators in the American Association. He later managed in the minors in the late 1940s and early 1950s. Today a glass bat hangs in the Corning Glass Museum in Corning, NY, as a tribute to Eddie Murphy. The regulation-sized, cut-glass bat was commissioned by the manager of the White Mills, PA, team Murphy played for in 1907 and 1908. It was presented to Murphy before the second game of the 1913 World Series as a token of appreciation for his baseball achievements.

Teams:
Philadelphia Athletics AL (1912–1915)
Chicago White Sox AL (1915–1921)
Pittsburgh Pirates NL (1926)

Born:
October 2, 1891
Hancock, NY

Died:
February 21, 1969
Dunmore, PA

▷ Batted: LH

▷ Threw: RH

▷ Position: OF

▷ Career BA: .287

Rebel Oakes

Rube Oldring

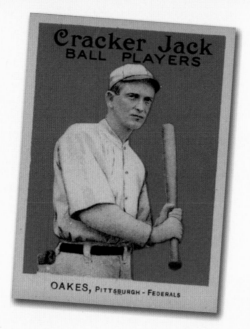

His name conjures up an image of a group of trees trying to overthrow the government, but Rebel Oakes seldom overthrew anyone in his seven big-league seasons. A gifted outfielder, Oakes led the National League in putouts with 364 in 1911. He was also one of baseball's top base stealers with 163 career swipes for the National League's Reds and Cardinals, and the Pittsburgh Rebels of the Federal League.

In 1914, Oakes became one of several players to jump to the rival Federal League and he enjoyed his best season as a professional with the Pittsburgh Rebels, reaching career highs in at-bats, hits, runs, home runs, RBI, OBP and slugging. The team was named after player-manager Oakes, who posted a 147–145 record in his two seasons at the helm. He played one final season with the Rebels in 1915 but his numbers dipped dramatically and his Major League career was finished along with the demise of the Federal League. Oakes played and managed in the minors for a few years before quitting the game for good in 1921.

A native of Louisiana, Ennis Telfair Oakes was a southerner through and through, hence the fitting nickname.

He was the first-ever Major League player from Louisiana Tech and a pesky thorn in the side of opponents, getting on base, annoying fielders and pitchers, pilfering bases, and creating run-scoring opportunities. In short, he was playing 1981 Oakland A's style "Billyball" long before Billy Martin ever came along. Despite his endless hustle, Oakes never played for a pennant winner. In fact, only his first and last teams, the 1909 Reds and the 1915 Rebels, had winning records. Oakes was the kind of player every team needs, a peppy, slap hitter with a non-stop motor and endless drive.

A slick-fielding outfielder that could hit and run with the best, Rube Oldring had a successful yet injury-prone Major League career which was spent mostly with the Athletics. His best offensive year was 1910 when he batted .308, but a leg injury kept him from playing in the World Series that year. Oldring led the American League in fielding percentage in 1910, 1911 and 1913. The fleet-footed Oldring also snagged 197 stolen bases over his career.

An integral part of the 1911 and 1913

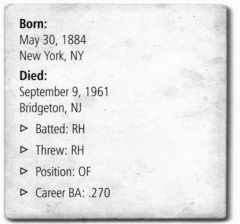

Born:
May 30, 1884
New York, NY

Died:
September 9, 1961
Bridgeton, NJ

▷ Batted: RH

▷ Threw: RH

▷ Position: OF

▷ Career BA: .270

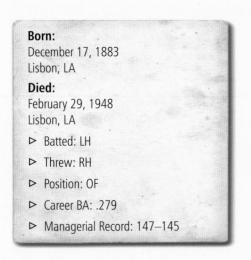

Born:
December 17, 1883
Lisbon, LA

Died:
February 29, 1948
Lisbon, LA

▷ Batted: LH

▷ Threw: RH

▷ Position: OF

▷ Career BA: .279

▷ Managerial Record: 147–145

Ennis Telfair Oakes

Teams:
Cincinnati Reds NL (1909)
St. Louis Cardinals NL (1910–1913)
Pittsburgh Rebels FL (player-manager: 1914–1915)

Reuben Henry Oldring

World Champion A's teams, Oldring also helped the A's take the AL pennant in 1914. In Game 4 of the 1913 Series, he made an incredible shoestring catch to hold runners on base. That catch is considered one of the greatest in World Series history. Oldring was so popular with the fans in 1913 that he was voted the Athletics' top player and was presented with a brand new Cadillac. Plagued with injuries off and on throughout his playing years, Oldring was also not in the best playing shape on occasion, which of course resulted in more injuries. As a matter of fact, Connie Mack once suspended both Oldring and his teammate Chief Bender for a little too much carousing.

After his MLB playing days, Oldring went on to manage and play in the minors through 1926. He finally hung them up and retired at age 42 to become a gentleman farmer in New Jersey. Oldring is credited with making many contributions to various youth baseball programs. As a matter of fact, the Rube Oldring Field, part of the Dreams Park Little League Complex in Cooperstown, NY, was dedicated to Oldring in 1997 for his many contributions to youth baseball.

Teams:
New York Highlanders/Yankees AL (1905, 1916)
Philadelphia Athletics AL (1906–1916, 1918)

Edd Rousch

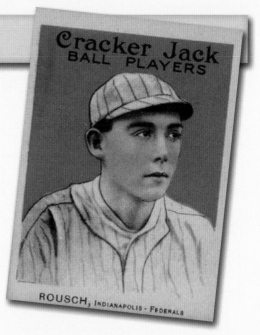

Between 1914 and 1927, Hall of Famer Edd Roush could basically hit .300 in his sleep. In 1917 and 1919, he led the National League, batting .341 and .321 respectively. Sandwiched between those two sterling campaigns was 1918, a season that saw Roush hit .333 and lead the NL in slugging and OPS. Roush was a man for all leagues. He broke into the Bigs with the American League's White Sox, then hopped to the Federal League and hit .325 and .298 for the Indianapolis Hoosiers and Newark Pepper. Roush then joined the National League's Giants for a cup of coffee before moving to the Reds midway through the 1916 season. Pitching legend Christy Mathewson also headed to Cincy in that deal.

Roush would spend the next 11 seasons with the Reds, and returned for one more season in 1931 after a three-year return to the Giants. Roush's numbers with Cincinnati stack up with baseball's best. He hit .331 with 1,784 hits, and had an OBP of .377 while slugging .462. In 1919, Roush led the Reds to the World Series against his old White Sox mates. He batted just .214 but Cincy beat the Pale Hose in eight games. That was, of course, the Series of the Black Sox where several members of the Chicago club tanked the Fall Classic. Throughout the remainder of his life, Roush was defensive about the controversial outcome of the Series.

Roush's .323 career batting average was not created by bloopers and spray hits. He was one of the game's best doubles

Teams:
Chicago White Sox AL (1913)
Indianapolis Hoosiers FL (1914)
Newark Pepper FL (1915)
New York Giants NL (1916, 1927–1929)
Cincinnati Reds NL (1916–1926, 1931)

Edd J. Roush

and triples hitters throughout his career. Playing predominantly in the Deadball Era, the energetic, and at times nasty, left-handed hitter used the entire field at the plate. In addition, he was viewed by his peers as one of the game's best outfielders with the uncanny ability to throw and catch with either hand. He was also known as a tough nut in salary negotiations. In retirement, Roush worked in local politics and banking, and was elected to the Hall of Fame in 1962. He was, in short, one of the greatest players of his generation.

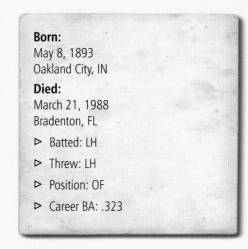

Born:
May 8, 1893
Oakland City, IN
Died:
March 21, 1988
Bradenton, FL
▷ Batted: LH
▷ Threw: LH
▷ Position: OF
▷ Career BA: .323

Wildfire Schulte

Burt Shotton

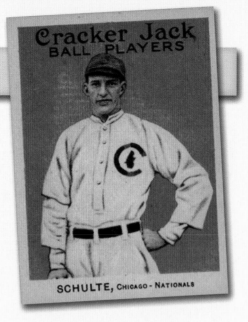

Frank M. Schulte

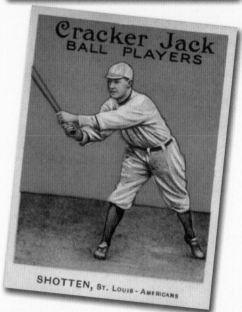

Frank "Wildfire" Schulte was a very solid player with a classic nickname. Some claim a star-struck Schulte saw Lillian Russell perform in the play "Wildfire" and teammates teased him with the nickname. Others maintain that he owned a racehorse with the same name, and it just carried over to Schulte. In any event, he was the complete player. Signed by the Cubs out of the New York State League, Schulte made an auspicious debut in September 1904, banging out three hits.

Among his banner years with the Cubs, Schulte lived up to his nickname in the 1911 season when he batted .300, led the league in RBI with 107, and assaulted National League pitching with 21 home runs, a remarkable feat during the Deadball Era. That year Schulte became the first player to top the 20 mark in doubles (30), triples (21), stolen bases (23), and home runs (21). Over the years only three other players have earned a place in the 20-20-20-20-club. The other three members? Willie Mays, Jimmy Rollins and Curtis Granderson. Schulte's 1911 season was so spectacular that he won the Chalmers Award as MVP of the National League. The speedy Schulte also stole 233 bases over his stellar career.

A bit eccentric, Schulte refused to use the heavy bats of the era, favoring a thin-handled 40-ounce bat instead, and would typically break about 50 bats each season. He also believed that if he found a hairpin on the street, it would predict his batting success, and he was often seen searching the sidewalks for hairpins before a game. Wildfire Schulte had the distinction of leading the NL in home runs in 1910 and 1911, played on four NL pennant teams (1906, 1907, 1908, 1910) and two World Series Champions (1907, 1908). By the way, he owns a .321 batting average in the World Series. Not too shabby. As his career declined, he was dealt to Pittsburgh, Philadelphia and Washington, where he ended his Major League career with the Senators. Frank played and managed for another five years in the bushes until 1923. Three days before the World Series in 1949 Wildfire Schulte's flame went out permanently. He was 67 years old.

Teams:

Chicago Cubs NL (1904–1916)
Pittsburgh Pirates NL (1916–1917)
Philadelphia Phillies NL (1917)
Washington Senators AL (1918)

Burt "Barney" Shotton was a skilled outfielder and overall was a pretty good manager. As a player in the American League, the mild-mannered Shotton had some very solid seasons. In 1916 he batted .283 and led the league in plate appearances, at-bats and walks. Nicknamed after famous race car driver Barney Oldfield, Shotton was pretty fast himself, swiping 293 bases over his 14-year career.

He got his feet wet as a manager while playing for the Cards when Branch Rickey, a fanatic about observing the Sabbath, used Shotton as his replacement for every Sunday game. As he honed his managerial skills, Shotton still produced well as a player. After his playing days, he coached for a few seasons in the Cardinals organization. In 1928, Shotton got his first real shot at managing, when he took over the helm for the Philadelphia Phillies. Although he stayed on as skipper until 1933, his Philly tenure was not terribly successful and he twice lost at least 100 games. Once he was relieved as manager, Shotton coached in the Reds and Indians systems.

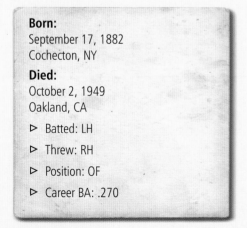

Born:
September 17, 1882
Cochecton, NY

Died:
October 2, 1949
Oakland, CA

▷ Batted: LH

▷ Threw: RH

▷ Position: OF

▷ Career BA: .270

Burton Edwin Shotton

His big break came at age 62, when his old friend Branch Rickey brought him on board to replace the fiery Leo Durocher who had been suspended by the Dodgers in 1947. Shotton won two pennants with the Dodgers (1947, 1949) who were led by the likes of Pee Wee Reese, Carl Furillo, Dixie Walker and their brilliant rookie, Jackie Robinson. Some people attribute Shotton's success directly to the pool of talent he inherited, but many believe that his calming influence had a positive impact on his younger players. No matter how you look at it, Barney Shotton's Dodgers won two pennants. When the Dodgers fell two games short of first place in 1950, scribes and fans alike felt that Shotton's passive demeanor kept the team from winning another pennant. Shotton was relieved of his duties after that fateful season but dabbled in baseball until 1960 in various capacities, and passed away at age 77 in 1962.

Teams:
St. Louis Browns AL (1909–1917)
Washington Senators AL (1918)
St. Louis Cardinals NL (1919–1923)
Philadelphia Phillies NL (manager: 1928–1933)
Brooklyn Dodgers NL (manager: 1947–1950)

Born:
October 18, 1884
Brownheim, OH
Died:
July 29, 1962
Lake Wales, FL
▷ Batted: LH
▷ Threw: RH
▷ Position: OF
▷ Career BA: .271
▷ Managerial Record: 697–764

Amos Strunk

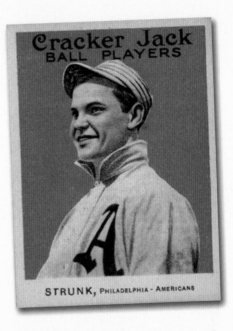

Crazy fast, graceful, outstanding defensively, dependable offensively, and injury prone are some of the words that describe the career of Amos Strunk. Nicknamed "The Flying Foot" and "Lightning," he was the type of runner who could create havoc for the opposition. Base stealing was not his forte but Strunk was so fast that he would sometimes score from second base on a squeeze play following the guy at third. Connie Mack loved him from the day he was called up to the Bigs in 1908.

From a defensive standpoint, some considered him the best outfielder in baseball, even better than Cobb. Strunk led American League outfielders in fielding percentage four times, and played in five World Series with two teams, the A's and the Red Sox. Unfortunately, he did not fare well in those Series, batting only .200 in 65 at-bats. When he was healthy though, he was an outstanding contact hitter. In 1916, Strunk batted .316 on the worst team in modern baseball history. That was the year Connie Mack dismantled his exceptional team, and the A's proceeded to lose an amazing 117 games. Wonder how the karma was in that locker room.

Plagued with injuries throughout his career, Strunk was hurt in 12 of his 17 seasons. In 1921, he did manage to bat a tidy .332 after being traded to the White Sox, but in 1924 he sustained a serious head injury when he collided with teammate Roy Elsh in the outfield during

Teams:
Philadelphia Athletics AL (1908–1917, 1919–1920, 1924)
Boston Red Sox AL (1918–1919)
Chicago White Sox AL (1920–1924)

Amos Aaron Strunk

spring training, essentially ending his MLB playing days. Strunk then became a player-manager in the New York-Penn League but hung up the spikes in 1925. After baseball, Amos Strunk moved on to a 50-year career in the insurance business and dabbled in photography.

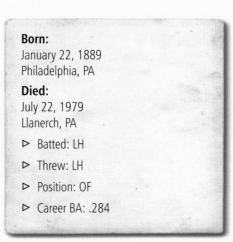

Born:
January 22, 1889
Philadelphia, PA
Died:
July 22, 1979
Llanerch, PA
▷ Batted: LH
▷ Threw: LH
▷ Position: OF
▷ Career BA: .284

Bobby Veach

Tillie Walker

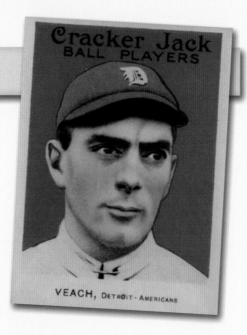

VEACH, DETROIT-AMERICANS

Bobby Veach is probably the most glaring example of a player who, for some reason, has been shortchanged when it comes to entry into the hallowed Halls of Cooperstown. With a .310 lifetime batting average and over 2,000 career hits, Veach batted over .300 ten times, had 3,754 putouts, led the American League in RBI on three different occasions (1915, 1917, 1918), and was the first Tiger to hit for the cycle. Veach stole 195 bases over his 14 years in the majors and was an outstanding outfielder. Why isn't he in the Hall? Perhaps it's because he was overshadowed by three outfielders he played alongside at one time or another. Yes, future Hall of Famers Ty Cobb, Sam Crawford and Harry Heilmann were all Veach's stable mates in the outfield.

Although an integral part of the Tigers' juggernaut, he suffered once Cobb took the helm and decided to take Veach down a peg or two. Cobb could never understand Veach's cordial attitude toward the opposing teams, and thought he did not take the game seriously. As manager, Cobb made life miserable for Veach, who in turn put up great numbers to prove Cobb wrong. In 1924, Cobb was finally able to get Veach out of the picture by selling him to the Red Sox. Looking back though, as a Tiger, Veach had some marvelous years. Noted baseball historian Bill James ranked the 1915 Tigers' outfield of Cobb, Veach and Sam Crawford as the greatest of all time.

By the way, Veach is the only player to ever pinch hit for Babe Ruth. He did some mop up work for the Yanks and Senators at the end of his campaign and then went back to the minors where he had some outstanding seasons. He finally left baseball behind in 1930 to buy into the coal business. Interestingly, Veach started out working in the Kentucky coal mines as a high school kid, so his retirement career brought him full circle. He died at the age of 57 in 1945 of what some suspect was lung cancer. Although overshadowed by his contemporaries, Veach was an outstanding player who belongs in the Hall.

Robert Hayes Veach

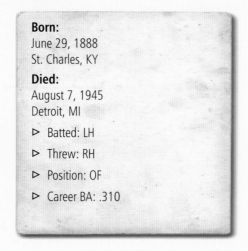

Born:
June 29, 1888
St. Charles, KY

Died:
August 7, 1945
Detroit, MI

▷ Batted: LH

▷ Threw: RH

▷ Position: OF

▷ Career BA: .310

Clarence "Tillie" Walker was an interesting character who transitioned out of the Deadball Era with success as a power hitter. With a rifle for an arm, Walker led the American League with assists six times. On the other hand, he was so wild that he led the league in errors four times. Offensively, Walker was one of the first power hitters of the new era. After smacking a league-leading 11 home runs in 1918, and 10 more in 1919; his home run production exploded over the next three seasons when he hit 17, 23 and 37 homers in 1920, 1921 and 1922, respectively. Great numbers, but there was another guy who dwarfed them. George Herman Ruth happened to hit 29, 54 and an amazing 59 home runs in the 1919, 1920 and 1921 seasons.

Walker really did have some nice years with the bat but developed a bad reputation of putting himself and his stats ahead of his team. He became very grouchy if things were not going

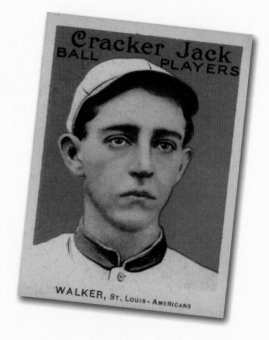

WALKER, ST. LOUIS-AMERICANS

Teams:

Detroit Tigers AL (1912–1923)

Boston Red Sox AL (1924–1925)

New York Yankees AL (1925)

Washington Senators AL (1925)

Clarence William Walker

well for him offensively. Most of his managers thought he was a defensive liability because of his wildness, even though he could hit. In Boston, Walker replaced Tris Speaker in center field and played on the 1916 Red Sox World Series Championship team. Once in Philadelphia, Walker became a home-run machine while the Athletics struggled, finishing in eighth place during his first four seasons with the team.

After his last Major League season in 1923, the 36-year-old Walker moved on to the minors where he played through 1929. He later became a Minor League umpire and manager. Walker became a highway patrolman in Tennessee after his baseball years and died in 1959.

Teams:

Washington Senators AL (1911–1912)
St. Louis Browns AL (1913–1915)
Boston Red Sox AL (1916–1917)
Philadelphia Athletics AL (1918–1923)

Born:
September 4, 1887
Telford, TN

Died:
September 21, 1959
Unicoi, TN

▷ Batted: RH

▷ Threw: RH

▷ Position: OF

▷ Career BA: .281

Jimmy Walsh

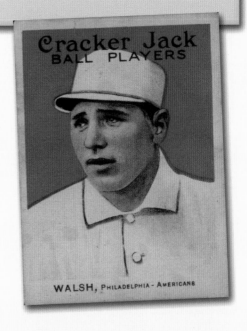

Irish Jimmy Walsh certainly had Hall of Fame numbers. With a .316 lifetime batting average, 2,699 hits, and 15 seasons with a better than .300 average over a 19-year career, there is no doubt about Walsh's qualifications. Unfortunately those were his Minor League stats. In the majors, it was not quite the same. With a .232 career batting average and 410 hits banged out over a period of seven years, Walsh does not quite make the cut for entry into the hallowed halls of Cooperstown.

One of the few professional ballplayers born in Ireland, young Jimmy Walsh arrived in America in 1895 and settled in Syracuse, New York. He took a liking to baseball almost immediately and became somewhat of a legend on the sandlots. After bouncing around in the New York State League and the Eastern League for nearly five years, Walsh got his chance in 1912 with Connie Mack's Philadelphia A's after batting a lofty .354 for Jack Dunn's Orioles in the International League. Unfortunately, he never quite made the grade at the Major League level. Although Walsh did play in both the 1914 and 1916 World Series, over his MLB career he played sporadically and had trouble hitting. From all accounts, he had difficulty hitting the curve ball.

Walsh was finally sent back to the bushes where his career really took off. He played great baseball in the International League over the next 10 years. Between 1920 and 1927, Walsh had some phenomenal seasons batting over .300 with a high water mark of .388 in 1926, and he quickly became an International League legend. A fun-loving, quiet guy, Walsh led a quiet life after baseball, working as foreman for the Syracuse

James Charles Walsh

Department of Public Works. He died in 1962 while playing golf, his second love. He was elected to the International League Hall of Fame in 1958, and was later inducted into the Syracuse Baseball Hall of Fame and the Buffalo Bisons Hall of Fame. Not bad for a guy who struggled in the Bigs.

Born:
August 24, 1887
Rathroe, County Tipperary, Ireland

Died:
July 3, 1962
Syracuse, NY

▷ Batted: RH

▷ Threw: RH

▷ Position: OF

▷ Career BA: .232

Teams:

Philadelphia Athletics AL (1912–1913, 1914–1916)
New York Yankees AL (1914)
Boston Red Sox AL (1916–1917)

Zack Wheat

One of the premier hitters of his generation, Zack Wheat's statistics still dominate the record books of the Dodgers' organization. He played 18 seasons (1909–1926) for the Brooklyn Superbas, Robins, and Dodgers before finishing his career with the Philadelphia A's in 1927. Statistically, the latter part of Wheat's career is even more impressive than his prime. He reached double figures in home runs four times after the age of 30. In 1922, at age 34, Wheat set career highs in home runs (16) and RBI (112), while batting .335. Three years later, he was still raking the ball slugging .541 and batting .359 with 14 roundtrippers and 103 RBI.

Between 1915 and 1919, Brooklyn featured the Zack and Mack attack as Wheat's brother Mack joined the team. Truth be told, the attack was pretty one-sided. Mack Wheat's best year for the Robins was in 1919 when he hit .205 with eight RBI. Zack Wheat's mother was full-blooded Cherokee, and his father was a direct descendant of the Puritans who founded Concord, MA. Wheat himself forged a unique family history, marrying his second cousin Daisy in 1912. She eventually became his agent and negotiated yearly raises for Wheat with a hard-line style that included regular holdouts.

While he had a subpar 1916 World Series in Brooklyn's loss to the Red Sox, Wheat rebounded in the 1920 Fall Classic batting .333, but the Robins were defeated in seven games by Cleveland. Wheat's lifetime .317 batting average was highlighted by two consecutive seasons of hitting .375 (1923 and 1924). As the Deadball Era came to a close, the man they called "Buck" saw his bat come alive with four consecutive seasons of plus-.500 slugging from 1922 to 1925. He won his only batting title in 1918, but registered three seasons of 200 hits or more.

After his final season in Philly, Wheat retired to a life of farming in his home state of Missouri, and later owned a hunting and fishing resort on the Lake of the Ozarks. Elected to the Hall of Fame in 1959 by the Veterans Committee, Wheat will forever be remembered as one of the all-time great Dodgers.

Zachariah Davis Wheat

Teams:

Brooklyn Superbas/Dodgers/Robins NL (1909–1926)
Philadelphia Athletics AL (1927)

Born:
May 23, 1888
Hamilton, MO

Died:
March 11, 1972
Sedalia, MO

▷ Batted: LH

▷ Threw: RH

▷ Position: OF

▷ Career BA: .317

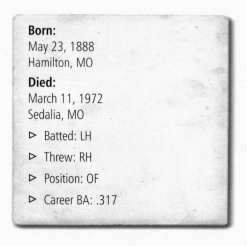

Possum Whitted

George "Possum" Whitted was one of those players that anyone would want on their team. Steady and dependable is how one could describe the play of old Possum. How did he get the nickname? Evidently Whitted had many of the characteristics of a possum: casual, retiring, solitary, a strong swimmer, docile unless disturbed, and nocturnal (he loved to stay up late at night). He is also credited with saving a man from drowning in a Louisiana river in 1915.

Born:
February 4, 1890
Durham, NC

Died:
October 15, 1962
Wilmington, NC

▷ Batted: RH

▷ Threw: RH

▷ Position: OF/3B/1B

▷ Career BA: .269

George Bostic Whitted

Whitted came up for a short stint with the Cards in 1912 and stayed with them into the 1913 season. After he was traded to Boston in 1914, Whitted settled in to really begin a nice tidy run. That year, he contributed to the Braves "Last to First" finish and their subsequent wipeout of Connie Mack's Athletics in four straight games to take the Series. The following year, Whitted was traded again, this time to the Phillies for Sherry Magee, and he wound up batting a sparkling .281, helping the Phillies to the pennant. Although they lost to the Red Sox, Possum got to play in yet another World Series. Offensively, his best season was 1917 when he batted .280 with 155 hits. From a defensive perspective, he was an above-average outfielder who would not embarrass any team.

Whitted joined the war effort in 1918 to serve Uncle Sam and returned to the Bigs in 1919. In August of that year he was traded to the Pirates for a young player named Casey Stengel. Whitted's playing days ended in 1922 with one at-bat with Brooklyn. He went on to play and manage in the minors until 1931, and continued on as a Minor League manager until 1937. When all is said and done, Whitted was one of those guys who would affectionately be referred to as a "Dirt Dog." Baseball needs more like Possum Whitted.

Teams:

St. Louis Cardinals NL (1912–1914)
Boston Braves NL (1914)
Philadelphia Phillies NL (1915–1919)
Pittsburgh Pirates NL (1919–1921)
Brooklyn Robins NL (1922)

Chief Wilson

John Owen Wilson

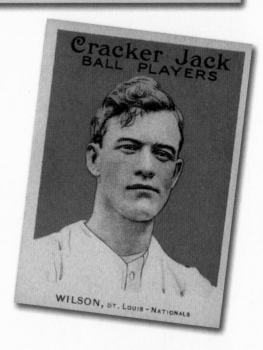

A slick-fielding player known for his strong throwing arm, Owen "Chief" Wilson had a memorable nine-year career with both the Pirates and the Cardinals. After working his way up through the Texas League and the Western League, "Tex" Wilson made his debut as a starter for the Pirates in 1908 batting a paltry .227, but was very steady defensively. With his tremendous arm, he was usually near the top of the leaderboard when it came to assists. In 1909, Wilson began to come into his own offensively, batting a respectable .272. That same year, the Pirates won the World Series but Wilson's postseason contributions were negligible.

He turned it up with the bat over the next two years hitting his high water mark with a .300 in 1911 and leading the league with 107 RBI. In 1912, Owen Wilson set two marks that are still Major League records today. He became the only player to hit an amazing 36 triples in one season, and the only player to hit a triple in five consecutive games. Both records have lasted a century. One would think the outfielders would have played him a little deeper, since the bulk of his triples were not in the gap but were line shots over the head of opposing outfielders.

After the 1913 season, Chief Wilson was dealt to the Cards in an eight-player swap and played out his career there with some solid seasons both offensively and defensively. In 1914 he led the league with 34 assists and his .983 fielding percentage. Wilson led the league again in 1915 with a .984 fielding percentage. Like many others, Wilson went back to the minors briefly before he retired to his ranch near Bertram, Texas. With his triples record, Chief Wilson left a lasting mark on our National Pastime. By the way, the nickname "Chief" came from Fred Clarke, his Pirates' manager, who said that Wilson looked like a chief of the Texas Rangers.

Teams:

Pittsburgh Pirates NL (1908–1913)
St. Louis Cardinals NL (1914–1916)

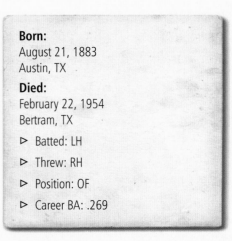

Born:
August 21, 1883
Austin, TX

Died:
February 22, 1954
Bertram, TX

▷ Batted: LH

▷ Threw: RH

▷ Position: OF

▷ Career BA: .269

8

EASTERLY, Kansas City - Federals

THE BACKSTOPS

The catchers listed in this chapter were all pretty darn good. Some were great field generals, some were good hitters, some were very good defensively and some were great clubhouse guys. The catcher is the backbone of any good defense. His hitting is usually secondary to his field and leadership skills. Many catchers go on to coach and manage. You have to be part defensive coordinator by calling balls and strikes, and part psychologist to keep your pitcher focused and prepared to throw any pitch at any given time. The group in this chapter includes just one Hall of Famer, Ray Schalk, but some of the players here were innovators when the game was still in its infancy stages. They opened the gates for the greats like Cochrane, Dickey, Campanella, Berra and Bench. Meet the backstops of the Cracker Jack Collection.

MEYERS, New York - Nationals

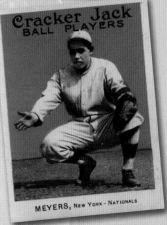

O'NEILL, Cleveland - Americans

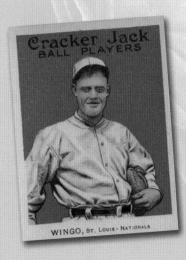

WINGO, St. Louis - Nationals

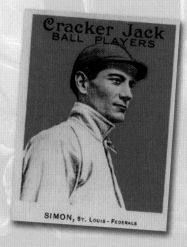

SIMON, St. Louis - Federals

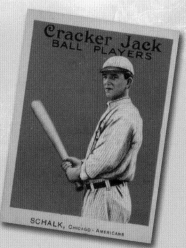

SCHALK, Chicago - Americans

RARIDEN, Indianapolis - Federals

Jimmy Archer

Walter Blair

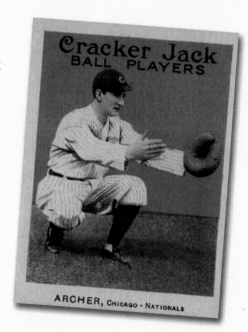

Thought by many to have the best throwing arm of his era, Jimmy Archer made his money by pegging out would-be base stealers and by his patented snap throw from the squat. This talent may have come from tragedy. As a teenager in Canada, Archer worked in a Toronto barrel cooperage, and severely injured his arm when he fell into a vat of scalding oak sap. Although the injuries healed with time, the tendon in his right arm contracted. This physiological twist of fate enabled him to perfect the snap throw.

A Chicago Cub from 1909 until 1917, Archer led the National League in assists for a catcher in 1912 and was consistently in the top five in that category. In 1910, he threw out more than 54 percent of the runners who attempted to steal, best in the NL. At 5-foot, 10-inches, and 168 pounds, Archer was built low to the ground and was also perennially in the top five in fielding percentage, putouts, and games played as a catcher.

Born in Dublin, Ireland, Archer did not have the luck of the Irish in the postseason. He played for the Tigers in 1907 when the team lost to the Cubs in the World Series. Three years later, he was on the Cubs as they lost to Philadelphia in the Series. Archer hit just .143 in World Series play. Jimmy Archer's career ended in 1918, and he retired to a life of competitive bowling and softball. He was inducted into the Canadian Baseball Hall of Fame in 1990 and will forever be remembered for making "snap" decisions behind the plate.

Primarily a backup catcher who was considered good defensively, Walter "Heavy" Blair had a fairly undistinguished career as a Major League ballplayer. Blair played baseball at Bucknell University before launching his professional career with the Williamsport Millionaires of the Tri-State League. The New York Highlanders saw something in the young collegian and brought him up to the Bigs in 1907, where he settled in as their backup catcher for the next four seasons.

A weak hitter, Blair's best offensive season was 1914 when he batted .243 for the Buffalo Buffeds of the Federal League. Most players who jumped to the upstart Federal League would see their offensive numbers go up, but Blair's stats remained flat. He did have the opportunity to manage the Buffalo Blues for two games in 1915, going 1–1. Between stints in the American League and Federal League, Blair played in the minors where he actually did quite well.

Born:
May 13, 1883
Dublin, Ireland

Died:
March 29, 1958
Milwaukee, WI

▷ Batted: RH

▷ Threw: RH

▷ Position: C

▷ Career BA: .249

James Patrick Archer

Teams:
Pittsburgh Pirates NL (1904, 1918)
Detroit Tigers AL (1907)
Chicago Cubs NL (1909–1917)
Brooklyn Robins NL (1918)
Cincinnati Reds NL (1918)

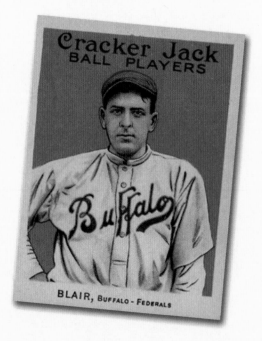

Walter Allen Blair

After the 1915 season, he became part-owner and manager of Harrisburg in the New York State League, before finally finding his niche as a coach at the collegiate level. In 1917 Blair coached at the University of Pittsburgh and then returned to coach at his alma mater. At Bucknell, Blair took an active role in promoting the athletic program and was heavily involved with the construction of Bucknell's Memorial Stadium as well as the Bucknell Golf Course. Walter "Heavy" Blair was elected into the Bucknell Hall of Fame in 1987.

Teams:

New York Highlanders AL (1907–1911)
Buffalo Buffeds/Blues FL (1914; player-manager: 1915)

Born:
October 13, 1883
Landrus, PA
Died:
August 20, 1948
Lewisburg, PA
▷ Batted: RH
▷ Threw: RH
▷ Position: C
▷ Career BA: .217
▷ Managerial Record: 1–1

Hick Cady

As a 26-year-old rookie, Forrest "Hick" Cady caught the eye of Red Sox manager Jake Stahl with his powerful, accurate throwing arm. Stahl brought him up to Boston in 1912 as backup catcher to Bill Carrigan. A talented defensive catcher, Cady quickly became the preferred batterymate of Red Sox pitching ace Smokey Joe Wood, but continued to serve as back up to Carrigan throughout his six seasons with the Sox.

Cady saw action in three World Series (1912, 1915, 1916) and caught in seven games in the 1912 Fall Classic. That year he batted a respectable .259 and in 1915 a solid .278. In one remarkable at-bat on June 29th during the 1912 Championship season, Cady managed to get *two hits* on *one at-bat*. Evidently he singled, which scored Jake Stahl from third base, but the umpire called a balk and the hit was negated. Cady went back into the batters box and promptly hit a double. Now that's a bit of unusual trivia for the record books. Defensively, Cady was dependable behind the plate with his high water mark being in 1915 when he accumulated 313 putouts and eight errors in 400 chances, and his .980 fielding percentage was second best in the league.

Tragedy struck in the 1917 offseason when Cady's shoulder was shattered in a car accident that killed one of his passengers. Although injured, Cady was still included in the January 1918 trade to the Philadelphia Athletics with two other players for the great Stuffy McInnis. Cady sat out the 1918 season in Philly while his

injuries healed. Although he saw active duty again in 1919 with the A's, his MLB playing days were numbered. Cady played in the minors through the 1924 season and later umpired in the Pacific Coast League. On March 3, 1946, Hick Cady died in a tragic hotel fire in Cedar Rapids, Iowa. Three championships in seven years. Not bad for a backup catcher.

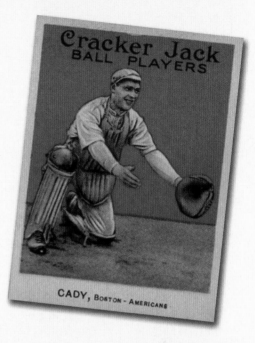

CADY, Boston - Americans

Forrest Leroy Cady

Born: Forrest Leroy Bergland

Born:
January 26, 1886
Bishop Hill, IL
Died:
March 3, 1946
▷ Cedar Rapids, IA
▷ Batted: RH
▷ Threw: RH
▷ Position: C
▷ Career BA: .240

Teams:

Boston Red Sox AL (1912–1917)
Philadelphia Phillies NL (1919)

Bill Carrigan

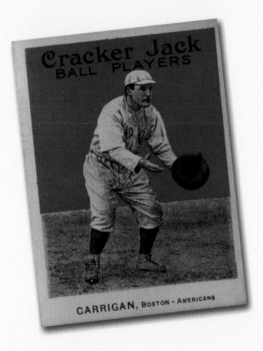

CARRIGAN, BOSTON - AMERICANS

Bill Carrigan and Terry Francona will forever be remembered as the only two managers in Red Sox history to date to win two World Series titles with Boston. A native of Lewiston, Maine, Carrigan came up to the Red Sox out of Holy Cross College, where he was converted from infield to catcher by future Hall of Famer, Tommy McCarthy. Nicknamed "Rough" because of his ability to block the plate with his body, Carrigan was a steady hitter and excellent defensively.

He played on the 1912 Red Sox Championship team, and in July 1913 the 29-year-old Carrigan took over the helm after manager Jake Stahl was fired. As player-manager, he led the Sox to a second-place finish in 1914, and then won back-to-back World Series in 1915 and 1916. Well-respected throughout the league as both a fiery competitor

and student of the game, Carrigan's leadership skills solidified the ball club. He was instrumental in convincing Red Sox ownership to acquire Babe Ruth from Baltimore as a pitcher. Although sometimes criticized for not using Ruth primarily as a hitter, Carrigan's plan was to develop his protégé into a premier pitcher because with Tris Speaker, Duffy Lewis and Harry Hooper, there was no need for Ruth in the outfield. In later years, Ruth maintained that Bill Carrigan was the best manager he ever had.

After two wildly successful seasons, Carrigan left baseball in 1916 to spend more time with his young family. He returned to Lewiston to launch a successful career in real estate and banking, but continued to get MLB offers every offseason. Carrigan was finally lured back to manage the Red Sox in 1927 but had no success. After finishing in eighth place three years in a row, Carrigan returned to his banking career in Maine. A member of the Holy Cross Hall of Fame and the Red Sox Hall of Fame, Carrigan will be remembered for his tough but cerebral approach to the game.

Born:
October 22, 1883
Lewiston, ME

Died:
July 8, 1969
Lewiston, ME

▷ Batted: RH

▷ Threw: RH

▷ Position: C

▷ Career BA: .257

▷ Managerial Record: 489–500

Team:
Boston Americans/Red Sox AL (1906, 1908–1912;
player-manager: 1913–1916; manager: 1927–
1929)

William Francis Carrigan

Red Dooin

Because of his slight build he wasn't taken seriously as a catcher at first, but Charles "Red" Dooin eventually enjoyed a stellar career as a Major League catcher. After attending Xavier University, Dooin worked as a tailor while playing the Minor League circuit in the late 1890s and finally got into the big leagues in 1902 with the Phillies. Although he was very small in stature, Dooin proved to be tough at the plate and was not afraid to mix it up with base sliders. Unfortunately, this resulted in a broken ankle in 1910 and a broken leg in 1911. When he was not injured, the feisty redhead was a steady, competent catcher who excelled at working with pitchers. Offensively, he was a marginal hitter, although he did manage to bat .328 in 1911 for the Phils with 247 at-bats.

Dooin took over as skipper of the Phillies in 1910. As player-manager, he led them to second place in 1913, and had an overall winning record north of .500. He is credited with developing future Hall of Fame pitcher Grover Cleveland Alexander, who had a fantastic rookie year in 1911. One of the early innovators of the game, Dooin was the first to wear lightweight, paper-mache shin guards under his stockings to prevent his legs from being slashed by spikes. Although Roger Bresnahan is credited with the invention, Dooin maintained that Bresnahan learned of the idea when he slid into home and collided with Dooin's reinforced stockings. Bresnahan developed the idea into padded shin guards worn over his stockings that he removed when not catching, whereas Dooin wore his shin guards throughout the game.

After injuries put an end to his career Dooin became a successful businessman, only to lose everything when the stock market crashed. In the offseason as a player, Dooin sang and acted in vaudeville. After his business ventures failed, his baritone voice came to the rescue and he enjoyed a lucrative career in vaudeville and on the radio. Player, manager, inventor, entertainer...Red Dooin was a very interesting guy.

Teams:
Philadelphia Phillies NL (1902–1909; player-manager: 1910–1914)
Cincinnati Reds NL (1915)
New York Giants NL (1915, 1916)

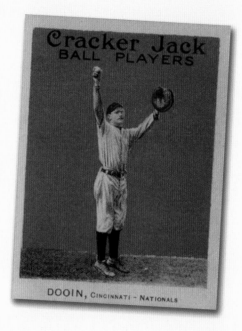

Charles Sebastian Dooin

Born:
June 12, 1879
Cincinnati, OH

Died:
May 14, 1952
Rochester, NY

▷ Batted: RH

▷ Threw: RH

▷ Position: C

▷ Career BA: .240

▷ Managerial Record: 392–370

Ted Easterly

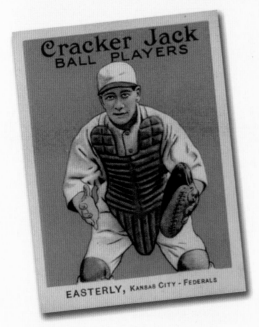

One of the premier pinch hitters of the Deadball Era, Ted Easterly got his start in the Pacific Coast League playing for Los Angeles at the single-A level. The young catcher with the big bat quickly caught the eye of the Cleveland Naps who brought Easterly up in 1909 after just over a year in the minors. As backup catcher for the Naps, Easterly topped a .300 batting average three seasons in a row, from 1910 through 1912, and led the league in pinch hits in 1912. His best season with the Naps was 1911 when he batted .324 in 287 at-bats. Easterly was a good defensive catcher with a strong arm who could also manage pitchers.

In 1914, he jumped to the new Federal League and had a great season in the weaker league batting .335 with 146 hits in 436 at-bats. That year he wound up third in his quest for the batting title. The Federal League collapsed after the 1915 season and, like many players that jumped to the Feds, Ted was not welcomed back to the majors. He found himself back in the Pacific Coast League playing for his old Minor League team in Los Angeles. Easterly kicked around the PCL and the Texas League for a few seasons, but did not play much at that point in his career, batting .259 in 78 games for Sacramento and .310 in only 54 games for Beaumont in the Texas League. After the 1920 season, Easterly called it quits and returned to California. He passed away in 1951 at age 66.

Born:
April 20, 1885
Lincoln, NE

Died:
July 6, 1951
Clearlake Highlands, CA

▷ Batted: LH

▷ Threw: RH

▷ Position: C

▷ Career BA: .300

Theodore Harrison Easterly

Teams:
Cleveland Naps AL (1909–1912)
Chicago White Sox AL (1912–1913)
Kansas City Packers FL (1914–1915)

There is a special place in our hearts for Ted Easterly. In our first book, *The T206 Collection: The Players & Their Stories*, we mention that we started collecting T206 cards after finding a Ted Easterly card while rummaging through a box of memorabilia in a Cooperstown, NY antique store. The Easterly card not only got us interested in the storied T206 Collection, but in the Deadball Era itself. That Easterly card is still our favorite. It is in poor condition, but it has a special meaning for us. Thanks Ted!

Hank Gowdy

Coming up to the Giants for a short stint at first base at the end of the 1910 season, Texas Leaguer Hank Gowdy was advised by manager John McGraw to switch to catcher for more playing time as Fred Merkle was already entrenched at first base. After four at-bats early in the 1911 season, Gowdy moved to the Boston Rustlers to back up manager Fred Tenney at first base. The next season his team had a new name and a new manager, and Gowdy finally made the switch to catcher.

Manager George Stallings sent him to the minors to hone his skills in 1913, which was the turning point in his career. Gowdy did so well that he became the regular backstop for the Braves later that season. An integral part of the Braves amazing run to the World Series Championship in 1914, Gowdy proceeded to eat up American League pitching and batted a gaudy .545 in the Series. After a few successful seasons in Boston, his life changed forever in June of 1917. Hank Gowdy became the first Major League ballplayer to enlist during World War I. He served in the famed Rainbow Division, carrying the flag for the Fighting 42nd infantry and seeing fierce hand-to-hand combat in the trenches against the Germans. Gowdy returned from the conflict a famous and beloved war hero, and went on a speaking tour before continuing on with his baseball career.

After the Braves traded him to the Giants in 1923, Gowdy played in two World Series although he famously muffed a play in the 12th inning of Game 7 of the 1924 Series that cost the Giants the win. After he was released in 1925, Gowdy played in the minors before returning to coach and play with the Braves in 1929 and 1930. He coached for the Giants and Reds in the 1930s, and served Uncle Sam again during World War II. Major Gowdy served as the chief athletic officer at Fort Benning, where the playing field is now named after him. Hank Gowdy earned his place in baseball history as a very good catcher who distinguished himself as one of baseball's first war heroes.

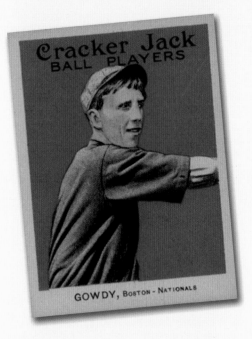

GOWDY, Boston - Nationals

Born:
August 24, 1889
Columbus, OH

Died:
August 1, 1966
Columbus, OH

▷ Batted: RH

▷ Threw: RH

▷ Position: C

▷ Career BA: .270

Henry Morgan Gowdy

Teams:
New York Giants NL (1910–1911, 1923–1925)
Boston Rustlers/Braves NL (1911–1917, 1919–1923, 1929–1930)

Bill Killefer

Chief Meyers

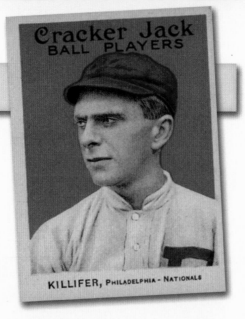

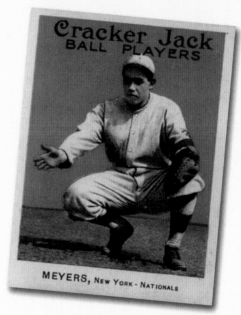

Several great batterymates have gained fame over the course of baseball history; Grove and Cochrane, Paige and Gibson, Ford and Berra, Carleton and McCarver. There are, of course, many more. Two that tend to be overlooked are Grover Cleveland Alexander "Old Pete" and Bill Killefer "Reindeer Bill." Killefer was an outstanding catcher who caught Alexander 250 times. With cat-like reflexes and a powerful, accurate throwing arm, he was a skilled defensive catcher with a knack for calling a great game.

Coming up from Houston of the Texas League, Killefer made his debut with the St. Louis Browns in the American League, but was released after the 1910 season. He was dispatched to the Eastern League where, under the tutelage of his future brother-in-law George Stallings, he developed into a fine catcher. Once Killefer was established as a front line catcher, he would at one time or another lead the league in fielding percentage, assists, baserunners caught stealing, putouts and double plays. In a nutshell, Bill Killefer was one of the best at that position. Unfortunately, he is sometimes overlooked when discussing the real "greats" because of his weak batting skills. After many years as batterymates, Killefer and Alexander went

over to the Cubs together in 1918. This proved to be the infusion that the Cubs needed to win the pennant, but they lost to the Red Sox in the World Series.

By 1921, injuries sustained over Killefer's long career caught up with him, greatly reducing his playing time. Always popular with his teammates, cheers were heard in the clubhouse when Killefer was named manager of the Cubs late that season. He skippered the Cubs through 1925 with a 300–293 record. He then coached for the Cardinals and the Browns before managing the Browns from 1930 through 1933. He remained in baseball for many years, managing in the minors, coaching for the Dodgers and Phillies, and scouting for the Dodgers, Phillies and Indians. Killefer developed a reputation for mentoring young pitchers and catchers and, as a scout, was instrumental in signing Larry Doby, the first black player in the history of the American League. Between playing, managing, coaching and scouting, Bill Killefer enjoyed a remarkable 48-year run in baseball.

One of the more captivating players of the Cracker Jack Collection, John Tortes "Chief" Meyers was a man of many talents who made his mark on our National Pastime. A Native American from the Cahuilla Tribe, Meyers attended Dartmouth College in 1905 and did very well academically. When Dartmouth officials discovered that he never completed high school, they offered him admittance if he would complete a prep program. Instead, Meyers signed with Harrisburg of the Tri-State League and was on his way to becoming one of the best catchers of the Deadball Era.

As he worked his way up through the Minor League ranks dealing with the racism that was prevalent at the time, Meyers' experience in the Northwestern League and the American Association was difficult, to say the least. His persistence and hard work paid off and in 1909 he made the New York Giants team. After getting his feet wet the first year, Chief Meyers, as he became known, developed into the best-hitting catcher in baseball.

Born:
October 10, 1887
Bloomingdale, MI

Died:
July 3, 1960
Elsmere, DE

▷ Batted: RH

▷ Threw: RH

▷ Position: C

▷ Career BA: .238

▷ Managerial Record: 524–622

William Killefer

Teams:

St. Louis Browns AL (1909–1910; manager:
1930–1933)

Philadelphia Phillies NL (1911–1917)

Chicago Cubs NL (1918–1920; player-manager:
1921; manager: 1922–1925)

John Tortes Meyers

In 1911 he batted .332 and in 1912 he not only batted .358 but his .441 on-base percentage led the league. For three consecutive years Meyers was a candidate to win the Chalmers award as the Most Valuable Player. From a defensive standpoint, he was better than average and worked very well with his pitchers.

As his popularity increased Meyers played the vaudeville circuit in the offseason, demonstrating pitching and catching techniques with his batterymate Christy Mathewson. Outside of the diamond, Meyers was considered an intellectual who frequented museums and enjoyed engaging in political debate. Going into the 1915 season, the wear and tear of catching began to take its toll and Meyers' skills began to diminish. He spent 1917 between Brooklyn and Boston before joining the U.S. Marine Corps to serve in World War I. Upon his return, Meyers played and managed in the minors until 1920. After leaving the game, he served as police chief and later worked as an Indian Supervisor for the Department of the Interior.

Teams:
New York Giants NL (1909–1915)
Brooklyn Robins NL (1916–1917)
Boston Braves NL (1917)

Born:
July 29, 1880
Riverside, CA
Died:
July 25, 1971
San Bernardino, CA
▷ Batted: RH
▷ Threw: RH
▷ Position: C
▷ Career BA: .291

Otto Miller

Lowell Otto Miller

OTTO MILLER, Brooklyn - Nationals

Otto "Moonie" Miller was a so-so catcher who played his entire career with Brooklyn of the National League. Over the 13 years that Miller played, his team changed names three times, going from the Superbas to the Dodgers, and then renaming themselves the Robins after manager Will Robinson. They later settled on the Dodgers, but that was several years after Miller had retired from the team.

Nicknamed for his round face, "Moonie" came up to the Superbas after two seasons in the minors. Known mostly for his defensive play, Miller had a career .973 fielding percentage, which was not bad. From an offensive standpoint, Miller's best year was 1920 when he batted .289 with 301 at-bats. That year his defensive stats as catcher led the National League in putouts with 418, range factor with 5.43, and fielding percentage with .986. Miller had the opportunity to play on two Brooklyn pennant-winning teams in 1916 and 1920, and actually played a role in an historical baseball event. In the fifth inning of Game 5 of the 1920 World Series, he was part of the only unassisted triple play in World Series history. Clarence Mitchell was at the plate and hit a line drive to Cleveland's second baseman Bill Wambsganss who stepped on second to retire Pete Kilduff and tagged out poor Miller who was barreling in from first.

Team:
Brooklyn Superbas/Dodgers/Robins NL (1910–1922)

Like many other players of that era, Miller went back to the minors after his Major League playing days were over. He eventually managed the Atlanta Crackers of the Southern Association and later the Kingsport Indians of the Appalachian League. Miller then returned to the Dodgers as coach and also did a bit of coaching for the Red Sox.

Born:
June 1, 1889
Minden, NE
Died:
March 29, 1962
Brooklyn, NY
▷ Batted: RH
▷ Threw: RH
▷ Position: C
▷ Career BA: .245

Les Nunamaker

Steve O'Neill

Born and raised in Nebraska, Les Nunamaker was the son of pioneers who helped settle Hamilton County. He came up to the big leagues by way of the Haskel Indians, Dubuque Dubs and the Lincoln Railsplitters. Nunamaker caught for Grover Cleveland Alexander when they both played for a town team in St. Paul, Minnesota, and it was through Alexander that he got a chance to catch in the big leagues.

The best years of his career were with the Yankees. On August 3, 1914, during his first season in New York, Nunamaker threw out three Detroit Tigers at second base in the same inning. He got Hugh High, Sam Crawford, and Bobby Veach in succession; a notable feat that set a Major League record he still holds today. In 1916, Nunamaker batted .296 for the pinstripes. Although he was considered a durable, steady backstop and above average defensively, Nunamaker split catching duties with various other teammates for most of his career. He had the good fortune of playing on two World

Leslie Grant Nunamaker

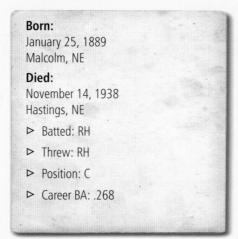

Born:
January 25, 1889
Malcolm, NE
Died:
November 14, 1938
Hastings, NE
▷ Batted: RH
▷ Threw: RH
▷ Position: C
▷ Career BA: .268

Series Championship teams. While with the Red Sox in 1912 he did not see any Series action, but with Cleveland in 1920, Nunamaker got some playing time and delivered one hit in his two at-bats.

After a Major League career that spanned 12 years and four teams, Les Nunamaker became player-manager for several Minor League teams, finishing up with the Lincoln Links back in his home state of Nebraska through the 1931 season. He finally retired to Hastings, Nebraska, where he worked with his brother in the family business, the Pioneer Cash Market. He died in 1938, at age 49, after being ill for several months.

Teams:
Boston Red Sox AL (1911–1914)
New York Yankees AL (1914–1917)
St. Louis Browns AL (1918)
Cleveland Indians AL (1919–1922)

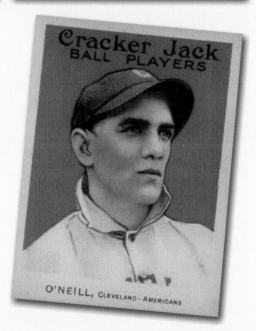

O'NEILL, CLEVELAND - AMERICANS

From all accounts, Steve O'Neill was one of the most respected men to ever play the game. More than that, he was beloved by players and fans. At his funeral, Commissioner Ford Frick called O'Neill "A man with no enemies in baseball." Considering that his career spanned five decades, that is an amazing accomplishment.

O'Neill was one of four brothers who made it to the big leagues after starting out in the coal mines of Pennsylvania. Throughout his 17-year playing career, O'Neill was considered one of the best

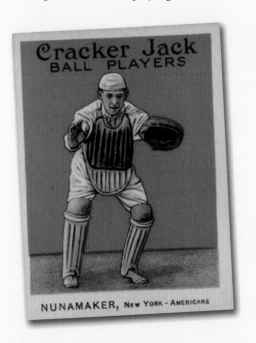

NUNAMAKER, New York - Americans

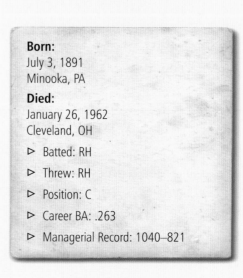

Born:
July 3, 1891
Minooka, PA
Died:
January 26, 1962
Cleveland, OH
▷ Batted: RH
▷ Threw: RH
▷ Position: C
▷ Career BA: .263
▷ Managerial Record: 1040–821

Stephen Francis O'Neill

catchers in baseball. With Cleveland in 1920, he caught all seven games and batted .333 in the World Series helping propel the Indians to the Championship. A steady .263 lifetime hitter and an outstanding defensive specialist, O'Neill's real strength was managing. He worked his way up from managing in the International League, and then skippered the Indians, Tigers, Red Sox and Phillies. In 1945, his Detroit Tigers won the World Series. O'Neill never had a losing record with any organization that he managed and ranks 51st on the all-time wins list.

His influence on players was legendary. One of the greatest mentors the game has ever known, O'Neill is credited with helping the career of Bob Feller and Lou Boudreau, among others. A caring mentor outside the lines as well, he once gave a lift to a young hitchhiker who ran away from home. As the story goes, he told the hitchhiker that no one can run away from their problems, and gave him money so he could get back home. Many years later that hitchhiker sent flowers to O'Neill's funeral to honor the man he had never forgotten. Although O'Neill has been considered for entry into the Hall of Fame more than once, at this time he has not yet been inducted. Whether or not he ever gets into the Hall, Steve O'Neill will always be remembered as an exceptional manager and a great man.

Teams:
Cleveland Naps/Indians AL (1911–1923; manager: 1935–1937)
Boston Red Sox AL (1924; manager: 1950–1951)
New York Yankees AL (1925)
St. Louis Browns AL (1927–1928)
Detroit Tigers AL (manager: 1943–1948)
Philadelphia Phillies NL (manager: 1952–1954)

Frank Owens

Frank Walter Owens

One of few Canadian-born catchers to play in the Major Leagues, Frank Owens had a lengthy career in the minors around his sporadic stints in the American League and the Federal League. In 1905, the 19-year-old Owens came up for a short stint with the Boston Americans, batting .000 in his two at-bats in his first and only game with Boston. After three seasons with the Memphis Egyptians in the Southern Association, he made it back to the Bigs in 1909 to catch 57 games for the White Sox, and batted a paltry .201. He was sent down to the Minneapolis Millers in the American Association where he honed his skills for four seasons before getting his big break with the fledgling Federal League.

Statistically speaking, Owens was not strong although his numbers went up in the inferior Federal League. In 1915 he finished third in the league in putouts and range factor, and fourth in assists as catcher. After the collapse of the Federal League, Owens returned to the Millers to catch for them through the 1920 season. After an attempt at managing the St. Joseph Saints in the Western League in 1921, it was back to Minneapolis for one final season.

Known more for his defense, Owens had a strong arm and was considered pretty good at calling a game. With

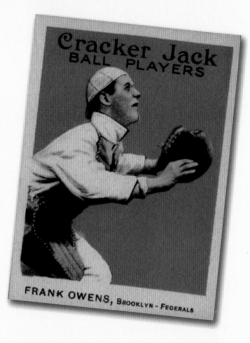

Minneapolis for 10 seasons, one of the longest tenures of any Millers catcher, Owens is deemed one of the best catchers in the history of the team. By the way, Frank Owens is not to be confused with the pitcher, Frank Owen, who played for the White Sox from 1903 to 1909.

Teams:
Boston Americans AL (1905)
Chicago White Sox AL (1909)
Brooklyn Tip-Tops FL (1914)
Baltimore Terrapins FL (1915)

Born:
January 26, 1886
Toronto, Ontario, Canada

Died:
July 2, 1958
Minneapolis, MN

▷ Batted: RH

▷ Threw: RH

▷ Position: C

▷ Career BA: .245

Bill Rariden

Ray Schalk

Even though he was a weak hitter, any manager would have loved "Bedford Bill" Rariden behind the plate. Keeping in mind that bunting was a key strategy during the Deadball Era, Rariden was exceptional because of his small frame and agility at throwing out baserunners. Actually, Rariden still holds the record for most assists in a season for a catcher (238), albeit for the Newark Pepper of the fledgling Federal League. From a defensive standpoint Rariden was quite good, leading the league as catcher in putouts in 1914, 1915, and 1916; assists in 1914 and 1915; and range factor in 1915 and 1916. The light-hitting Rariden had a decent offensive season in 1917 batting .271.

After the Federal League folded, Rariden caught most of the games for John McGraw's Giants. Although he did not shine offensively, he was stellar behind the plate and it is unfortunate that he is remembered for a mental mistake that cost the 1917 Giants the World Series. In Game 6, the Giants had future Hall of Famer Eddie Collins in a rundown from third base, but Rariden failed to cover the plate, which forced Giants third baseman Heinie Zimmerman to chase Collins down the line. There was speculation that

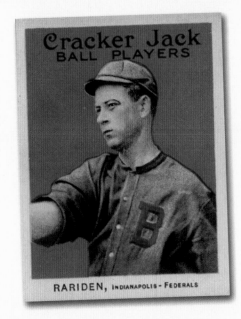

RARIDEN, INDIANAPOLIS - FEDERALS

Zimmerman allowed Collins to score because he bet against his own team and threw the game, but Zimmerman denied it. Rariden, on the other hand, simply made a bad play. Could Zimmerman have tagged out Collins? Some say that he certainly could. If Rariden were in position, however, the Zimmerman controversy would never have taken place. Bill Rariden also participated in another controversial World Series. This time he was on the winning side as the World Champ Cincinnati team the beat the 1919 Black Sox. Although he only batted .211 in the Series, he did a very nice job behind the plate.

If you were to list the essential qualities of a catcher, you might just need to write two words: Ray Schalk. Slightly built, Schalk was a 5-foot, 9-inch, 165 pound package of strength. In his 18-year Major League career, he was a catcher, period. Unlike other backstops, Schalk did not venture into the outfield or to first base as he aged. He knew just one home, and it was behind home plate.

For 17 years, he called pitches for the Chicago White Sox, and although his career ended in 1929 with the Giants, Schalk will forever be remembered as a South Sider. He never hit .300, never hit more than four home runs in a season, and never led the league in any major offensive category, yet he finished in the top 10 in MVP voting twice (1914 and 1922). This tells the story of Schalk's value.

If you want to talk stats, strap on the catcher's gear. Schalk led the American League in putouts every season between 1913 and 1920, and again in 1922. He didn't just block the plate, he guarded it like a sentinel. He was consistently among the best in assists and fielding percentage, and led the AL in games played for a

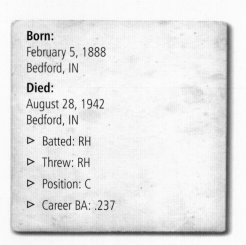

Born:
February 5, 1888
Bedford, IN

Died:
August 28, 1942
Bedford, IN

▷ Batted: RH

▷ Threw: RH

▷ Position: C

▷ Career BA: .237

William Angle Rariden

Teams:
Boston Doves/Rustlers/Braves NL (1909–1913)
Indianapolis Hoosiers FL (1914)
Newark Pepper FL (1915)
New York Giants NL (1916–1918)
Cincinnati Reds NL (1919–1920)

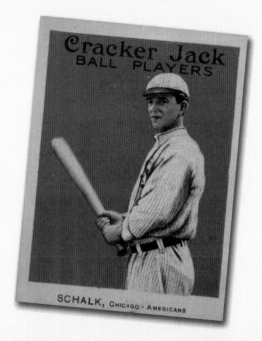

SCHALK, CHICAGO - AMERICANS

Raymond William Schalk

catcher seven times. Schalk's 30 steals in 1916 stood as the record for catchers until John Wathan swiped 36 in 1982. As a publicity stunt, he once caught a ball dropped from Chicago's 463-foot Tribune Tower.

Schalk, who was player-manager of the ChiSox in 1927 and 1928, got his nickname Cracker from his relentless cracking of the whip with pitchers. He caught four no-hitters, popularized the art of backing up bases, and boasted of scoring a putout at every base. He was also a leader in double plays for a catcher. Perhaps most importantly, Schalk was not involved in the 1919 Black Sox World Series scandal. This integrity extended into retirement as he founded Baseball Anonymous, a program that aided impoverished players; coached and scouted for the Cubs; managed in the minors; and coached at Purdue University. Schalk was inducted into the Hall of Fame in 1955. His plaque is filled with numerous factoids, but could simply read: Ray Schalk, a catcher's catcher.

Teams:
Chicago White Sox AL (1912–1926; player-manager: 1927–1928)
New York Giants NL (1929)

Born:
August 12, 1892
Harvel, IL
Died:
May 19, 1970
Chicago, IL
▷ Batted: RH
▷ Threw: RH
▷ Position: C
▷ Career BA: .253
▷ Managerial Record: 102–125

Wally Schang

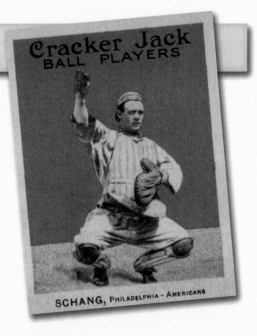

SCHANG, PHILADELPHIA - AMERICANS

From Bill Dickey to Yogi Berra to Gary Carter, there must be something about Hall of Fame catchers and the number eight. Wally Schang did not make it to Cooperstown, but his ability behind the plate over a 19-year career put him in that rarified air of baseball's top catchers. Schang, whose brother Bobby was also a big-league catcher, recorded 5,202 putouts and 1,420 assists for the A's, Red Sox, Yankees, Browns and Tigers.

An athletic catcher, Schang got a glove on many pitches that others would not have touched. For this reason, perhaps, he was often unfairly among the league leaders in errors and passed balls. Many baserunners tested the arm of Schang, and many failed as he whistled darts that nailed would-be base swipers. Schang did his job at the plate as well with a career batting average of .284 and 1,506 hits. Those, however, were not his only hits. Built like a steel barrel at 5-foot, 10-inches and 180 pounds, Schang presented a wide target for enemy hurlers. He was hit by pitches 107 times in his career and led the American League twice in that category. Between 1913 and 1917 alone, he was hit 51 times. Schang was a patient hitter who consistently walked more than he struck out. He is also the holder of a unique baseball first. In 1916, he became the first ever Major Leaguer to hit a home run from both sides of the plate in the same game.

Teams:
Philadelphia Athletics AL (1913–1917, 1930)
Boston Red Sox AL (1918–1920)
New York Yankees AL (1921–1925)
St. Louis Browns AL (1926–1929)
Detroit Tigers AL (1931)

In Philadelphia's 1913 World Series win over the Giants, Schang hit .357 with seven RBI. With the Red Sox in 1918, he batted .444 in the Series win versus Chicago. In 1923, Schang sparked a dynasty hitting .318 against the Giants as the Yankees won their first ever World Series. Schang had some postseason clunkers as well, but overall, he batted .287 in six Fall Classics. In retirement, Schang played and managed in the minors until 1946, and coached in Cleveland where he mentored a young prospect named Bob Feller. A real gamer, Schang proudly wore that number eight, which in no coincidence, rhymes with great.

Walter Henry Schang

Born:
August 22, 1889
South Wales, NY
Died:
March 6, 1965
St. Louis, MO
▷ Batted: Switch
▷ Threw: RH
▷ Position: C
▷ Career BA: .284

Mike Simon

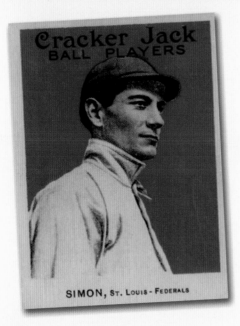

SIMON, St. Louis - Federals

Stocky, solid, and strong, Mike Simon hailed from Hayden, Indiana and attended Indiana University in Bloomington. In 1909, the brawny catcher went from a Hoosier to a Buc, joining the Pittsburgh Pirates for what would be a five-year run as a catcher. Playing behind starter George Gibson, Simon may not have been a rookie sensation, but he did enjoy immediate team success riding the Pittsburgh train to a 1909 World Series victory in seven games over the Detroit Tigers.

Simon backed up Gibson from 1909 until 1912. The latter season was a breakout one for Simon as he hit .301 in 42 games. Frustration had to be the watchword for Simon as George Gibson was no Josh Gibson. Simon sat behind a guy whose career batting average for the Pirates was just .238. There were, however, some fringe benefits to being part of the Bucs team. Simon got to share a dugout with Max Carey, one of the best players of his time, and of course, the one and only Honus Wagner, who was still very productive in his mid-30s for Pittsburgh.

Finally, in 1913, Simon leapfrogged over Gibson and became Pittsburgh's starting backstop. He set career highs in games, at-bats, and hits. Simon also hit his first and only big-league home run that season. His batting average dipped to .247, but he was reliable behind the dish with 393 putouts and 151 assists, good for second in the National League behind Philadelphia's Bill Killefer. Alas, Simon also led the NL in passed balls. 1913 would be Simon's last in Pittsburgh. He would finish out his pro career in the Federal League with the St. Louis Terriers and Brooklyn Tip-Tops. Simon was a hard-nosed player who gave his all and performed well when finally given the chance.

Born:
April 13, 1883
Hayden, IN

Died:
June 10, 1963
Los Angeles, CA

▷ Batted: RH

▷ Threw: RH

▷ Position: C

▷ Career BA: .225

Michael Edward Simon

Teams:

Pittsburgh Pirates NL (1909–1913)
St. Louis Terriers FL (1914)
Brooklyn Tip-Tops FL (1915)

Ed Sweeney

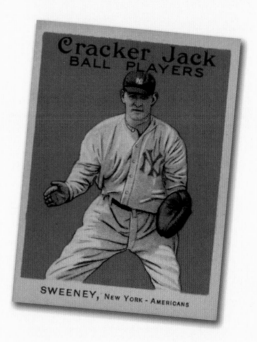

SWEENEY, New York - Americans

Known more for his effective handling of pitchers and defensive play than for his ability to swing a bat, Edward "Jeff" Sweeney was one of the first decent Highlanders/Yankees catchers. After just one season in the Southern Association with the Atlanta Crackers, Sweeney was signed by the Highlanders in 1908 at the age of 19, and saw action in 32 games but batted a paltry .146. As his skills developed, Sweeney earned more playing time, and by 1910 he took Red Kleinow's slot as starting catcher. His two best years were in 1912 and 1913 when he batted .268 and .265 respectively and played in 227 games between both seasons. As catcher, Sweeney led the league with his 548 putouts and 6.62 range factor in 1912 and his 180 assists in 1913.

One of the first players to make it to the Bigs from Loyola University in Chicago, Sweeney's playing time diminished in 1915 when he batted an anemic .190. He spent the next two

Edward Francis Sweeney

seasons with the Toledo Iron Men in the American Association before enlisting in the U.S. Navy to serve in World War I. Sweeney got one last shot in the majors in 1919 for the Pittsburgh Pirates, batting a miniscule .095 in just 17 games. He finished up his playing career in 1920 between the Seattle Rainiers of the Pacific Coast League and the Kansas City Blues of the American Association. He retired to Chicago to work as an electrical switchman, and died of lung cancer in 1947 at the age of 58.

Teams:

New York Highlanders/Yankees AL (1908–1915)
Pittsburgh Pirates NL (1919)

Born:
July 19, 1888
Chicago, IL

Died:
July 4, 1947
Chicago, IL

▷ Batted: RH

▷ Threw: RH

▷ Position: C

Career BA: .232

Ira Thomas

Ira Felix Thomas

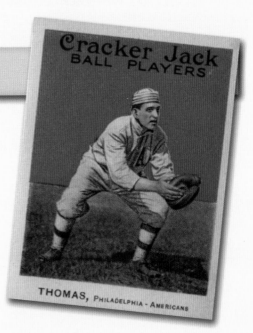

It is interesting that Ira Thomas was even included in the Cracker Jack Collection. Over the two-year period that the cards were released, Ira had exactly three at-bats with a batting average of .000. Why was he in the Collection? A very good catcher with a pretty good bat, Thomas came up from the Eastern League to hook up with the New York Highlanders in 1906 and saw limited action in 44 games, batting .200, but he was considered very strong defensively. Thomas was traded to the Tigers in 1908, and actually appeared in the World Series. As a matter of fact, he had the first pinch hit in World Series history.

In December 1908, Thomas was sold to the Philadelphia Athletics where he blossomed as both a team leader and good catcher. The A's were World Champs in 1910 and 1911, with Thomas appearing in four games of each Fall Classic. From an offensive standpoint he was just adequate, always hovering around the .250 mark, but his leadership skills, his ability to call a good game and to handle pitchers were Thomas' real strengths. He did not believe in drinking, smoking or the nightlife, which became a problem for his teammates because, of course, they enjoyed all of those things. Since Thomas set such a good example, Connie Mack decided to make him the team captain of the A's in 1914. This was unusual because

by that time his days as a player had pretty much ended, and Thomas was working as a base coach.

From all accounts, Connie Mack's decision led to dissension on the team. Although the Athletics won the pennant that year, they got swept in the Series. Mack dismantled his Philadelphia dynasty after that season but kept Thomas on as coach. Thomas loyally remained with the organization for many years, eventually becoming a well-respected scout, discovering Lefty Grove and George Ernshaw. Why is Ira Thomas in the Cracker Jack Collection? Could it be that Connie Mack had something to do with it? In any event, Ira Thomas was a team guy and a good catcher over the ten years that he played.

Teams:

New York Highlanders AL (1906–1907)
Detroit Tigers AL (1908)
Philadelphia Athletics AL (1909–1915)

Born:
January 22, 1881
Ballston Spa, New York

Died:
October 11, 1958
Philadelphia, PA

▷ Batted: RH

▷ Threw: RH

▷ Position: C

▷ Career BA: .242

Bert Whaling

Bert Whaling had an outstanding season as a catcher playing for the Seattle Giants in the Northwestern League in 1912. In 138 games played, he threw out an astounding 188 base runners. That in itself is the stuff of legend. Unfortunately, in the Major Leagues, Whaling never made it to starting catcher because of his weak hitting.

A California native, Whaling worked his way up through Portland of the Pacific Coast League and Seattle of the Northwestern League before finally getting his shot with the Braves of the National League in 1913. In his rookie year, Whaling led the league with a .990 fielding percentage while sharing catching duties with Bill Rariden. He spent the next two seasons as back up to Hank Gowdy and then it was back to the bushes. Whaling did get the opportunity to play on the 1914 World Champion "Miracle Braves" team that went from last to first after the month of July. That year his 54.5 baserunners caught stealing percentage was good enough to lead the National League.

Although considered a very good catcher, Whaling's hitting became his downfall, and he was traded to the

Vernon Tigers of the Pacific Coast League in 1916. Whaling served in the U.S. Navy during World War I, and returned to play the Minor League circuit until 1926. He went on to manage in the Arizona State League in 1928, leading the Phoenix Senators to the league championship. Whaling's .986 MLB career fielding average has us scratching our heads. There have been many weak-hitting catchers over the history of baseball, and Bert Whaling's defensive numbers are pretty darn good. It seems that this guy should have been in the big leagues longer than he was.

Albert James Whaling

Team:
Boston Braves NL (1913–1915)

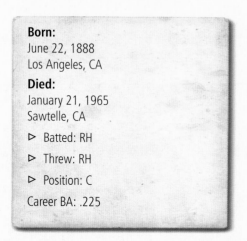

Born:
June 22, 1888
Los Angeles, CA

Died:
January 21, 1965
Sawtelle, CA

▷ Batted: RH

▷ Threw: RH

▷ Position: C

Career BA: .225

Art Wilson

As catchers go, Art "Dutch" Wilson was pretty darn good. Wilson came up to the big leagues in a reserve role for the Giants to back up Admiral Schlei and Chief Meyers. As backup catcher, Wilson did a nice job defensively, and he even chipped in with a .303 batting average in 109 at-bats in 1911. Wilson's big break came when he jumped to the Federal League and batted .291 and .305 respectively in 1914 and 1915. This gave him some exposure, and once the Federal League folded he was given the opportunity to get back into the National League.

As is sometimes the case, Wilson's baseball legacy is unfortunately attached to a single play. Dutch Wilson was the Cubs' catcher in the famous "double no-hitter" game that took place between his Chicago team and the Cincinnati Reds on May 2, 1917. That day, pitcher Hippo Vaughn of the Cubs and Fred Toney of the Reds hooked up for one of the most famous pitching duels of all time. Through the first nine innings, both men threw no-hitters in an amazing performance. With the game going into extra innings, both pitchers remained on the mound. In the tenth, Vaughn finally

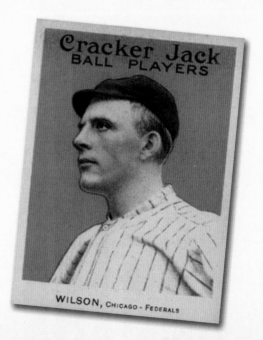

Arthur Earl Wilson

gave up a hit to infielder Larry Kopf, which broke up his no-hitter.

To add insult to injury, after a comedy of errors with dropped fly balls and poor defensive play, Jim Thorpe of the Reds laid down an inadvertent bunt, and with Kopf on third and a play at the plate, Wilson was instead concentrating on Thorpe running up the first base line. Wilson was not prepared when Vaughn fielded the bunt and made a clean throw to the plate, and the ball bounced off his chest protector. Kopf scored and the Reds won the game. Vaughn was disappointed, the fans were disappointed and Wilson was devastated. A pretty good catcher made a costly mental error. It happens. Sadly, Dutch Wilson always carried the baggage as the catcher that lost the "double no-hitter" game. If you look at his whole body of work, however, with a .261 lifetime batting average and a nice .972 fielding percentage, Wilson deserves a better legacy.

Teams:

New York Giants NL (1908–1913)
Chicago Chi-Feds/Whales FL (1914–1915)
Pittsburgh Pirates NL (1916)
Chicago Cubs NL (1916–1917)
Boston Braves NL (1918–1920)
Cleveland Indians AL (1921)

Born:
December 11, 1885
Macon, IL
Died:
June 12, 1960
Chicago, IL
▷ Batted: RH
▷ Threw: RH
▷ Position: C
▷ Career BA: .261

Ivey Wingo

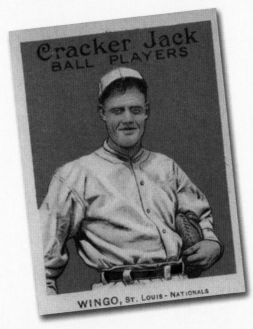

Longevity and durability were the calling cards of National League catcher Ivey Wingo. The fact that he played 17 years of Major League baseball during the Deadball Era as a catcher is an extraordinary feat, especially with all of the bunting that went on. Known for his offensive ability, Wingo was the catcher for the World Champion Cincinnati team that beat the infamous Black Sox in the 1919 World Series, and batted a sparkling .571 in that Fall Classic. With a .260 lifetime batting average, Wingo had a decent stick, banging out 1,039 hits over his career.

He was average defensively, but his durability is what his team liked. At one time or another, he led the league in assists, passed balls and baserunners caught stealing by a catcher. On the flip side, he also led the league in stolen bases allowed a few seasons, and with 234 career errors, Wingo still holds the record for most errors during the 20th century by a catcher. Maybe that had something to do with the sheer number of games that he caught, as Wingo retired holding the record for most games caught (1,231) by a National League catcher. In 1927 Wingo left Cincinnati to manage the Columbus Senators in the American Association, but returned to coach in 1929 and caught one last game as a Red. He coached his Reds one final season in 1936 before retiring to his beloved Georgia. Ivey Wingo was inducted into the Georgia Sports Hall of Fame in 1993.

Ivey Brown Wingo

Born:
July, 8, 1890
Gainesville, GA
Died:
March 1, 1941
Norcross, GA
▷ Batted: LH
▷ Threw: RH
▷ Position: C
▷ Career BA: .260
▷ Managerial Record: 1–1

Teams:

St. Louis Cardinals NL (1911–1914)
Cincinnati Reds NL (1915–1926, 1929; player-manager: 1916)

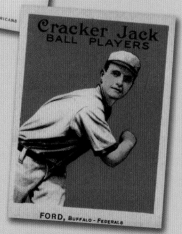

BUSH, Philadelphia - Americans

FORD, Buffalo - Federals

9

THE MOUNDSMEN

With such an extensive list of pitchers in the Cracker Jack Collection, there is a real mix of great, good, and fair. There are Hall of Famers such as Chief Bender, "Big" Ed Walsh and Rube Marquard along with commons like Jimmy Lavender, Tom Seaton and Cy Falkenberg, but all in some manner made their mark on the game. From spitballs to crossfire fastballs to "emery" balls, it was the Wild West of

baseball. The commissioner's office finally stepped in and began to outlaw certain pitches, but those restrictions did not apply to everyone. Some guys were actually allowed to throw certain pitches while others were not. The guys here were not on pitch counts and probably did not ice because ice was needed for the ice box.

Meet the moundsmen of the Cracker Jack Collection.

MULLEN, Indianapolis - Federals

MARQUARD, Brooklyn - Federals

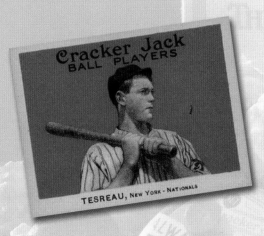

TESREAU, New York - Nationals

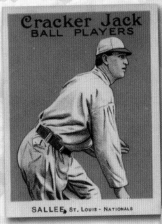

SALLEE, St. Louis - Nationals

REULBACH, Brooklyn - Nationals

Babe Adams

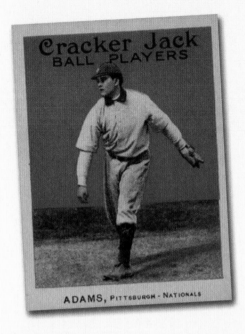

Charles Benjamin "Babe" Adams broke in with the St. Louis Cardinals in 1906, but his stay in redbird country would be brief. The Pirates purchased his contract in 1907, beginning a uniquely fickle romance between team and player. Adams won 111 games for Pittsburgh between 1909 and 1915, highlighted by two 20-plus win seasons. In 1916, Adams dipped to 2–9 and the Bucs, showing no loyalty at all, released him. In July of 1918, Pittsburgh reacquired Adams, and once again he delivered. Pitching into his early 40s, Adams won 69 games between 1919 and 1923. In 1924, Adams again saw his numbers drop, and once again the treacherous Pirates released him, this time for good in 1926.

To realize the extent of Pittsburgh's constant betrayal, one need only look at Adams' postseason record. As a rookie, he led the Bucs to the 1909 World Championship with three complete game wins versus Detroit. He also pitched a scoreless inning in the Pirates' 1925 Series win against Washington. Adams' 194–140 career record does not do justice to the singular talent he possessed. He was recognized as baseball's premier control pitcher, walking just 430 men in almost 3,000 career innings. That's a little more than one walk per nine-inning game. In retirement, Adams continued to use his keen eye in hunting and horseshoes. Adams was supposedly nicknamed "Babe" because an admiring female fan once gushed over his baby face, but he proudly took the ups and downs of his big-league career like a man.

Charles Benjamin Adams

Teams:

St. Louis Cardinals NL (1906)

Pittsburgh Pirates NL (1907, 1909–1916, 1918–1926)

Born:
May 18, 1882
Tipton, IN

Died:
July 27, 1968
Silver Spring, MD

▷ Batted: LH

▷ Threw: RH

▷ Position: P

▷ MLB Pitching Record: 194–140

▷ ERA: 2.76

Cy Barger

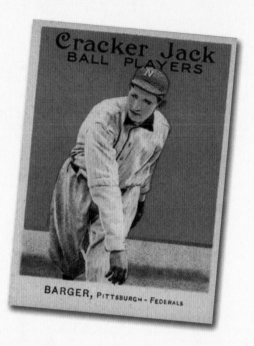

Named after the Greek god of love and a Venezuelan hero, Eros Bolivar "Cy" Barger never made it to baseball hero status. Although he had a lifetime pitching record that fell below the .500 mark, Barger was not all that bad. With a 15-year career spread between the Minor Leagues and the majors, Barger certainly had some bright spots.

Coming out of Transylvania University in Lexington, Kentucky, he first played pro ball in the New York State League in 1905, where it was quickly determined that Barger would be better suited as a pitcher. The following year he was 16–8 pitching for Lancaster in the Tri-State League and soon made it up to the New York Highlanders. Needing a little more seasoning, Barger went back to the minors to post some good seasons in the Eastern League with both his arm and his bat. In 1909 he won 23 games for the Rochester Bronchos, along with a tidy 1.00 earned-run average. He also had some success as a hitter with a .319 season one year and several where he batted north of .240.

Eros Bolivar Barger

When Barger got back into the majors again in 1910, he won 15 games for Brooklyn followed by an 11-win season. After going 17–9 for the International League's Newark Indians in 1913, Barger jumped back to the majors to pitch for the Pittsburgh Rebels of the newly formed Federal League. There, in 1915, he led the league in games finished with 19, and fielding percentage as pitcher with 1.00. After the Federal League folded, Barger was player-manager of the Memphis Chickasaws in the Southern Association through 1919 and, in 1921, he managed the St. Petersburg Saints in the Florida State League before retiring to his home state of Kentucky.

Teams:
New York Highlanders AL (1906–1907)
Brooklyn Superbas/Dodgers NL (1910–1912)
Pittsburgh Rebels FL (1914–1915)

Born:
May 18, 1885
Jamestown, KY

Died:
September 23, 1964
Columbia, KY

▷ Batted: LH

▷ Threw: RH

▷ Position: P

▷ MLB Pitching Record: 46–63

▷ ERA: 3.56

George Baumgardner

George Washington Baumgardner

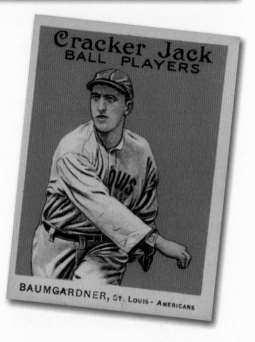

In *The T206 Collection: The Players & Their Stories*, we discuss the common player as the building block of our National Pastime. Without these stalwart players, there would be no baseball. Not everyone can become a superstar and enjoy the big salary that goes along with that status. The common player is similar to the postal worker, office worker, and laborer. Without them, nothing else will function properly.

George Baumgardner would be classified as a common. Over a career spanning five years, he went out and pitched for his team at an average or slightly below average level. Today Baumgardner would be slotted four or five in a pitching rotation. Back then, he was one of the better pitchers on some sorry St. Louis teams. A Barboursville, West Virginia, native, Baumgardner brought his country ways and work ethic to the majors when he came up to the Browns from the West Virginia League. He was a guy that, for a few seasons, ate up innings and was out there every start towing the rubber. His best year was 1914 when he went 16–14 with a 2.79 earned-run average, and led the American League in games finished with 23. Primarily a fastball pitcher, Baumgardner managed 102 Ks in 1912, his rookie season, which was his high-water mark.

Unfortunately, he played for a team that was just not that good. Had Baumgardner played for a better team, he would likely have better career stats. After his few seasons with the Browns, he played and managed in the South Atlantic League and the Southern Association through 1917, and then returned to a quiet life in Barboursville. Thankfully there have been thousands of George Baumgardners over the course of baseball history, for without them baseball simply would not exist.

Team:
St. Louis Browns AL (1912–1916)

Born:
July 22, 1891
Barboursville, WV

Died:
December 13, 1970
Barboursville, WV

▷ Batted: LH

▷ Threw: RH

▷ Position: P

▷ MLB Pitching Record: 38–49

▷ ERA: 3.22

Chief Bender

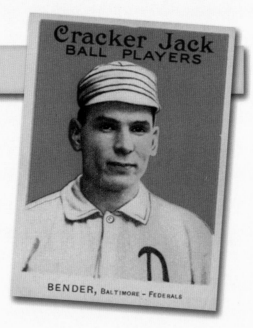

Cracker Jack
BALL PLAYERS

BENDER, BALTIMORE – FEDERALS

One of the innovators of the pitch known as the slider, Charlie "Chief" Bender was not just a great pitcher, he was also a great representative of our National Pastime. Bender's German-American father and Ojibwa mother settled in Crow Wing County, Minnesota, to raise their large family. When he was 12 years old, Bender was recruited to the famed Carlisle Indian School in Pennsylvania, where he developed his mental and baseball skills. Well-respected by peers and fans alike, Charlie Bender carried himself with grace and dignity, even when dealing with racial slurs. Known for his cerebral approach to the game and his ability to pitch under pressure, Bender was an integral part of the A's dynasty in the days of Connie Mack's $100,000 infield.

With 212 lifetime wins and a 2.46 lifetime ERA, Bender played on three World Series Champions and had two 20-win seasons. He led the American League in winning percentage in 1910, 1911 and 1914; and in saves in 1906 and 1913. A fairly good hitter, Bender also played both the infield and outfield on occasion. Although not overpowering, Bender was a crafty control pitcher who seemed to be at his best in important games.

After a short stint in the Federal League, Bender worked in the shipyards during World War I, managed in the minors into the 1940s, coached at the U.S. Naval Academy, and served as coach or scout for the New York Yankees, Chicago White Sox, New York Giants, and Philadelphia Athletics. Actually, as coach for the White Sox, Bender pitched one last inning for them in 1925. Always loyal to the A's, Bender went back to work for them as pitching coach when he was 61 years old.

Charlie Bender was elected to the Hall of Fame in 1953. Although Bender accepted his nickname, he always signed autographs as Charlie Bender. When in Cooperstown for Hall of Fame weekend a few years ago, this writer met a gentleman who was a huge Bender fan, and would only refer to him as Charlie. He maintained that the "Chief" moniker was racially derogatory, and although Bender always answered with a smile, he wanted to be known as Charlie.

Charles Albert Bender

Teams:
Philadelphia Athletics AL (1903–1914)
Baltimore Terrapins FL (1915)
Philadelphia Phillies NL (1916–1917)
Chicago White Sox AL (1925)

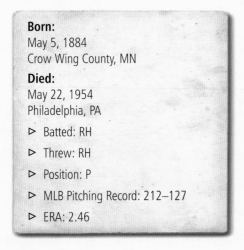

Born:
May 5, 1884
Crow Wing County, MN

Died:
May 22, 1954
Philadelphia, PA

▷ Batted: RH

▷ Threw: RH

▷ Position: P

▷ MLB Pitching Record: 212–127

▷ ERA: 2.46

Rube Benton

Besides pitching, Rube Benton was pretty good at drinking, living dangerously, and betting on anything, even two flies buzzing across a room. His 15-year career in the majors was saddled with controversy, bad behavior and innuendo. As a young pitcher from the Southern Association, Benton was considered a "can't miss" prospect.

With a good fastball and curve, he came into his own in 1912, winning 18 games for the Cincinnati Reds. Unfortunately, he also lost 20 games that year. For the next several years, Benton was a sub-.500 pitcher. During that period, he developed a reputation as a hard drinker who loved the nightlife, and it was not unusual for him to appear at the ballpark with a hangover. The Reds finally got tired of Benton's act, and he was waived. He was claimed by the Giants, but the Pittsburgh Pirates wired the Reds a higher offer and Benton wound up pitching one game for the Pirates before the league ruled in favor of the Giants. His one outing with the

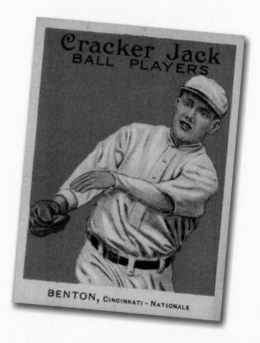

Cracker Jack
BALL PLAYERS

BENTON, CINCINNATI – NATIONALS

John Cleave Benton

Pirates was declared a "no game" to be replayed later on in the season.

For the Giants, Benton had greater success, going 16–8, 15–9 and 17–11 in his three best seasons with them. He toiled for Uncle Sam in 1918, missing most of the season. After the 1919 season, Benton admitted to betting on games along with Hal Chase. He was implicated in the Black Sox scandal but no wrongdoing was ever proven. Even though he was 5–2 in 1921, Benton was banned from the majors and sent down to the minors for being an "undesirable." Shockingly, Judge Kenesaw Mountain Landis overturned the ban because nothing was ever proven.

Benton pitched through the 1925 season for the Reds and finally packed it in. Still drinking and carousing, he spent the next eight years with the Minneapolis Millers in the minors, pitching until he was 43 years old. Benton met his fate in 1937 when he was killed in a head-on collision. At 47 years old, Rube Benton died liked he lived, in the fast lane.

Teams:
Cincinnati Reds NL (1910–1915, 1923–1925)
New York Giants NL (1915–1921)

Born:
June 27, 1890
Clinton, NC

Died:
December 12, 1937
Dothan, AL

▷ Batted: RH
▷ Threw: LH
▷ Position: P
▷ MLB Pitching Record: 150–144
▷ ERA: 3.09

Joseph Benz

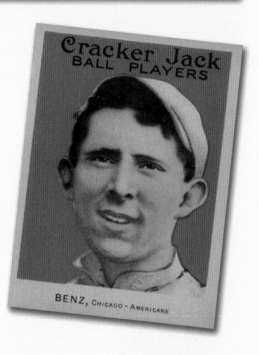

Known as the "Butcher Boy" because he worked in his father's meat market during the offseason, Joe Benz was a master of the spitball. From all accounts, Benz was one of the real good guys of the game. He spent his entire career with the White Sox and was considered a very reliable middle rotation guy who could eat up innings. Working his way up from the bushes, Benz made his debut with the White Sox in the latter part of the 1911 season. Going into the 1912 season, Benz became the workhorse of the Sox, devouring 238 innings and winning 13 games. The highlight of his career came in May of 1914 when he pitched a no-hitter against the Cleveland Naps. It was only the second no-hitter in White Sox history.

Benz was meticulous about staying in shape during the offseason, and could be counted on to show up at spring training camp in mid-season condition. Despite his focus on good health, he contracted typhoid fever, which affected his play early in the 1915 season, and in 1918 a bout of pneumonia shortened his playing time. Those serious illnesses, coupled with a hand injury and recurring arm problems over his tenure, hampered his ability to remain consistent. From 1916 through his one appearance in 1919, Benz' numbers tailed off dramatically. He was finally released by the White Sox after that one appearance, but remained a fixture in the Chicago area.

As a career White Sox pitcher, Benz became a well-liked celebrity of sorts,

Team:
Chicago White Sox AL (1911–1919)

Joseph Louis Benz

attending many charity events, sports banquets, and often playing in the old-timers' ball games. He worked as an engineer and a surveyor before operating a tavern in Chicago for many years. A genuinely nice guy, Joe Benz was always accommodating to fans and friends. He passed away as a result of a stroke in 1957 when he was 71 years old.

Born:
January 21, 1886
New Alsace, IN

Died:
April 22, 1957
Chicago, IL

▷ Batted: RH
▷ Threw: RH
▷ Position: P
▷ MLB Pitching Record: 77–75
▷ ERA: 2.43

Fred Blanding

Joe Boehling

Known as "Fritz," Fred Blanding was right down the middle in his career with 46 wins and 46 losses, all with the Cleveland Naps over a five-year span. A pitching phenom out of the University of Michigan, Blanding was one of those guys labeled a "can't miss." In 1910, he was a 20 game winner in the tough Texas League before making his debut with the Naps in September. In an auspicious first appearance, he led the Naps to a 3–0 shutout over the Senators and the great Walter Johnson.

Blanding only managed a 7–11 record during the 1911 campaign, and in what was considered a very classy gesture, he requested to be sent down to the minors for more seasoning because he was not carrying his own weight and felt guilty about the salary he was commanding. Confident of his ability, upper management refused to send him down. The next year Blanding proved them right with an 18-win season, followed by a 15-win season in 1913, but he was soon caught up in the controversy surrounding the upstart Federal League.

Frederick James Blanding

Born:
February 8, 1888
Redlands, CA

Died:
July 16, 1950
Salem, VA

▷ Batted: RH

▷ Threw: RH

▷ Position: P

▷ MLB Pitching Record: 46–46

▷ ERA: 3.13

BOEHLING, WASHINGTON - AMERICANS

Blanding accepted an offer to play in the new league in 1914, but reneged when the Naps offered him more money to stay on board. After the dust cleared and lawsuits ended, he was allowed to stay with the Naps, but had problems with his manager, Joe Birmingham, and decided not to return for the 1915 season.

Blanding may have lost his passion for baseball, but he discovered a passion for the automotive business as owner and operator of one of the earliest Ford dealerships in Michigan. Blanding also dabbled in baseball in the 1920s as president of the Lansing Senators of the Central League. After moving to Roanoke, Virginia, he continued in the automotive field, experiencing the success he lacked on the diamond. On the field, Fritz Blanding was average. Off the field, Fritz was a 20-game winner.

Team:
Cleveland Naps AL (1910–1914)

Some called him Joe, some called him John. We call him pretty good. Joe Boeling had a few good seasons in the majors playing for the Washington Senators, and then three very mediocre seasons with the Indians. Boeling started the 1912 season with the Worcester Busters of the New England League, going 14–8 for them and catching the eye of the scouts. Like today, a good left-handed starting pitcher was a real find, and the Senators grabbed him at the end

Born:
March 20, 1891
Richmond, VA

Died:
September 8, 1941
Richmond, VA

▷ Batted: LH

▷ Threw: LH

▷ Position: P

▷ MLB Pitching Record: 56–50

▷ ERA: 2.97

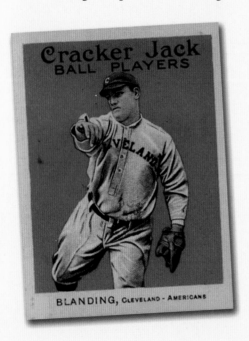

BLANDING, CLEVELAND - AMERICANS

John Joseph Boehling

of the season where he appeared in three games.

The next season, pitching alongside Walter Johnson, the 22-year-old southpaw went 17–7 for the Senators with a sparkling 2.14 ERA. As a matter of fact, he was sixth in the league that year in earned-run average. In 1914 Boehling came back to win 13 games and it was 14 wins the year after that. During the 1916 season, the wheels began to come off and Boeling was traded to the Indians. During his tenure with Cleveland, Boehling was 3–10 with the Tribe and was finally sent back down to the minors in July of 1917.

For the next few years he played in the Pacific Coast League only to resurface in 1920 to appear in three games and pitch a total of 13 innings for the Indians. The next season found Boehling back in the minors pitching for the Bridgeport Americans of the Eastern League and the Toronto Maple Leafs of the International League. That proved to be his last season as a professional ballplayer. Only 30 years old when he packed it in, Boehling worked with his brother in the grain and seed business and spent time coaching youth baseball. With a career win-loss percentage of .528 and a 2.97 ERA, there were a lot worse than Joe Boehling.

Teams:
Washington Senators AL (1912–1916)
Cleveland Indians AL (1916–1917, 1920)

Ad Brennan

Addison Foster Brennan

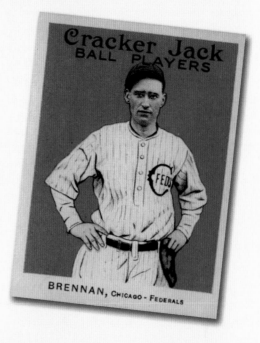

BRENNAN, Chicago - Federals

Addison "Ad" Brennan is another on the list of so-so pitchers in the Cracker Jack Collection. Coming up through the minors, Brennan started his career in 1909 with the Springfield Midgets of the Western Association, followed by a stint with the Wichita Jobbers of the Western League. After a brief call-up by the Phils in 1910, he was sent down to the Eastern League for a little more seasoning with the Buffalo Bisons but was called back up to Philadelphia for good that same year. With the Phillies, Brennan had a little success, going 11–9 in 1912 and 14–12 in 1913. His 2.39 ERA in 1913 was actually very good.

However, his claim to fame was more as a fighter than a pitcher. On June 30, 1913 the Phillies lost to John McGraw's powerful New York Giants in a gripping 11–10 game with Christy Mathewson besting Pete Alexander. At the time, both teams were in the hunt for the pennant, although the Giants eventually ran away with it. After the game, under the stands, as the Giants were going back to the clubhouse, some Philly fans started berating McGraw. Evidently when Brennan got involved it escalated into a pretty good fight and he decked McGraw with several punches. From all indications, Brennan was the antagonist in this one, but both McGraw and Brennan were suspended for five games. On top of that, Brennan was fined $100.

After that season, he jumped to the fledgling Federal League but had little success. Back in the minors with the Atlanta Crackers of the Southern Association, he went 16–8 in 1916 and 12–13 in 1917. Brennan resurfaced briefly with both the Senators and Indians of the American League in 1918, then faded into the sunset. Ad Brennan: 37–36 as a pitcher; 1–0 as a fighter.

Teams:
Philadelphia Phillies NL (1910–1913)
Chicago Chi-Feds/Whales FL (1914–1915)
Washington Senators AL (1918)
Cleveland Indians AL (1918)

Born:
July 18, 1887
La Harpe, KS
Died:
January 7, 1962
Kansas City, MO
▷ Batted: LH
▷ Threw: LH
▷ Position: P
▷ MLB Pitching Record: 37–36
▷ ERA: 3.11

Mordecai Brown

Joe Bush

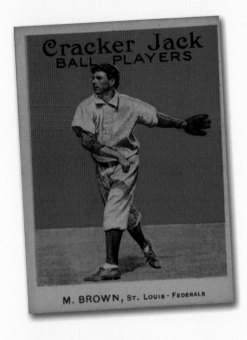

M. BROWN, St. Louis · Federals

One of the most dominant pitchers of the Deadball Era, "Three Finger" Mordecai Brown won at least 20 games on six different occasions and won at least 12 games over another five seasons. Brown turned a serious childhood injury to his throwing hand to his advantage, working to develop a mind-boggling curve ball that simply froze batters in their tracks. Besides earning him a nickname, Brown's injury also allowed him to throw a very deceptive change-up that baffled batters. Brown's battles against one of our All-Star pitchers, Christy Mathewson, were legendary.

He had a superb season in 1908 when he went 29–9 with a 1.47 ERA, and his 27 wins in 1909 led the National League. His amazing stats include leading the NL in saves four seasons running (1908–1911), shutouts twice (1906, 1910), complete games twice (1909, 1910), ERA (1906), and fielding percentage (1908). Although Brown pitched in many renowned World Series games, he always maintained that his best performance was in the one-game playoff after the Merkle debacle. As his career was winding down, Brown made a brief stop to the Federal League, managing the Terriers for part of the 1914 season, and then finished back in the National League.

After retiring, Brown pitched and managed in the minors until 1920, and later pitched in exhibition games. With 55 career shutouts, World Series Championships in 1907 and 1908, and all of those 20-plus win seasons, "Three Finger" Mordecai Brown was elected to the Hall of Fame in 1949. Unfortunately, the master of the deceptive pitch had passed away the previous year in 1948, and never got the opportunity to address his fans.

Mordecai Peter Centennial Brown

Teams:
St. Louis Cardinals NL (1903)
Chicago Cubs NL (1904–1912, 1916)
Cincinnati Reds NL (1913)
St. Louis Terriers FL (player-manager: 1914)
Brooklyn Tip-Tops FL (1914)
Chicago Whales FL (1915)

Born:
October 19, 1876
Nyesville, IN

Died:
February 14, 1948
Terre Haute, IN

▷ Batted: Switch
▷ Threw: RH
▷ Position: P
▷ MLB Pitching Record: 239–130
▷ ERA: 2.06
▷ Managerial Record: 50–63

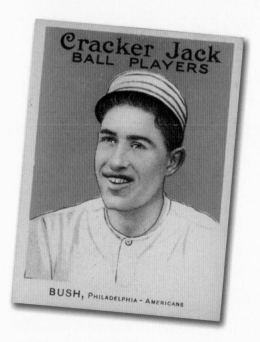

BUSH, Philadelphia – Americans

"Bullet" Joe Bush, so nicknamed because of the speed of his fastball, was a hero in Philadelphia after leading the Athletics to an unlikely win over the New York Giants in the 1913 World Series. Bush was 1–0 in that Series with a microscopic ERA of 1.00. His performance catapulted the A's to a 4–1 drubbing of New York.

Bush was a pitcher of extremes. His heroics helped win in 1913, but the very next year, his throwing error was the death knell as the A's lost the 1914 Series to the Braves. Similarly, Bush lost 24 games for the 1916 A's, and then won 26 for the Yankees in 1922. That season was a true sparkler for Bush. He finished fourth in MVP voting with an ERA of 3.31 and 20 complete games. In a 17-year career for seven different teams, Bush was 196–184. He won 15 or more games nine times, but control was always an issue. Bush walked more batters than he struck out eight times. He also led his league in wild pitches in 1916, 1923, and 1924.

Bush was known for releasing loud

Leslie Ambrose Bush

grunts as he unleashed a violent fastball. Word is that his twisting delivery was so effective that teammate Babe Ruth wanted other Yankees pitchers to adopt it. After leaving Philly in 1921, Bush pitched admirably for some bad Red Sox teams before joining the powerful Yanks in 1922 where he played in two World Series, winning one in 1923. Bush never repeated his 1913 Series heroics, going 1–5 in four subsequent Fall Classics. In 1922, he stopped George Sisler's then-record 41-game hitting streak, a mark that would remain untouched until Joe DiMaggio's 56 games in 1941.

A gifted ventriloquist, Bush once faked animal sounds while in a restaurant, scaring the clientele. When a constable arrived, Bush feigned the sound of a barking dog. As the officer looked away, Bush hightailed it out of there. Clearly, Bullet Joe was one heck of a ventriloquist, but on the mound, he was no dummy.

Teams:

Philadelphia Athletics AL (1912–1917, 1928)
Boston Red Sox AL (1918–1921)
New York Yankees AL (1922–1924)
St. Louis Browns AL (1925)
Washington Senators AL (1926)
Pittsburgh Pirates NL (1926–1927)
New York Giants NL (1927)

Born:
November 27, 1892
Ehime, MN
Died:
November 1, 1974
Fort Lauderdale, FL
▷ Batted: RH
▷ Threw: RH
▷ Position: P
▷ MLB Pitching Record: 196–184
▷ ERA: 3.51

Ray Caldwell

Raymond Benjamin Caldwell

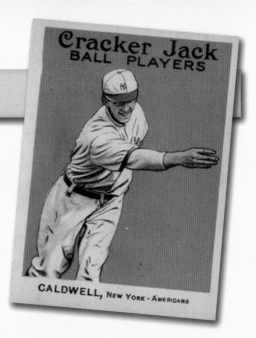

CALDWELL, NEW YORK - AMERICANS

If there was ever a player with unlimited potential for greatness, Ray "Slim" Caldwell was that player. Some say Caldwell could have been the greatest pitcher of his era. In 1914, sportswriter Grantland Rice remarked that Caldwell would be as great as Mathewson or Johnson had he not chosen the same path as Rube Waddell.

A fun-loving ladies man, notorious for drinking and after-hours carousing, Caldwell sometimes disappeared for extended periods of time, leaving his team in the lurch. Caldwell would show flashes of brilliance but then falter because of his alcohol abuse. The normal tactics of fines and suspensions did not keep him in line. In 1914, he finished 17–9 with a brilliant 1.94 ERA, but he could have easily won 20 had he not been benched and fined numerous times because of his off-field antics.

In 1915 he pitched more than 300 innings, and logged at least 200 innings another four times. An excellent hitter, Caldwell once hit home runs over three consecutive days. Caldwell was so good that the Senators offered Walter Johnson for him in 1914. Although he frustrated Yankees management, they stuck with their ace pitcher for years because of his great talent, but they finally had enough in 1919 and traded him to the Red Sox, where he lasted less than a season.

After joining the Tribe in 1919 he threw a no-hitter. That year, while pitching against the Phillies, Caldwell was struck by lightning in the bottom of the ninth with two outs. He was knocked unconscious but got up and pitched to get the final out. He won 20 in 1920 for the Indians but in 1921 Caldwell was up to his antics again, which ended his days in the MLB. He went on to pitch 12 years in the minors because no Major League team would touch him. Between the majors and minors, Caldwell won nearly 300 games. After all of the antics, Caldwell straightened up in retirement. He bought a farm, worked as a telegraph operator for the railroad, and later worked as a bartender with his fourth wife. Ray Caldwell was certainly one of the more colorful characters in the Cracker Jack Collection.

Teams:

New York Highlanders/Yankees AL (1910–1918)
Boston Red Sox AL (1919)
Cleveland Indians AL (1919–1921)

Born:
April 26, 1888
Croydon, PA
Died:
August, 17, 1967
Salamanca, NY
▷ Batted: LH
▷ Threw: RH
▷ Position: P
▷ MLB Pitching Record: 133–120
▷ ERA: 3.22

Nixey Callahan 1914

Howie Camnitz

A veritable baseball Jack-of-all-trades, Nixey Callahan was a pitcher, hitter, runner, fielder and a manager. He did everything except sell Cracker Jack. In 1894 Callahan signed with the Philadelphia Phillies, but was not quite ready for the big leagues. As a result, he was released after posting a 1–2 pitching record and batting only .238. Going down to the minors, he excelled as a pitcher, leading the Eastern League with 30 wins. When Callahan signed on with the Chicago Colts in 1897, he batted .292 and won 12 games on the mound, but he really came into his own in 1898 and 1899, winning at least 20 games both years and hitting a very respectable .262 and .260 respectively.

Callahan fashioned his pitching style after Clark Griffith, going for control over speed. In 1901, Callahan jumped ship to the crosstown White Sox in the new American League going 15–8 as a pitcher and batting .331 in 118 at-bats. He made history when, on September 20, 1902, he pitched the first no-hitter in AL history. Callahan transitioned to the outfield in 1903 and played very well while also managing the Sox, but in 1905

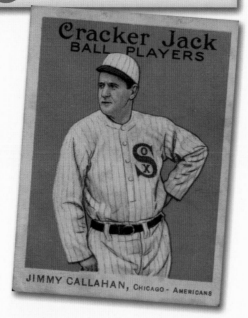

JIMMY CALLAHAN, CHICAGO - AMERICANS

he decided to quit Major League baseball to run his own semi-pro team. He felt that with his promotional skills as well as his managerial abilities, his team would be a winner. He was right, and as a result the White Sox wanted him back as president. Believe it or not, Callahan chose to play and manage instead.

Ever the promoter, Callahan was one of the organizers of the Sox and Giants exhibition tour of the world after the 1913 season. After managing for two seasons, Callahan went to the front office in 1915 before signing on as manager of the Pirates. He wrapped up his MLB career in 1917 and went on to develop a very successful commercial contracting business in Chicago. Nixey Callahan was certainly a man of many talents.

James Joseph Callahan

Teams:

Philadelphia Phillies NL (1894)

Chicago Colts/Orphans NL (1897–1900)

Chicago White Sox AL (1901–1913; player-manager: 1903–1904, 1912–1913; manager: 1914)

Pittsburgh Pirates NL (manager: 1916–1917)

Three time 20-game winner, Howie "Red" Camnitz, enjoyed a pretty good run with the Pirates. The redheaded 22-year-old curveball whiz came up to the Pirates after going 26–7 for Vicksburg in the Cotton States League, but his rookie year was not auspicious. He played in just 10 games, going 1–4 before he was sent back to the minors to learn how to protect his signature pitch. Apparently Camnitz overused the curveball so batters could hit off him easily. After 17 wins in 1905 and 22 in 1906 for the Toledo Mud Hens, Camnitz got the call to rejoin the Pirates.

From that point his career took off. He had worked to perfect and protect his out pitch, a big sweeping curveball that would freeze batters in their tracks. In 1909 he posted a sparkling 25–6 record with an anemic 1.62 earned-run average, helping the Pirates to the pennant. Camnitz did not perform well in the Series, and there was speculation that he was either ill or drinking. Whatever it was, it affected his play during the 1910 season, but Camnitz

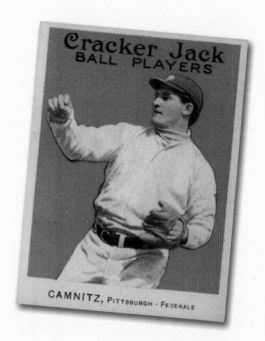

CAMNITZ, PITTSBURGH - FEDERALS

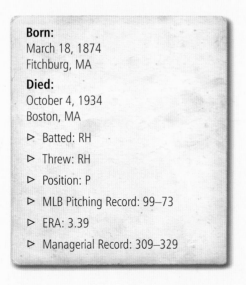

Born:
March 18, 1874
Fitchburg, MA

Died:
October 4, 1934
Boston, MA

▷ Batted: RH

▷ Threw: RH

▷ Position: P

▷ MLB Pitching Record: 99–73

▷ ERA: 3.39

▷ Managerial Record: 309–329

Samuel Howard Camnitz

was back in form in 1911 with 20 wins, and followed that with 22 in 1912. A real workhorse, Camnitz threw at least 240 innings per year over a span of seven seasons.

By the time he jumped ship to the Pittsburgh Rebels of the Federal League in 1914, he had seen better days as a pitcher. His curveball became erratic, his walks began to soar, and he played out the string as a very mediocre pitcher. Camnitz had a penchant for socializing, and was never in the best of shape, which some believe led to the mediocrity. The Rebels released him early in the 1915 season because of his conditioning, and Camnitz was out of the game for good. He returned home to Kentucky where he had a successful 40-year career in the automotive sales business.

Teams:

Pittsburgh Pirates NL (1904, 1906–1913)
Philadelphia Phillies NL (1913)
Pittsburgh Rebels FL (1914–1915)

Born:
August 22, 1881
Covington, KY
Died:
March 2, 1960
Louisville, KY
▷ Batted: RH
▷ Threw: RH
▷ Position: P
▷ MLB Pitching Record: 133–106
▷ ERA: 2.75

Carl Cashion 1914

Sometimes referred to as Jay, Carl Cashion had a brief and unspectacular Major League career. After attending both Davidson College and Erskine College, Cashion had a short two-season tour with the Greenville Spinners in the Carolina Association, where he divided his time between pitching and the outfield. Although primarily a pitcher in the majors, Cashion played a bit in the outfield and actually continued on in the minors as an outfielder after his MLB days were done.

Cashion's claim to fame was the six-inning no-hitter that he threw in the second game of a doubleheader on August 20, 1912, against the Cleveland Indians. The game was called after six innings so the Indians could catch a train to Boston. With an overall Major League record of 12–13, his best season was 1912 when he went 10–6. According to *Baseball Magazine*, Cashion had a fastball that "flashed across the plate." Unfortunately, he lacked control and placed second in the league in wild pitches in 1912.

Cashion was really a non-factor for three of his four years with the Senators, winning two and losing seven. He did play a little outfield with a total of 153

Team:

Washington Senators AL (1911–1914)

CASHION, WASHINGTON - AMERICANS

Jay Carl Cashion

at-bats and a .242 batting average. In 1915 Cashion went down to the Minneapolis Millers of the American Association where he fared much better as an outfielder. As a matter of fact, he batted .327 in 1915 with 297 at-bats. Not much is known about Carl Cashion after the 1918 season. We do know that he died at the young age of 44 in 1935.

Born:
June 6, 1891
Mecklenberg, NC
Died:
November 17, 1935
Lake Millicent, WI
▷ Batted: LH
▷ Threw: RH
▷ Position: P
▷ MLB Pitching Record: 12–13
▷ ERA: 3.70

Larry Cheney

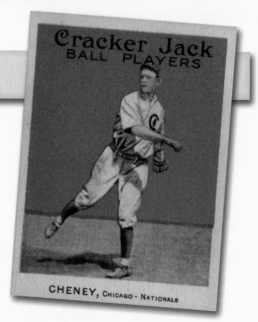

CHENEY, Chicago - Nationals

One of the wildest pitchers of the era, Larry Cheney was quite good when he could control the ball. Cheney once admitted that in his early days as a pitcher, he was never sure where the ball was going. Called up to the Cubs in 1911, Cheney's thumb was injured fielding a line drive by Zack Wheat in his third appearance, which forced him to change his pitching style, and the rest is history.

Needing to develop an overhand delivery because his thumb was too weak to grip the ball properly, he perfected his spitball which became a devastating pitch. The delivery and trajectory actually allowed the ball to rise as it approached the plate, which really affected the timing of some hitters. In 1912, his first full season, Cheney led the National League with 26 wins and 28 complete games, but also led the league with 18 wild pitches. He became one of the most dominant pitchers in the league over the next two years, with 21 wins in 1913 and 20 wins in 1914, but continued to lead the league in wild pitches. A real workhorse, Cheney logged more than 300 innings per season over that three-year period.

To go along with his awesome spitball, Cheney terrorized hitters because of his wildness. His 26 wild pitches in 1914 is still a Cubs record today. That wildness finally got him traded in 1915 because his new manager, Roger Bresnahan, believed that Cheney had no mound discipline. With the Brooklyn Robins in 1916, Cheney had one more very good season, winning 18 games. That year he appeared in the World Series but really had no impact. Cheney spent 1919 between Brooklyn, Boston and Philly, getting very little playing time, and his Major League career was over. Like many players during that time period, Cheney went back down to the minors for several seasons with pretty good success. He finally retired to operate an orange grove in Florida, which evidently had a good effect on him since he lived to the ripe old age of 82.

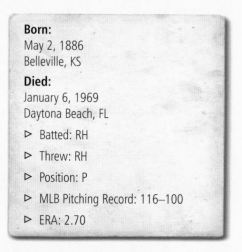

Born:
May 2, 1886
Belleville, KS

Died:
January 6, 1969
Daytona Beach, FL

▷ Batted: RH

▷ Threw: RH

▷ Position: P

▷ MLB Pitching Record: 116–100

▷ ERA: 2.70

Laurence Russell Cheney

Teams:
Chicago Cubs NL (1911–1915)
Brooklyn Robins NL (1915–1919)
Boston Braves NL (1919)
Philadelphia Phillies NL (1919)

Eddie Cicotte

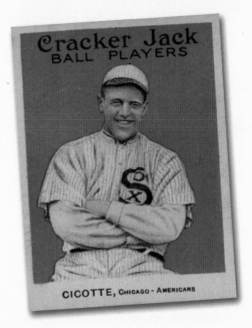

CICOTTE, Chicago - Americans

More remembered for scandals than sliders, Ed Cicotte was one of the nastiest men to ever toss the horsehide. Aptly nicknamed "Knuckles," the fiery Cicotte became notorious as one of the eight Chicago White Sox players who threw the 1919 World Series.

Before his socks turned black, Cicotte was a devastating hurler. In a 14-year career, he posted an ERA of under 2.00 five times. This frugality was mixed with ferocity as Knuckles whiffed over 100 batters in a season eight times. Cicotte was little more than a .500 pitcher in four and a half seasons with the Red Sox. He continued that trend after being sold to Chicago in 1912. Things changed in 1916 as the 32-year-old Cicotte went 15–7 with a 1.78 ERA. It was a sign of things to come.

He broke out in 1917, leading the American League with 28 wins, a 1.53 ERA, and a Herculean 346.2 innings pitched. In the 1917 World Series, Cicotte was 1–1 with 13 Ks and an ERA

Edward Victor Cicotte

of 1.57 as Chicago beat the Giants in six games. In that Series, Cicotte surrendered 23 hits in 23 innings pitched. In fact, he gave up nearly 3,000 hits in his career, but allowed just over 1,100 runs.

Cicotte was 29–7 in that fateful 1919 season and 1–2 in the tainted World Series loss. He would win 21 games in his final season of 1920 before being banned for life by Commissioner Kenesaw Mountain Landis. Ultimately, Cicotte's legacy of awesome pitching is forever tarnished by awful decision-making.

Teams:

Detroit Tigers AL (1905)

Boston Red Sox AL (1908–1912)

Chicago White Sox AL (1912–1920)

Born:
June 19, 1884
Springwells, MI

Died:
May 5, 1969
Detroit, MI

▷ Batted: Switch

▷ Threw: RH

▷ Position: P

▷ MLB Pitching Record: 208–148

▷ ERA: 2.38

Ray Collins

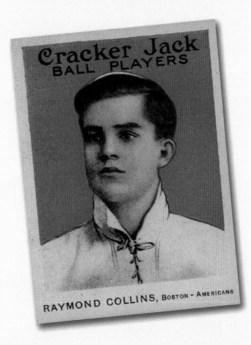

RAYMOND COLLINS, Boston - Americans

One of the first elite pitchers of the Boston Red Sox, Ray Collins was known for his outstanding control. A graduate of the University of Vermont, Collins made his Boston debut in relief against Cleveland, facing the great future Hall of Famer, Cy Young. That game is noteworthy for the first unassisted triple play in baseball history made by Naps shortstop, Neal Ball.

Collins had exceptional command, delivering his fastball with pinpoint accuracy. In 1910, his real first season as part of the Red Sox rotation, Collins won 13 games with a remarkable 1.62 ERA. In 1912, the Sox inaugural season at Fenway Park, he blossomed as the number two pitcher in the rotation behind Smokey Joe Wood, who compiled an incredible 34–5 mark. Collins held his own with 13–8 and a 2.53 ERA. That year the Sox were in the World Series and Collins

Team:

Boston Red Sox AL (1909–1915)

faced Christy Mathewson in Game 2 of the Series. The game was actually called because of darkness after 11 innings, and Collins was not involved in the decision. The 1913 and 1914 seasons proved to be Collins' best as he won 19 and 20 games, respectively. His performance slipped to 4–7 in 1915 and the proud Ray Collins promptly retired at the age of 29 because he felt that he had lost his edge.

Collins led a very productive life after his playing days ended. As a true Vermonter whose great-great-grandfather was a captain with Ethan Allen's Green Mountain Boys, Collins bled Vermont green. He returned to Vermont to run the family dairy farm but also coached baseball at his alma mater, served in the Vermont House of Representatives, and served for many years on the board of trustees of the University of Vermont. Ray Collins, one of the early good ones, passed away at age 82 in 1970.

Ray Williston Collins

Born:
February 11, 1887
Colchester, VT

Died:
January 9, 1970
Burlington, VT

▷ Batted: LH

▷ Threw: LH

▷ Position: P

▷ MLB Pitching Record: 84–62

▷ ERA: 2.51

Doc Crandall

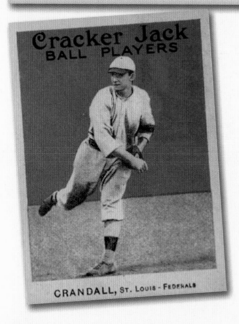

CRANDALL, St. Louis - Federals

Crandall was a specialist before specialists ever existed. He was one of baseball's best relievers, and while his save numbers are not comparable to those of recent times, he led the National League in games finished every season between 1909 and 1913. Crandall also won 67 games during his time with the Giants. It's no wonder that a check into the origin of Crandall's nickname reveals that noted scribe Damon Runyon called him "Doc" because he always came into the game in an emergency situation. Crandall and the Giants went to three straight World Series (1911–1913), and each time they lost, twice to Philadelphia and once to Boston. Overall, Doc was 1–0 in postseason play with an ERA of 1.69.

After his time in the majors, Crandall tore up the Pacific Coast League as a starter for the Los Angeles Angels, putting together a 249–163 record over 14 Minor League seasons. He was inducted into the Pacific League Hall of Fame in 1943. In retirement, Crandall coached in the minors and served a short stint as pitching coach for the Pittsburgh Pirates. We hold him in high regard as one of the forefathers of today's big time closers.

B etween 1909 and 1913, opposing batters could do a lot of things to New York Giants pitcher James Otis "Doc" Crandall. They could hit against him. Crandall surrendered more hits than innings pitched in 1911, 1912, and 1913. They could hit home runs against him. Crandall led the National League in home runs allowed with 10 in 1910, and gave up the same amount of gopher balls in 1911. They could even score against him. Crandall allowed over 80 runs scored four times in those five seasons. What opposing batters could not do to Otis Crandall was to beat him late in the game.

Born:
October 8, 1887
Wadena, IN

Died:
August 17, 1951
Bell, CA

▷ Batted: RH

▷ Threw: RH

▷ Position: P

▷ MLB Pitching Record: 102–62

▷ ERA: 2.92

James Otis Crandall

Teams:

New York Giants NL (1908–1913)

St. Louis Cardinals NL (1913)

St. Louis Terriers FL (1914–1915)

St. Louis Browns AL (1916)

Boston Braves NL (1918)

Al Demaree

DEMAREE, Philadelphia - Nationals

A s pitchers go, Al Demaree was pretty good. As sports cartoonists go, Al Demaree was very good. He spent five seasons in the minors, working his way up to the Class A league playing for the Chattanooga Lookouts and Mobile Sea Gulls of the Southern Association. His 24–10 season for Mobile in 1912 finally attracted MLB attention and Demaree made it to the big leagues with the New York Giants as a late call-up in September that year.

His coming out year was 1913 when the 28-year-old rookie had a 13–4 record with a nifty 2.21 ERA. That was the same year that the Giants won 101 games and the National League Pennant, only to lose the Series to the Philadelphia Athletics. After Demaree was traded to the Phillies in 1915, he proceeded to win 14 games and followed that with 19 wins in 1916. For the next few years, Demaree bounced around the National League. He played for the Cubs, returned to the Giants for one season, and finished up with the Boston Braves. Over that period of time he was basically a .500 pitcher. He eventually wound up back in the minors playing in the Pacific Coast League and American Association right through 1924.

Albert Wentworth Demaree

Demaree always had a flair with the pencil and during his tenure in the minors, at the end of his career, he dabbled in drawing. Demaree went on to become one of the most celebrated sports cartoonists in the country. His work was syndicated in over 200 newspapers nationwide and was published in the *Sporting News* for thirty years. He passed away in 1962 at the age of 77. Strangely enough, Al Demaree died penniless after being robbed of his life savings. He is buried in an unmarked grave in Costa Mesa, California. A very sad ending for a very talented guy.

Teams:

New York Giants NL (1912–1914, 1917–1918)
Philadelphia Phillies NL (1915–1916)
Chicago Cubs NL (1917)
Boston Braves NL (1919)

Born:
September 8, 1884
Quincy, IL

Died:
April 30, 1962
Los Angeles, CA

▷ Batted: LH

▷ Threw: RH

▷ Position: P

▷ MLB Pitching Record: 80–72

▷ ERA: 2.77

Jean Dubuc

Jean Joseph Octave Dubuc

The French-speaking Jean "Chauncey" Dubuc first pitched at the Seminary of St. Theresa in Montreal, where he was studying to become a priest. Realizing that he was not cut out for the cloth, Dubuc returned home to Vermont and played for St. Michaels College before transferring to Notre Dame University in Indiana. There Dubuc excelled as pitcher for an outstanding Notre Dame team. The following year he got caught pitching for a semi-pro team and lost his amateur status, ending his days as a college hurler. Immediately catching the eye of the Cincinnati Reds, Dubuc signed in 1908 but was released after two seasons because he needed to hone his skills.

He returned to Montreal, where he played for two years with the Royals, while also starting a successful bowling alley and pool hall business. After a 21-win season in 1911, Dubuc was claimed by Detroit where he had five very good seasons, winning 71 games for the Tigers over that span. Playing alongside the likes of Ty Cobb, Dubuc developed his "slow pitch" and became successful using this variation of the change-up. After working in the minors again in 1917, Dubuc signed with the Red Sox and appeared in the 1918 World Series. John McGraw then signed him to play the 1919 season for the Giants.

Things got a little murky from that point. Evidently, Dubuc was still friendly with former teammate and notorious gambler "Sleepy" Bill Burns. During the Black Sox trial it was noted that Burns gave Dubuc a tip to bet on the Reds because the Series was fixed. Before Judge Landis could hand out banishments, Dubuc quit the MLB and returned to Canada, staying out of the spotlight. He resurfaced in 1922 to play and manage in the minors for several years.

Whether he really knew anything about the fix is still in question. We do know that Dubuc went on to become a very well-respected coach for Brown University. He also scouted for the Tigers and is credited with signing future Hall of Famers Birdie Tebbetts and Hank Greenberg. By 1937, Dubuc left sports to go into sales, and later retired to Florida. "Chauncey" Dubuc was one interesting character.

Teams:

Cincinnati Reds NL (1908–1909)
Detroit Tigers AL (1912–1916)
Boston Red Sox AL (1918)
New York Giants NL (1919)

Born:
September 15, 1888
St. Johnsbury, VT

Died:
August 28, 1958
Fort Myers, FL

▷ Batted: RH

▷ Threw: RH

▷ Position: P

▷ MLB Pitching Record: 85–76

▷ ERA: 3.04

Cy Falkenberg

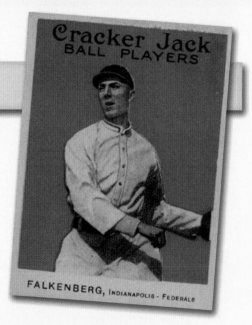

FALKENBERG, INDIANAPOLIS - FEDERALS

Most likely Cy Falkenberg would not have found success in the majors without his trick "emery pitch." Coming out of the University of Illinois with a mathematics degree, the young Falkenberg signed with the Eastern League Worcester Hustlers, but was soon acquired by the Pittsburgh Pirates. After winning only one game in 10 appearances in 1903, he was dropped from the team and sent back to the minors. Falkenberg was picked up for the 1905 season by the Washington Senators and had a pretty good season, compiling a 7–2 record, but struggled over the next two years, losing 20 games in 1906 and 17 games in 1907. Falkenberg hooked up with the Naps in 1908, only to deliver a string of four mediocre seasons.

He was finally sent back to the Minor Leagues after the 1911 season, and it was there that his career took a turn for the better. Sometime during that stretch Falkenberg developed a trick pitch called the emery pitch, or emery ball. A few other pitchers secretly used emery paper to scuff up the baseball. The rough surface would allow the pitcher to really take command of his pitches, utilizing deadly curveballs. It was sort of an unwritten

rule that umpires would look the other way. Back with the Naps in 1913, Cy proceeded to rack up 23 wins with a neat 2.22 earned-run average. That year, Falkenberg also became an unofficial spokesman for what is today the Players' Union. It is interesting that he got involved with labor negotiations and pay raises the year he won 23 games.

Unable to come to terms on a new contract, Falkenberg jumped to the Federal League where in 1914 he won 25 games for the Hoosiers and led the league in strikeouts, innings pitched, and games played. His skills began to wane in 1915, and the league folded after that season. Unfortunately, when he returned to the American League in 1917, the emery ball had been banned, and his career ended with only two wins for the Athletics. An accomplished bowler, Cy Falkenberg moved to San Francisco and opened a bowling alley after he retired from baseball.

Frederick Peter Falkenberg

Teams:

Pittsburgh Pirates NL (1903)
Washington Senators AL (1905–1908)
Cleveland Naps AL (1908–1911, 1913)
Indianapolis Hoosiers FL (1914)
Newark Pepper FL (1915)
Brooklyn Tip-Tops FL (1915)
Philadelphia Athletics AL (1917)

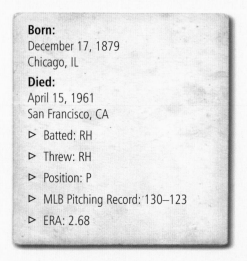

Born:
December 17, 1879
Chicago, IL
Died:
April 15, 1961
San Francisco, CA
▷ Batted: RH
▷ Threw: RH
▷ Position: P
▷ MLB Pitching Record: 130–123
▷ ERA: 2.68

Ray Fisher

Born in Middlebury, Vermont, and a graduate of Middlebury High School and Middlebury College, Ray Fisher's impact on baseball would go far beyond the Green Mountain State. From 1910 until 1917, Fisher pitched for the New York Highlanders, who were renamed the Yankees in 1913. He enjoyed his best season in 1915, posting an 18–11 record with an ERA of 2.11.

During the offseason, Fisher returned to Middlebury College as athletic director and Latin professor. His love of the collegiate life would remain a constant. In 1917, Fisher battled pleurisy, missing a month of the season, but the irrepressible spitballer would return and post a 2.19 ERA. He served in the U.S. Army in 1918 and ended his career with a two-year stint in Cincinnati. In 1919, he recorded a 14–5 record with an ERA of 2.17, helping Cincy to a World Championship.

After a 1921 salary dispute put him on baseball's Permanent Ineligible List, Fisher moved from the Reds to the Maize and Blue. He became the head baseball coach

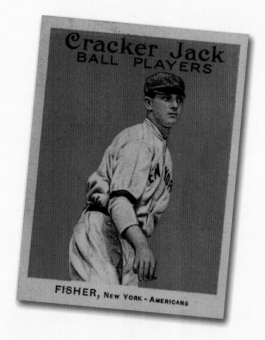

FISHER, NEW YORK - AMERICANS

Ray Lyle Fisher

at the University of Michigan, a position he would hold until 1958. Fisher guided the Wolverines to the 1953 NCAA Championship and won over 600 games. He was inducted into the Michigan Sports Hall of Fame, the American Association of College Baseball Coaches Hall of Fame, and the University of Michigan Hall of Honor. In 1980, Fisher was finally reinstated into baseball, but it really did not matter. He had already secured his legacy as a reliable pitcher and, more importantly, a leader of men.

Teams:
New York Highlanders/Yankees AL (1910–1917)
Cincinnati Reds NL (1919–1920)

Born:
October 4, 1887
Middlebury, VT
Died:
November 3, 1982
Ann Arbor, MI
▷ Batted: RH
▷ Threw: RH
▷ Position: P
▷ MLB Pitching Record: 100–94
▷ ERA: 2.82

Russ Ford

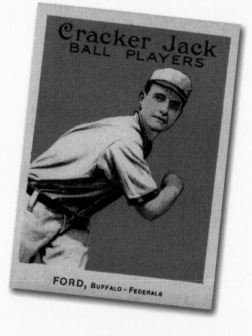

Considered the master of the trick pitch, Russ Ford could throw the knuckle ball, spitball and his signature pitch, the emery ball. For the first half of the century, Ford was considered the greatest pitcher ever to come out of Canada. Making his debut in 1905 with the Cedar Rapids Rabbits of the Illinois-Indiana-Iowa League, Ford won 16 games followed by a 22 win season in 1906. For the next few years, he moved around the Southern Association and Eastern League making a name as one of the toughest pitchers to hit in the minors.

In 1909 he came up with the Highlanders for one game at the very end of the season. However, in 1910, Ford put together a fabulous rookie year winning 26 games and losing only six, with a sparkling 1.65 earned-run average and over 200 Ks. Ford followed up with another impressive season in 1911 going 22–11. His out pitch, the emery ball, was just too difficult to hit. While in the minors, Ford discovered that scuffing the ball with emery paper made it nearly impossible to hit. He disguised it as a spitball, but eventually other pitchers

Born:
April 25, 1883
Brandon, Manitoba, Canada
Died:
January 24, 1960
Rockingham, NC
▷ Batted: RH
▷ Threw: RH
▷ Position: P
▷ MLB Pitching Record: 99–71
▷ ERA: 2.59

Russell William Ford

learned his technique and started to doctor the ball as well.

We will never know if Russ Ford would have been just average had he not learned how to master the emery ball. He developed arm trouble in 1912 and lost 21 games. In 1913, his team was renamed the Yankees, but he had another poor season, losing 18 games. Ford got on the winning track again in 1914 with 21 victories for the Buffalo Buffeds in the new Federal League. After one more season in the majors, Ford returned to the minors through 1917 and was then out of baseball. Russ Ford was elected to the Canadian Baseball Hall of Fame in 1989.

Teams:
New York Highlanders/Yankees AL (1909–1913)
Buffalo Buffeds/Blues FL (1914–1915)

Vean Gregg

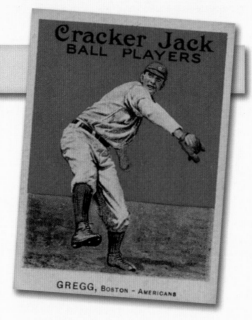

GREGG, Boston - Americans

Sylveanus "Vean" Gregg came out of the gate like a house afire. Probably the most dominant lefty in the majors from 1911 to 1913, Gregg won 63 games during his first three seasons with the Cleveland Naps in the American League, and is the only pitcher in the 20th century to win at least 20 games in his first three years. The Naps signed the 26-year-old Gregg after his incredible performance for the Portland Beavers in the Pacific Coast League where he won 32 games, racked up 383 innings pitched, and struck out 379 batters in 1910. Tall and lanky, Gregg had a deceptive fastball that would fool hitters, but his big sweeping curveball was his signature pitch.

Unfortunately, Gregg developed arm problems from overuse and struggled after the 1913 season. After his trade to the Red Sox in 1914, his arm woes continued. He actually pitched so infrequently that, even though his team appeared in the 1915 and 1916 World Series, he was not voted a full share of the Series winnings. Gregg was again traded, this time to the Philadelphia A's where he continued to struggle. He finally dropped out of baseball in 1918 to work his ranch in Alberta, Canada.

The story does not end there. After resting his arm for three years, Gregg decided to give the game another try and hooked up with the Seattle Indians of the Pacific Coast League in 1922. He won an amazing 61 games over the next three years and, incredibly, returned to the majors at age 40 to play for Clark Griffith's Washington Senators. He went 2–2 for Washington in 1925 before returning to the minors for a few more years. He then returned home to Washington state where he played semi-pro ball, hunted, fished, and ran his sporting goods and luncheonette business "The Home Plate." Voted the greatest lefty in Cleveland Indians history, Vean Gregg is a member of the Pacific Coast League Hall of Fame. Had it not been for his arm miseries, Gregg could possibly have been one of the greatest pitchers of the Deadball Era.

Sylveanus Augustus Gregg

Teams:

Cleveland Naps AL (1911–1914)

Boston Red Sox AL (1914–1916)

Philadelphia Athletics AL (1918)

Washington Senators AL (1925)

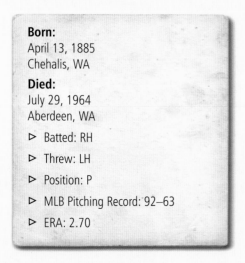

Born:
April 13, 1885
Chehalis, WA

Died:
July 29, 1964
Aberdeen, WA

▷ Batted: RH

▷ Threw: LH

▷ Position: P

▷ MLB Pitching Record: 92–63

▷ ERA: 2.70

Bob Groom

In a decade of baseball, Bob Groom saw the pinnacles and pitfalls of big-league pitching. An Illinois native, Groom broke in with the Washington Senators in 1909 just in time to play on a team that lost 110 games. The Senators were one of the worst teams in baseball history, and Groom took the brunt of it going 7–26 despite a decent 2.87 ERA. Some of his woes were self-inflicted, as he walked a league-high 105 batters.

Not one Washington starter batted over .300, and the club managed to accomplish the unthinkable—they made the great Walter Johnson look bad. That season, The Big Train lost 25 games. After two consecutive 17-loss seasons, Groom posted a 24–13 record in 1912 and the Senators won 91 games. Groom struck out 179 batters with an ERA of 2.62. He would lose 20 games for the St. Louis Terriers of the Federal League in 1914 and drop 19 games for the St. Louis Browns in 1917. Both marks led the league. Despite these poor records, Groom did garner

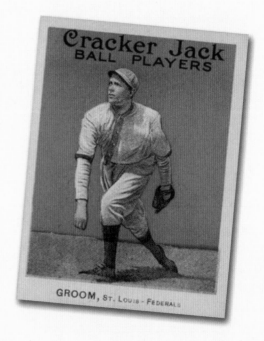

GROOM, St. Louis - Federals

Robert Groom

respect among his peers. No less than Ty Cobb once named Groom to a list of the toughest pitchers in the game.

After the 1918 season, Groom returned home to Belleville to run the family coal business, staying involved in the game by managing several amateur teams. Groom was a hard-throwing right-hander who could really make the ball dance. Sadly, his teams most often fell short. In fact, he played on three second place clubs in 10 years. I guess you could say that this was one Groom who was also a bridesmaid.

Teams:

Washington Senators AL (1909–1913)
St. Louis Terriers FL (1914–1915)
St. Louis Browns AL (1916–1917)
Cleveland Indians AL (1918)

Born:
September 12, 1884
Belleville, IL

Died:
February 19, 1948
Belleville, IL

▷ Batted: RH

▷ Threw: RH

▷ Position: P

▷ MLB Pitching Record: 119–150

▷ ERA: 3.10

Earl Hamilton

A durable yet inconsistent pitcher, lefty Earl Hamilton played 14 seasons in the majors, with one pocket of brilliance and plenty of mediocrity over that span. Coming out of the gate for the St. Louis Browns in 1911, the 19-year-old rookie found himself in the rotation and lost 12 games with only five victories. Over the next four seasons, Hamilton gave the underperforming Browns over 200 innings per season with sub-.500 results. He won 16 games in 1914, but unfortunately lost 18 games that year. One of the highlights of Hamilton's career took place on August 30, 1912, when he tossed a no-hitter against the Detroit Tigers, winning 5–1. The Tigers managed to score on a walk to Ty Cobb followed by an error.

The pocket of brilliance we referred to occurred in 1918, the first year Hamilton pitched for the Pittsburgh Pirates. That season, he started six games for the Pirates, recorded a 6–0 record with an astounding .083 earned-run average, and gave up only five earned runs. The patriotic Hamilton left the team in the middle of the season to join the U.S. Navy and fight overseas in World War I, thus ending his incredible streak. In 1919, he returned to Pittsburgh only to resume his pre-1918 mediocre pitching. Hamilton had one more decent season in 1922 when he went 11–7 for the Pirates, and finished out his career with the Philadelphia Phillies in 1924.

With his career wins falling 32 games below .500, Earl Hamilton could say that the six-game streak in 1918 made it all worthwhile. He continued to pitch in the minors until 1933 and transitioned to the front office as owner of the Ponca City Angels/St. Joseph Angels in the Western Association through 1939 and the Stockton Fliers in the California League in 1941.

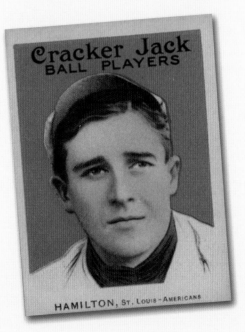

HAMILTON, ST. LOUIS - AMERICANS

Teams:

St. Louis Browns AL (1911–1916, 1917)
Detroit Tigers AL (1916)
Pittsburgh Pirates NL (1918–1923)
Philadelphia Phillies NL (1924)

Earl Andrew Hamilton

Born:
July 19, 1891
Gibson, IL

Died:
November 17, 1968
Anaheim, CA

▷ Batted: LH

▷ Threw: LH

▷ Position: P

▷ MLB Pitching Record: 115–147

▷ ERA: 3.16

Claude Hendrix

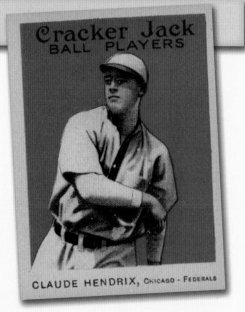

CLAUDE HENDRIX, Chicago - Federals

Had his career not been tainted by allegations of gambling and throwing a game, Claude Hendrix would go down in history as one of the better pitchers of the Deadball Era. A superb hitting pitcher who was a master of the spitball, Hendrix attended Wichita State University where he excelled as an athlete. He quickly made the jump to pitch in the Western League and continued on in the minors for a few years.

Hendrix finally caught the eye of the Pittsburgh Pirates in 1911 where he was befriended by Honus Wagner. In 1912 the 23-year-old Hendrix exploded as a star pitcher, compiling a 24–9 record and leading the National League with his .727 winning percentage. He also hit a blistering .322 in 121 at-bats that year. The success continued in 1913 when Hendrix placed among league leaders in strikeouts, even though he was one game under .500 as a pitcher. After jumping to the Chicago Chi-Feds in the new Federal League in 1914, Hendrix led the league with 29 wins and a great 1.69 earned-

run average. Once the Federal League folded, he went crosstown to join the National League Cubs and in 1918 his 20 wins helped lead them to the NL Pennant. Curiously enough, because his manager elected to go with a rotation of lefthanders, he did not appear in the Series as a pitcher.

In 1920, the career of Claude Hendrix took a negative turn when he was implicated in throwing a game between the Cubs and Phillies. The owner of the Cubs, Bill Veeck, received word that Hendrix bet against the Cubs in a game in which he was scheduled to pitch. He was immediately scratched from the lineup and was later released from the club. This episode opened the door for an investigation into gambling in baseball, which led to the eventual unraveling of the 1919 Black Sox debacle. Hendrix continued playing ball with various semi-pro teams and then went into the restaurant business. He died at age 55 in 1944, never exonerated from the gambling accusations that dogged him.

Teams:
Pittsburgh Pirates NL (1911–1913)
Chicago Chi-Feds/Whales FL (1914–1915)
Chicago Cubs NL (1916–1920)

Claude Raymond Hendrix

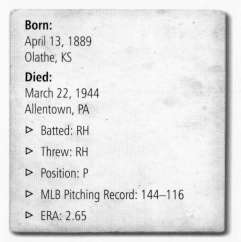

Born:
April 13, 1889
Olathe, KS
Died:
March 22, 1944
Allentown, PA
▷ Batted: RH
▷ Threw: RH
▷ Position: P
▷ MLB Pitching Record: 144–116
▷ ERA: 2.65

Bill James

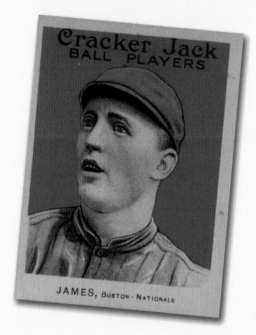

JAMES, Boston - Nationals

"Seattle Bill" James burst into the baseball galaxy like a shooting star, but faded away just as quickly. Pitching for the Seattle Indians of the Northwestern League in 1912, the young phenom posted a 29–7 record while acquiring his nickname. He was quickly signed by the Boston Braves, and in his first season with the woeful Braves, James was 6–10 with a 2.79 earned-run average; not all that bad for a rookie.

In 1914, James rose to the top of the baseball world to become a dominant pitcher. That year the Braves shocked everyone when they charged from last place to win the National League pennant and then swept the World Series. For a stretch of almost three months, James rattled off 19 wins and led the league in a variety of categories. In Game 2 of the World Series, James faced the legendary "Gettysburg Eddie" Plank and pitched a masterful two-hitter. James won a second game in the Series when he appeared in relief in extra innings. He racked up a sparkling 26–7 record along with a solid

William Lawrence James

1.90 earned-run average that season and was labeled as the next great pitching star to come down the line.

Unfortunately, Bill developed shoulder problems over the course of the winter and when he reported to spring training, he could not get the ball over the plate. He appeared in 13 games in 1915, pitching only 68 total innings, and was forced to retire from Major League baseball because of the shoulder ailment. From 1919 through 1925, James moved around the minors playing in the Texas League, Pacific Coast League, and the Southern Association. Sadly, "Seattle Bill" James never regained the form that made him the talk of baseball for one season. He coached a bit, settled into married life and lived out his days quietly, but he would never forget that one shining season.

Team:

Boston Braves NL (1913–1915, 1919)

Born:
March 12, 1892
Iowa Hill, CA

Died:
March 10, 1971
Oroville, CA

▷ Batted: RH

▷ Threw: RH

▷ Position: P

▷ MLB Pitching Record: 37–21

▷ ERA: 2.28

George Kaiserling

George Kaiserling is not the most famous person from Steubenville, Ohio. The blue-collar city along the Ohio River was home to the likes of entertainer Dean Martin, famous sports handicapper Jimmy "The Greek" Snyder and another pretty fair Major League pitcher, Hall of Famer Rollie Fingers. Nonetheless, Kaiserling deserves his place among the luminaries of Steubenville.

He played two years in the Federal League, 1914 with the Indianapolis Hoosiers and 1915 when the Hoosiers moved to Newark, NJ, and became known as the Pepper. Indy took the Federal League Championship in 1914 and the 19-year-old Kaiserling won 17 games with an ERA of 3.11. The ace of that staff won 25 games and his name was Cy, Falkenberg, not Young. Earl Moseley also chipped in with 19 wins for that terrific pitching rotation. The club also featured a 27-year-old future Hall of Famer named Bill McKechnie.

Kaiserling was a legitimate prospect with 20 complete games and over 275 innings pitched. Control was an issue as Kaiserling walked 72 batters and led the league in hit batsmen with 17. The next season, with fifth place Newark, Kaiserling's record dipped to 15–15, but he improved his ERA to 2.24. He had 16 complete games, five shutouts, and even recorded two saves. Sadly, 1915 would be Kaiserling's final MLB season. He played for the Toledo Iron Men of the American Association in 1916 and the Chattanooga Lookouts of the Southern Association

Teams:

Indianapolis Hoosiers FL (1914)
Newark Pepper FL (1915)

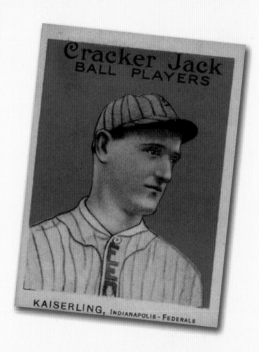

George Kaiserling

in 1917, but never had the chance to earn his way back to the big leagues. In March 1918, at the age of 24, he died of pulmonary tuberculosis. Still, along with Dean, Jimmy and Rollie, George Kaiserling should be remembered as one of Steubenville's all-time greats.

Born:
May 12, 1893
Steubenville, OH

Died:
March 2, 1918
Steubenville, OH

▷ Batted: RH

▷ Threw: RH

▷ Position: P

▷ MLB Pitching Record: 32–25

▷ ERA: 2.68

Ray Keating

Elmer Knetzer

For a few brief shining moments in 1912, New York Highlanders pitcher Ray Keating appeared to be the first coming of Babe Ruth. The rookie right-hander hit .375 with six hits in 16 at-bats. This early promise at the plate went unfulfilled, as Keating would never again hit higher than .241. On the hill, however, Keating did have one unique quality; he was one of the most notorious spitballers of his time. Keating whistled the wet one past many an opposing hitter. It also got him into trouble. Two times in his career, Keating had more walks than strikeouts.

Even though he had 11 wild pitches in 1914, that season, strangely enough, was probably his best. He cobbled together an 8–11 record, but had an ERA of 2.96, 14 complete games, and a career-high 109 Ks. In Keating's seven seasons in the Big Apple, the club never finished higher than fourth. Not much changed when Keating was sold to the Boston Braves in 1919. That team finished sixth, and Keating won seven games on a staff whose best pitcher was Dick Rudolph, with a 13–18

Raymond Herbert Keating

Born:
July 21, 1893
Bridgeport, CT
Died:
December 28, 1963
Sacramento, CA
▷ Batted: RH
▷ Threw: RH
▷ Position: P
▷ MLB Pitching Record: 31–51
▷ ERA: 3.29

record. In 1920, the Braves sold Keating to Los Angeles of the Pacific Coast League where he found better success. Keating continued on in the PCL through the 1931 season playing mostly for the Sacramento Senators for whom he had 20 wins in 1927 and 27 wins in 1928.

Give Keating credit. He remained steadfast in his spitballing. Baseball banned the spitter in 1919, but Keating was given amnesty. He continued to snub his nose, or in this case his mouth, at the game's new rules. Keating and his spitball lived moistly ever after in the PCL, compiling a 174–156 record over his 13 Minor League seasons.

Teams:
New York Highlanders/Yankees AL (1912–1916, 1918)
Boston Braves NL (1919)

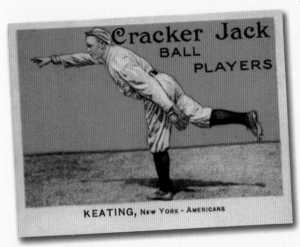

KEATING, New York - Americans

E. E. KNETZER, Pittsburgh - Federals

While with the Lawrence Colts of the New England League, Elmer Knetzer attracted the attention of Brooklyn Superbas scouts and the 23-year-old rookie was signed midway through the 1909 season. He appeared in five games that year compiling a weak 1–3 record. The next year, Knetzer fared better appearing as a spot starter as well as a reliever and winning seven games. His best year in the National League was 1911, when he won 11 games for the

Born:
July 22, 1885
Carrick, PA
Died:
October 3, 1975
Pittsburgh, PA
▷ Batted: RH
▷ Threw: RH
▷ Position: P
▷ MLB Pitching Record: 69–69
▷ ERA: 3.15

Elmer Ellsworth Knetzer

Dodgers. Knetzer had the bad luck to pitch on some lousy teams. During his four seasons in Brooklyn, the team never finished better than sixth place in the league.

When the new Federal League formed, Knetzer signed with his hometown Pittsburgh Rebels and it was there that he hit his stride going 20–12 followed by an 18–14 season. This will give you some indication of the skill level in the new league compared to both the American and National Leagues. After the Federal League folded, Knetzer signed on with the Boston Braves but saw little action, appearing in just two games and losing both. From Boston he went to the Cincinnati Reds where he pitched for two more years with no success and finally called it a career. In between his stints with the Reds, Knetzer hooked on with the Columbus Senators of the American Association. All in all, Elmer Knetzer hovered around the .500 mark as a pitcher. In retirement, he went well beyond the .500 mark, living to the ripe old age of 90.

Teams:
Brooklyn Superbas/Dodgers NL (1909–1912)
Pittsburgh Rebels FL (1914–1915)
Boston Braves NL (1916)
Cincinnati Reds NL (1916–1917)

Jimmy Lavender

James Sanford Lavender

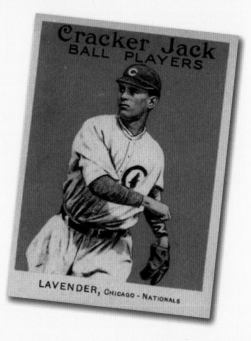

After a late start to baseball, Georgia native Jimmy Lavender enjoyed a few moments of fame over a fairly lackluster career. As a Minor Leaguer, Lavender threw plenty of innings with plenty of wins and losses. Over a five-year span from 1907 through 1911, he won 82 games, lost 94 and pitched somewhere in the vicinity of 1,500 innings. Primarily a spitball pitcher, Lavender's durability is what finally got him to the majors. After a 19-win season in 1911 for the Providence Grays in the Eastern League, the Chicago Cubs took a chance on Lavender. The 28-year-old rookie had a good first year posting a 16–13 record, throwing over 250 innings in 1912.

On the mound on July 8, 1912, against New York Giants' ace Rube Marquard, Lavender made a name for himself when he threw a five-hitter to end Marquard's 19-game winning streak. At the time, that was the longest winning streak by any pitcher in baseball history. This marked the high point of Lavender's career. Over the next four seasons, Lavender would go 41–55. One other notable bright spot in his career was on August 31, 1915, when he tossed a 2–0 no-hitter against the New York Giants. Jimmy Lavender ended his career with the Philadelphia Phillies in 1916 at 33 years old and never looked back. After baseball, he retired to his home in Georgia and worked in a textile mill, living comfortably to the age of 75.

Teams:
Chicago Cubs NL (1912–1916)
Philadelphia Phillies NL (1917)

Born:
May 26, 1884
Barnesville, GA
Died:
January 12, 1960
Cartersville, GA
▷ Batted: RH
▷ Threw: RH
▷ Position: P
▷ MLB Pitching Record: 63–76
▷ ERA: 3.09

Rube Marquard

Erskine Mayer

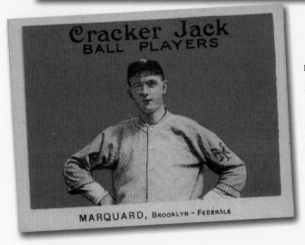

MARQUARD, Brooklyn - Federals

MAYER, Philadelphia - Nationals

Rube Marquard won 103 games between 1908 and 1915, not too shabby. Unfortunately, he was on the same New York Giants staff as Christy Mathewson, who won 195 in that same time span. Both men would culminate their legacies in the Hall of Fame, but for Marquard, the early road to Cooperstown was rocky. In 1908, the Giants paid a then-astronomical sum of $11,000 to sign Marquard, but the young pitcher was mocked by sportswriters as he won just nine games in his first three seasons. Thanks to coach Wilbert Robinson, Marquard blossomed in 1911, posting a record of 24–7 with a league-leading 237 Ks. His confidence at an all-time high, Marquard won 26 games in 1912, highlighted by a still-record 19-game winning streak.

Like many of baseball's cherished records, there was a twist to Marquard's mark. His streak began in April against the Brooklyn Dodgers and opposing pitcher Nap Rucker. It reached 19 games in July against, you guessed it, Nap Rucker and the Dodgers. Marquard actually won three more games than Mathewson in 1912, and followed that up with 23 more wins in 1913. Marquard became the toast of the Big Apple, and he took a fairly big bite out of it, endorsing numerous products and even starring in his own silent movie, "Rube Marquard Wins." He performed on the Broadway stage and had a scandalous affair with married actress Blossom Seeley, who eventually became his first of three wives.

Marquard's curtain began to fall in 1914 when he went 12–22. He tossed a no-hitter against Brooklyn on April 15, 1915, which, ironically, would be his next stop as he bolted the Giants in August that year. His record more up and down than the Cyclone roller coaster at Coney Island, Marquard moved to the Reds in 1921 and won 17 games. After four mediocre seasons with the Boston Braves, Marquard left the majors to play and manage in the minors, finally retiring in 1933 at age 46. A true character who reveled in telling stories of his colorful baseball life, Marquard was elected to the Hall of Fame by the Veterans Committee in 1971.

Steve Carlton won 238 more games than Erskine Mayer, but the two have a lot in common. In 1914, Mayer was a good pitcher on a bad team, winning 21 games for the sixth place Philadelphia Phillies. Carlton would meet the same fate 58 years later going 27–10 for the last place 1972 Phils. Both men deserved better. In 1914, only one Phillies regular, Beals Becker, hit over .300. It was for this reason that Mayer also lost 19 games that season.

In 1915, Mayer's team caught up with his arm. The Phillies took the National League flag as Mayer won 21 games with a 2.36 ERA. In the World Series versus the Red Sox, Mayer surrendered 16 hits in two starts as Boston eliminated Philly in five games. Those two seasons proved to be the pinnacle of his career. However, even at his best, Mayer was always overshadowed by teammate Grover Cleveland Alexander. On July 1, 1918, Mayer was traded to Pittsburgh for Elmer Jacobs. With the Pirates, he would complete his last great season in the big

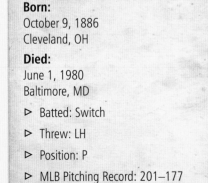

Born:
October 9, 1886
Cleveland, OH

Died:
June 1, 1980
Baltimore, MD

▷ Batted: Switch

▷ Threw: LH

▷ Position: P

▷ MLB Pitching Record: 201–177

▷ ERA: 3.08

Richard William Marquard

Teams:

New York Giants NL (1908–1915)
Brooklyn Robins NL (1915–1920)
Cincinnati Reds NL (1921)
Boston Braves NL (1922–1925)

Jacob Erskine Mayer

Born: James Erskine Mayer

leagues, fashioning a 16–7 record with 18 complete games. In Mayer's final season of 1919, he returned to the World Series with the ChiSox. Although Mayer was not involved, the fix was in and the Black Sox fell in disgrace.

Mayer's genealogy is more interesting than his career. His great-grandfather worked for German statesman Otto Von Bismarck, and his uncle captained the river boat that inspired the stories of a young author named Samuel Clemens, also known as Mark Twain. Mayer himself was no writer, but from time to time he did author a gem or two on the hill.

Teams:

Philadelphia Phillies NL (1912–1918)
Pittsburgh Pirates NL (1918–1919)
Chicago White Sox AL (1919)

Born:
January 16, 1890
Atlanta, GA
Died:
March 10, 1957
Los Angeles, CA

▷ Batted: RH

▷ Threw: RH

▷ Position: P

▷ MLB Pitching Record: 91–70

▷ ERA: 2.96

George McQuillan

George Watt McQuillan

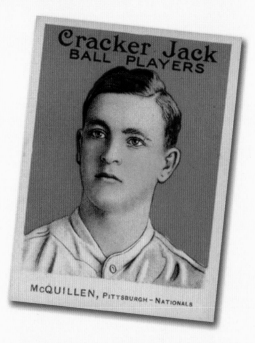

Had he paid more attention to honing his pitching skills than drinking and extracurricular escapades, George McQuillan could have been one of the best. After a very successful Minor League campaign, McQuillan made the jump to the big leagues in a very impressive manner, posting a 4–0 record with a miniscule 0.66 ERA. He pitched 25 consecutive innings, coming out of the gate without allowing an earned run, a record that stood for over 100 years. In 1908, as a starter for the Phillies, McQuillan posted a 23–17 record and pitched a whopping 359 innings. For his first few years in the majors, he was considered one of the best pitchers in baseball and the possible heir apparent to Christy Mathewson.

Things went awry for McQuillan after he took a liking to the bottle. He became inconsistent as a pitcher, was out of condition, and developed venereal disease due to extramarital escapades. The Phillies finally had enough and shipped him out after the 1910 season. The Cincinnati Reds tried to rehabilitate him, but the George McQuillan that showed up to play the 1911 season was no longer a promising young pitcher.

Teams:

Philadelphia Phillies NL (1907–1910, 1915–1916)
Cincinnati Reds NL (1911)
Pittsburgh Pirates NL (1913–1915)
Cleveland Indians AL (1918)

Things only got worse and the Reds dispatched him to the minors, where he pitched for Columbus of the American Association. In 1913, he resurfaced with Pittsburgh in the National League and had three mediocre seasons. He played for Cleveland in 1918, his final year in the majors, posting an unproductive 0–1. McQuillan continued in the minors until 1926, but never regained the form that was supposed to catapult him to stardom. Instead he chose a path that led to his baseball demise. McQuillan died at age 54 in 1940, a talent wasted.

Born:
May 1, 1885
Brooklyn, NY
Died:
March 30, 1940
Columbus, OH

▷ Batted: RH

▷ Threw: RH

▷ Position: P

▷ MLB Pitching Record: 85–89

▷ ERA: 2.38

Willie Mitchell

Earl Moore

The first player from Mississippi State University to make it to the majors, Willie Mitchell was also the first American League pitcher to strike out Babe Ruth. Mitchell won 13 games for the San Antonio Bronchos of the Texas League in 1909 before he was called up to finish the season with the Cleveland Naps. The 19-year-old rookie won just one of the three games he appeared in, but sported a nifty 1.57 earned-run average.

The following year, Mitchell went 12–8 and was a big part of the Naps rotation. However, in 1911 he struggled, winning only 7 games and losing 14, and he was relegated to the bullpen for the 1912 season. Mitchell had his best year in 1913 posting a 14-win season to go along with his 1.91 ERA. For the next several years he hovered around the .500 mark and was finally traded to the Detroit Tigers in 1916. Mitchell had one more good MLB year, going 12–8 in 1917. The next two seasons were rather unproductive and his Major League career came to an end in 1919.

Like many others, Mitchell went back to the minors. While playing for the

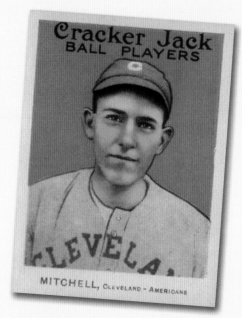

MITCHELL, Cleveland - Americans

Vernon Tigers of the Pacific Coast League in 1920, he had a sparkling 25–13 record. Mitchell bounced around the circuit for a few more years and called it a wrap after playing for the Topeka Senators in the Western Association for the 1924 season. Willie Mitchell was inducted into the Mississippi Sports Hall of Fame in 1966 and the Mississippi State Sports Hall of Fame in 1970. He passed away in 1973 at age 83.

He called himself the "Steam Engine in Boots," but Earl Moore was more like the not-so-little engine that could. Throughout his 14-year career, he battled injuries, rheumatism, pleurisy, and just plain bad luck. Moore's sidearm delivery earned him the nickname "Crossfire." Others called him "Big Ebbie" due to his 6-foot, 195 pound frame. Names aside, the man could bring it. Between 1903 and 1905 Moore struck out 418 batters for the Cleveland Naps. Along the way, he defeated some of the best pitchers of all time, including Cy Young and Rube Waddell.

In 1905, Moore was struck in the left foot by a wicked line drive back to the mound. It would take four years, time in the Minor Leagues, and stops with the Highlanders and Phillies for him to recover. Moore won 80 games in his first five seasons, but just 83 over his final nine. Fifty-five of those wins came for the Phils between 1909 and 1911. Moore's control issues led to five seasons of 100 or more walks.

William Mitchell

Teams:
Cleveland Naps/Indians AL (1909–1916)
Detroit Tigers AL (1916–1919)

Born:
December 1, 1889
Pleasant Grove, MS

Died:
November 23, 1973
Sardis, MS

▷ Batted: RH

▷ Threw: LH

▷ Position: P

▷ MLB Pitching Record: 83–92

▷ ERA: 2.88

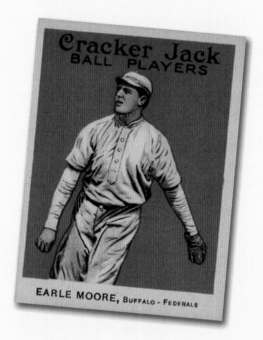

EARLE MOORE, Buffalo - Federals

Alonzo Earl Moore

His career was a portrait of highs and lows. During his rookie year, Moore threw the American League's first-ever nine-inning no-hitter, but lost the no-no and the game in the tenth. He won 20 games and led the AL with a 1.74 ERA in 1903, but missed the last month of the season due to injury. Through all this adversity, Moore persevered. We think that counts for something and rate him as one of the most relentless hurlers of the Deadball Era.

Teams:

Cleveland Blues/Bronchos/Naps AL (1901–1907)
New York Highlanders AL (1907)
Philadelphia Phillies NL (1908–1913)
Chicago Cubs NL (1913)
Buffalo Buffeds FL (1914)

Born:
July 29, 1877
Pickerington, OH

Died:
November 28, 1961
Columbus, OH

▷ Batted: RH

▷ Threw: RH

▷ Position: P

▷ MLB Pitching Record: 163–154

▷ ERA: 2.78

George Mullin

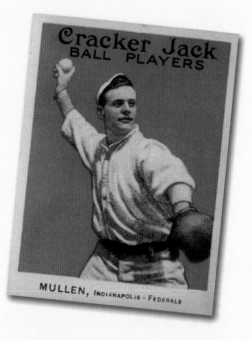

MULLEN, INDIANAPOLIS - FEDERALS

One of the better pitchers in the Cracker Jack Collection, and considered one of the Tigers' all-time best, Mullin won at least 20 games on five different occasions and still leads the Tigers in several categories, including innings pitched for a season (382), career innings (3,394) and complete games (42). Mullin also had the distinction of pitching a no-hitter against the St. Louis Browns on July 4, 1912, his 32nd birthday.

From 1903 through 1911, Mullin was considered one of the most dominant pitchers in the American League, amassing 183 wins. Over that same period, the workhorse Mullin pitched over 300 innings an incredible six times. His 29–8 season in 1909 was by far his best. A master of the fastball, part of the Mullin mystique was that he was a bit wild, hitting batters 131 times over his career. He was also a master of the stall, fidgeting and talking to himself on the mound to distract batters.

Mullin starred in the World Series from 1907 through 1909, although the Tigers did not fare well. He pitched an amazing six complete games over that span in the

Born:
July 4, 1880
Toledo, OH

Died:
January 7, 1944
Wabash, IN

▷ Batted: RH

▷ Threw: RH

▷ Position: P

▷ MLB Pitching Record: 228–196

▷ ERA: 2.82

George Joseph Mullin

Series. Mullin also ranks seventh all time in assists, and had a pretty good bat to boot, with a career .262 batting average. He once even pinch hit for Ty Cobb. In his later years, Mullin jumped to the Federal League winning 14 games his first year with the Indy Hoosiers. After the 1915 season with the Newark Pepper, Mullin called it quits. He played and coached in the minors through 1921 and later worked as a police officer. "Wabash George" Mullin was one heck of a pitcher.

Teams:

Detroit Tigers AL (1902–1913)
Washington Senators AL (1913)
Indianapolis Hoosiers FL (1914)
Newark Pepper FL (1915)

Marty O'Toole

Gene Packard

This is the classic story of the phenom, penciled in as the next great pitcher, who fizzled out before he even got started. Marty O'Toole was the "Can't Miss Kid" who happened to miss. Chalk it up to his arm burning out before he really got started in the majors. O'Toole put up incredible numbers coming up through the Minor Leagues. Beginning in 1906, he pitched a great many innings and racked up an impressive number of wins. That year the 17-year-old prodigy won 19 games, and in 1908 he pitched over 300 innings and won 31 games.

O'Toole was well on his way to super stardom when he was signed by the Cincinnati Reds, but he was only up for a short period, as he needed more seasoning. Back in the minors, playing in the American Association, he annihilated batters, dominating in most pitching categories. A bidding war ensued for his services in the majors, and in 1911, the Pittsburgh Pirates paid a whopping $22,500 for the "Can't Miss Kid."

Martin James O'Toole

Born:
November 27, 1888
William Penn, PA
Died:
February 18, 1949
Aberdeen, WA
▷ Batted: RH
▷ Threw: RH
▷ Position: P
▷ MLB Pitching Record: 27–36
▷ ERA: 3.21

Sadly, from there it was all down hill for O'Toole. He developed arm problems quickly, a result from overuse in the minors. His fastball disappeared and O'Toole developed a spitball, but it was not very effective. The sportswriters taunted O'Toole, referring to him as the $22,500 lemon. Unfortunately, his career with the Pirates never really materialized. O'Toole made a brief stop with the New York Giants, before returning to the minors where he actually put together a few good seasons in the Western League. After his playing days were over, he owned a pool hall, worked as a salesman for Boeing Aircraft during World War II and passed away soon after in 1949. The phenom never quite lived up to expectations.

Teams:

Cincinnati Reds NL (1908)
Pittsburgh Pirates NL (1911–1914)
New York Giants NL (1914)

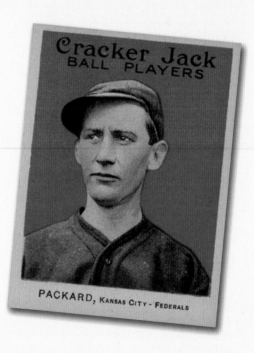

PACKARD, KANSAS CITY - FEDERALS

If you look at his entire body of work, Gene Packard was basically a journeyman pitcher. Remove the two 20-win seasons in the fledgling Federal League, and you have a pitcher that hovered around the .500 mark during his career in the National League. Packard had a noteworthy appearance on August 3, 1918, when he gave up 12 runs in a game and did not take the loss, a pretty difficult feat to say the least. When he jumped ship to the Kansas City Packers in the new Federal League, he had his

Born:
July 13, 1887
Colorado Springs, CO
Died:
May 19, 1959
Riverside, CA
▷ Batted: LH
▷ Threw: LH
▷ Position: P
▷ MLB Pitching Record: 85–69
▷ ERA: 3.01

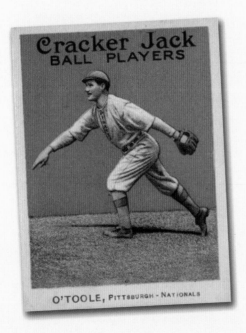

O'TOOLE, PITTSBURGH - NATIONALS

Eugene Milo Packard

best seasons going 20–14 in 1914 and 20–12 in 1915. The skill level of the new league was no match for the established American or National leagues, and Packard could not continue his success when he returned to the majors.

There is some controversy that has come to light about Packard. In 1918, the Red Sox played the Cubs in the World Series. This particular season was shortened because of the outbreak of World War I. There was, and still is, speculation that the Cubs threw that series, and that Packard was involved as go-between for the gamblers and the Cubs' players involved in the scheme. Keep in mind that although he played for the Cardinals at the time, he was a former Cub with strong ties to many of his former teammates.

Baseball officials never officially looked into the 1918 Series and Packard was never charged with any wrong doing, but the speculation remains. Written documentation that surfaced years later and player interviews both indicate that it is very likely the 1918 Series was tainted, and that Packard had a hand in it. Some even believe this is how the Black Sox got the idea to fix the 1919 Series. In any event, Packard wisely disappeared into oblivion after finishing up his career with the Phillies in 1919.

Teams:
Cincinnati Reds NL (1912–1913)
Kansas City Packers FL (1914–1915)
Chicago Cubs NL (1916–1917)
St. Louis Cardinals NL (1917–1918)
Philadelphia Phillies NL (1919)

Hub Perdue

Herbert Rodney Perdue

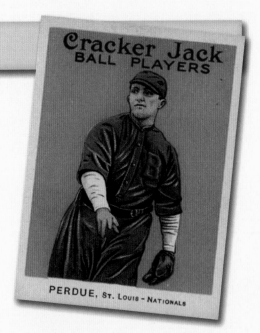

PERDUE, St. Louis - Nationals

Hub Perdue began his baseball career in 1911 with the Boston Rustlers, a club that featured an aging 44-year old pitcher named Cy Young playing in his last big-league season. The Boston team would change its name to the Braves beginning in 1912. That year, Perdue was 13–16 with a 3.80 ERA for a team that lost 101 games and finished in eighth place. The following year, the Braves were 69–82, but Perdue rose above the level of his teammates posting a 16–13 record with a 3.26 ERA.

Beyond any statistics, Perdue's most interesting facet may have been his nickname. He was known as "The Gallatin Squash," a moniker given to him by celebrated sportswriter Grantland Rice. The name was a combination of geography and agriculture. Perdue's home was in Gallatin, Tennessee, and his first name, Hub (shortened from Herbert), reminded Rice of a Hubbard Squash, ergo, the Gallatin Squash. Unfortunately, squash is exactly what many opposing hitters did to Perdue's pitches, specifically in 1912, when he surrendered a league-leading 11 home runs. It would be nice to say that Perdue balanced his penchant for surrendering long balls by hitting a few of his own. Sadly, this is not true. In 300 career at-bats, he managed just 42 hits and no home runs.

Perdue did have one unique aspect to his career beyond his nickname. He is one of the few men in Major League baseball history ever to be traded for a marsupial, well sort of. In 1914, the Braves dealt Perdue to the Cardinals for a player named Possum Whitted. Perdue won a total of 14 games in St. Louis in 1914 and 1915. While he was never more than an average hurler in the majors, Perdue attained a higher rank in an equally famous organization after his playing career ended. In June of 1924, he was sworn in as an Apprentice in the Freemasons of Bethpage Lodge in Tennessee. Within two months, he had risen to the level of Sublime Degree of Master Mason. For a guy whose career record was 51–64, it must have been nice to finally rise from sub-.500 to sublime.

Teams:
Boston Rustlers/Braves NL (1911–1914)
St. Louis Cardinals NL (1914–1915)

Born:
June 7, 1882
Bethpage, TN

Died:
October 31, 1968
Gallatin, TN

▷ Batted: RH
▷ Threw: RH
▷ Position: P
▷ MLB Pitching Record: 51–64
▷ ERA: 3.85

Ed Reulbach

Nap Rucker

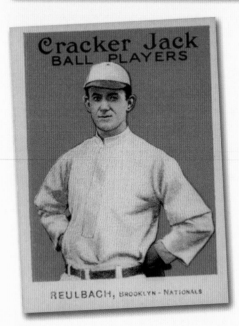

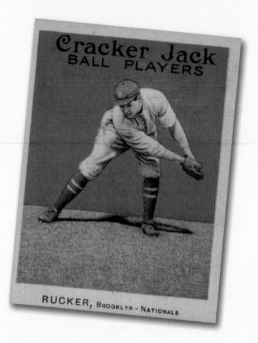

Before his death in 1961, Ed Reulbach held the distinction of being the last living Cub to have won a World Series. He joined the Cubbies in 1905 and quickly impressed with 18 wins and an ERA of 1.42. The following year, he contributed 19 wins to a league-leading 1.75 team ERA which earned the Cubs a trip to the World Series. In the Fall Classic, Reulbach pitched a complete game one-hitter, but the Cubs fell to the crosstown rival White Sox in six games. He was the National League win-loss percentage leader for three seasons (1906–1908) and enjoyed two winning streaks of 14 games or more.

On September 26, 1908, "Big Ed" Reulbach surpassed these impressive accomplishments with one that may never be duplicated. He pitched two complete game shutouts in one day against the Brooklyn Superbas. Sadly, 97 wins and two World Series Championships in his first five seasons were not enough to get Reulbach to Cooperstown. In 1910, his ERA rose while his innings pitched tumbled. That season, his only child became seriously ill with diphtheria and Reulbach missed multiple games to be with his son.

His career would last another seven seasons with stops in Brooklyn, Boston, and the Newark Pepper of the Federal League. During the latter part of his career, Reulbach helped found the Baseball Players' Fraternity to help fight for higher player salaries, and he even tried to convince MLB players to abstain from alcohol. After his retirement, he nearly sacrificed his own well-being to care for his sickly son, who passed away in 1931. The accomplishments of fellow Cub pitcher Mordecai "Three Finger" Brown were more notable, but "Big Ed" Reulbach was a big part of the Cubs' successful run in the early years of the 20th century.

Edward Marvin Reulbach

Teams:

Chicago Cubs NL (1905–1913)
Brooklyn Superbas/Robins NL (1913–1914)
Newark Peppers FL (1915)
Boston Braves NL (1916–1917)

Born:
December 1, 1882
Detroit, MI

Died:
July 17, 1961
Glens Falls, NY

▷ Batted: RH

▷ Threw: RH

▷ Position: P

▷ MLB Pitching Record: 182–106

▷ ERA: 2.28

During Nap Rucker's 10 years in Brooklyn, his team's name changed from the Superbas to the Dodgers back to the Superbas and then to the Robins. What did not change was Rucker's ERA, which consistently hovered just over 2.00. Rucker was the quintessential hard-luck loser putting together records like 17–19 in 1908, 17–18 in 1910, and 18–21 in 1912. To put it mildly, he got little support from a predominantly weak Brooklyn bunch. Only in his final year of 1916 did Brooklyn reach the World Series, and of course, they lost in five games to the Red Sox.

Rucker's 1908 campaign was highlighted by 199 strikeouts and a September no-hitter against the Boston Doves, where he fanned 14. In 1909 he topped that with 201 strikeouts, 16 of which came in one game vs. the Cardinals, a record that would stand for 24 years. His 17–18 mark in 1910 belied a great season, as Rucker led the National League in complete games, shutouts, and

George Napoleon Rucker

innings pitched. Rucker won 22 games in 1911, but lost 18 despite a solid 2.71 ERA. Fittingly, his final career record was 134–134.

Before joining Brooklyn, Rucker played on an Augusta, Georgia, Minor League team that featured future White Sox great Eddie Cicotte and a fellow Georgian teenager named Ty Cobb, Rucker's roommate. One night, Rucker decided to take a bath before Cobb got home. When he arrived, the fuming Cobb, accustomed to being first at bathing and everything else, nearly killed the soap-soaked Rucker. The incident would be prophetic. Just like his time in Brooklyn, Nap Rucker was clean despite the chaos around him. In retirement, Rucker was a successful Georgia businessman and politician while also scouting for the Dodgers, and was inducted into the Georgia Sports Hall of Fame in 1967.

Team:

Brooklyn Superbas/Dodgers/Robins NL (1907–1916)

Born:
September 30, 1884
Crabapple, GA

Died:
December 19, 1970
Alpharetta, GA

▷ Batted: RH

▷ Threw: LH

▷ Position: P

▷ MLB Pitching Record: 134–134

▷ ERA: 2.42

Dick Rudolph

Richard Rudolph

RUDOLPH, Boston - Nationals

At just 5-foot, 9-inches and 160 pounds, Dick Rudolph packed a punch as a Major League pitcher. With great control and a pretty good spitter, Rudolph was dominant over a three-year period in the National League. As a Fordham University student, Rudolph dreamed of pitching in the majors. The best pitcher in the Eastern League from 1907 through 1910, he finally got his chance in the majors with the New York Giants. In his first start, Rudolph was pummeled in an 8–2 Giants loss, and was promptly sent back to the minors for more seasoning. He would not get another chance to pitch in the Bigs for two seasons.

Over that next two years Rudolph led the International League in wins, prompting the Boston Braves to take a chance on the 25-year-old. Rudolph did not disappoint, winning 14 games his first year. He followed that in 1914 with his best season, winning 26 games. That year he led the Braves to an improbable World Series Championship, besting Chief Bender in Game 1 and Bob Shawkey in Game 4 of the Series. Rudolph's pitching dominated NL hitters in 1915 and 1916. In his first five seasons in Boston he ate up innings, averaging nearly 300 during that period.

After the 1917 season, Rudolph developed arm issues, and pitched only sporadically for the balance of his career.

Although he pitched his last game in 1927, Rudolph was predominately a coach for the Braves during his last eight seasons. He managed in the minors through 1930 and left the game to work as an undertaker with his brother. Rudolph later returned to baseball as a concessions supervisor at Yankee Stadium and freshman baseball coach at Fordham University, his alma mater. For that shining period between 1914 and 1916, the diminutive Rudolph was a true giant on the mound.

Born:
August 25, 1887
New York, NY

Died:
October 20, 1949
Bronx, NY

▷ Batted: RH

▷ Threw: RH

▷ Position: P

▷ MLB Pitching Record: 121–109

▷ ERA: 2.66

Teams:
New York Giants NL (1910–1911)
Boston Braves NL (1913–1920, 1922–1923, 1927)

Reb Russell

Although his name sounds like a Civil War hero, "Reb" Russell fought his battles on the mound. A control pitcher, Russell enjoyed a terrific rookie season with the White Sox in 1913. He was 22–16 with a miniscule 1.90 ERA. The wily lefty started a league-leading 52 games and surrendered just two home runs, pretty impressive for a fly-ball pitcher. His 122 strikeouts were offset by only 79 walks. Unfortunately, he would win just 58 games over the next six seasons in Chicago. He did post a 15–5 record with a 1.95 ERA in the team's World Championship season of 1917, but in the World Series he gave up two hits, two runs, and recorded no outs in a brief appearance.

Nicknamed "Reb" for his Mississippi roots, Russell was adept at pitching out of jams. His nerves were unflappable, but his body was not. In 1914, an ankle injury put him on the shelf, and three years later he struggled through left-arm injury woes. By 1918, the control that made Russell one of the game's best southpaws was gone, but Russell was not. Always a decent hitter, Russell put up excellent offensive numbers in the minors and was acquired by the Pirates in 1922. Over the

RUSSELL, CHICAGO - AMERICANS

next two seasons, he played outfield and hit .323 with 21 home runs and 133 RBI in 154 games, an amazing comeback.

Russell was released for good after the 1923 season, but true to his name, he fought hard and was a dedicated baseball combatant. He continued on, playing the outfield in the Minor Leagues until he was 41 years old, retiring in 1930 with a Minor League career .329 batting average. Ironically, Russell passed away on September 30, 1973, the 50th anniversary of his final Major League game.

Born:
March 12, 1889
Jackson, MS
Died:
September 30, 1973
Indianapolis, IN
▷ Batted: LH
▷ Threw: LH
▷ Position: P
▷ MLB Pitching Record: 80–59
▷ ERA: 2.33

Ewell Albert Russell

Teams:
Chicago White Sox AL (1913–1919)
Pittsburgh Pirates NL (1922–1923)

Slim Sallee

In some ways, "Slim" Sallee's career mirrored that of Hall of Famer Rube Waddell. Both talented southpaws had battles with the bottle and would sometimes disappear for weeks at a time. With his crossfire fastball, Sallee had moments of brilliance during his 14-year career. He was labeled a phenom while pitching for several independent teams as well as the Birmingham Barons of the Southern Association.

With a 20-win season under his Minor League belt, Sallee's contract was bought by the St. Louis Cardinals in 1908, but

Born:
February 3, 1885
Higginsport, OH
Died:
March 22, 1950
Higginsport, OH
▷ Batted: RH
▷ Threw: LH
▷ Position: P
▷ MLB Pitching Record: 174–143
▷ ERA: 2.56

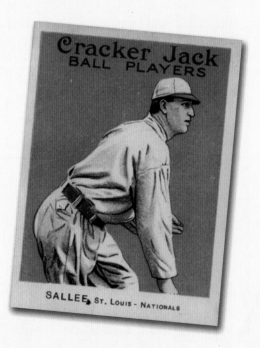

SALLEE, ST. LOUIS - NATIONALS

Harry Franklin Sallee

his drinking habits became obvious right away. Sallee would disappear for several days on a drinking binge and then return to pitch a gem. His manager, Roger Bresnahan, suspended and fined him repeatedly during his first few years in St. Louis. Finally late in the 1911 season Sallee vowed to curtail his bad habits and really contribute to the team. Over the next several years, he did not disappoint, becoming the big stopper on some pretty weak teams.

After Sallee was signed by the Giants he saw great success, winning 18 games and the pennant in 1917. He then played for the Reds so he could be closer to home, enjoying the best year of his career in 1919, compiling 21 wins to help lead Cincinnati to the World Series. That was the infamous Black Sox Series, but Sallee pitched well for the Reds, winning one and losing one. Because of his age, he became a reliever in 1920 and hooked up with the Giants again, helping them to a pennant in 1921.

That proved to be Sallee's final MLB season. He invested wisely in several thriving business ventures in his hometown of Higginsport but lost them in the Ohio River flood of 1937. He then worked as a bartender in Cincinnati for several years. In 1947 Sallee coached the Higginsport town team to the county championship. He died in 1950 after suffering a heart attack. Had Sallee devoted more time to his craft than to drinking in his early days, he would likely have been a dominant Deadball Era pitcher.

Teams:
St. Louis Cardinals NL (1908–1916)
New York Giants NL (1916–1918, 1920–1921)
Cincinnati Reds NL (1919–1920)

Jim Scott

"Death Valley Jim" Scott was one of the fastest guns in the west, or in his case, the Midwest. The 6-foot, 1-inch, 235 pound hurler played nine seasons with the Chicago White Sox and was known for mixing junk with a hard fastball and for a blistering pickoff move to first base. According to legend, Scott got his nickname from an erroneous reference to his native Deadwood, South Dakota, or from the fact that he shared a train ride with a notorious criminal named Death Valley Scott.

After leaving Wesleyan University medical school to pursue a baseball career, Scott went 12–12 in 1909, his rookie year with the White Sox. In 1910, he lost 18 games but led the American League in games finished with 17. Three years later, he won 20 games, but lost 21 with a miniscule ERA of 1.90. He actually finished 14th in MVP voting that season. Scott had a no-hitter through nine innings in 1914, but lost his shot at history, and the game, in the tenth. His best year was 1915 when he went 24–11 with a 2.03 ERA and a league-leading seven shutouts.

Scott was a spitballer, but he used a full arsenal to register 945 career Ks.

Born:
April 23, 1888
Deadwood, SD
Died:
April 7, 1957
Jacumba, CA
▷ Batted: RH
▷ Threw: RH
▷ Position: P
▷ MLB Pitching Record: 107–114
▷ ERA: 2.30

SCOTT, Chicago - Americans

James Scott

In 1917, he ended Ty Cobb's 35-game hitting streak, and the White Sox won the World Series, but Scott left the club mid-season to serve in World War I. After his return, Scott pitched in the Pacific Coast League and Southern Association until 1927, putting together a 155–108 Minor League record. He then worked as an umpire until 1932. In retirement, Scott worked in the film industry, and reportedly joined a religious cult. He passed away in 1957, but as he faded off into the sunset, no one would soon forget the legend of "Death Valley Jim."

Team:
Chicago White Sox AL (1909–1917)

Tom Seaton

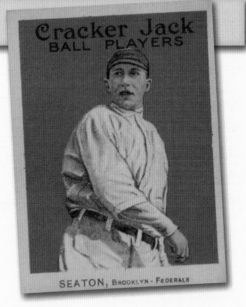

Another controversial player, Tom Seaton was a very good pitcher but concerns about his character arose later in his career. While playing in the Northwestern League and the Pacific Coast League, Seaton honed his pitching skills, developing a big sweeping curveball and an excellent command of his fastball. Signed by the Phillies in 1912, Seaton had a successful breakout year going 16–12 with a 3.28 earned-run average. In 1913, he was, without a doubt, the best pitcher in the National League, compiling a 27–12 record to go along with a nifty 2.60 ERA. He also led the league that year with 322 innings pitched and 168 Ks.

The new Federal League offered Seaton a boatload of money in 1914 to sign with the Brooklyn Tip-Tops, and his first campaign was very successful. A workhorse again, Seaton pitched over 300 innings to compile a 25–14 record, but soon after developed shoulder problems. After the Federal League folded, Seaton was signed by the Cubs but was just not the same pitcher. He most likely developed a rotator cuff problem which

Thomas Gordon Seaton

Born:
August 30, 1887
Blair, NE

Died:
April 10, 1940
El Paso, TX

▷ Batted: Switch

▷ Threw: RH

▷ Position: P

▷ MLB Pitching Record: 92–65

▷ ERA: 3.12

was not successfully treated due to medical technology of that time. After a few lackluster seasons he was sold to a Minor League team.

Seaton played in the Pacific Coast League and had some pretty good seasons for the San Francisco Seals. While in the PCL, rumors started to circulate, implicating that Seaton bet on or against various teams that he played for. Charges were not brought against him, and wrong doing was never proven, but in the wake of the 1919 Black Sox scandal, Seaton was promptly released from his Pacific Coast League team. He hooked up with a Southern League team only to be released again because of the rumors. No longer welcome in professional baseball, Tom Seaton played semi-pro Industrial League ball until 1927 and then faded from the baseball scene. He retired to El Paso, where he worked for a smelting company as foreman and made a name for himself as the best bowler in the area. After battling lung cancer, Seaton died in 1940 at age 52.

Teams:
Philadelphia Phillies NL (1912–1913)
Brooklyn Tip-Tops FL (1914–1915)
Newark Pepper FL (1915)
Chicago Cubs NL (1916–1917)

Bob Shawkey

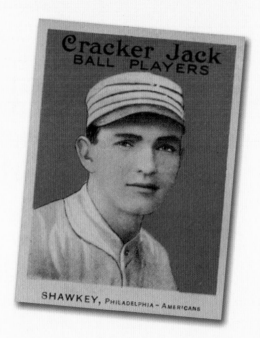

After the Philadelphia Athletics were upset by the "Miracle" Boston Braves in the 1914 World Series, A's manager Connie Mack did a little housecleaning. Among those jettisoned was Bob Shawkey, sold to the Yankees for $3,500 midway through the 1915 season. Mack did not make many mistakes during his brilliant career, but Shawkey was definitely one of them. Over the next 13 seasons in New York, Shawkey would win 20 or more games four times. He went 24–14 in 1916 and was a terrific relief pitcher, leading the American League with 24 games finished and eight saves.

Shawkey missed most of the 1918 season to serve in the Navy during World War I. Upon his return in 1919, he repeated the feat of winning 20 games while leading the league in saves. That same year, Shawkey faced his old Philly mates and recorded 15 strikeouts, a Yankee record that stood until Ron Guidry fanned 18 in 1978. In essence, Shawkey's right arm helped launch a dynasty. In the Yankees first three

James Robert Shawkey

pennant-winning seasons (1921–1923), Shawkey won 54 games. In 1923, New York's first World Championship season, he was a 16-game winner on a staff that included Joe Bush, Sam Jones, Waite Hoyt and Herb Pennock. That year he got the win over Boston in the first-ever game at Yankee Stadium.

Shawkey would eventually manage the Yanks for one season in 1930, leading them to 86 wins and a third-place finish. He continued on in baseball, coaching, scouting and managing in the minors through the 1950 season, after which he coached at Dartmouth College until 1956. When Yankee Stadium was renovated in 1976, an 85-year-old Shawkey once again threw out the first pitch. It is no exaggeration to say that Bob Shawkey was one of the most significant pitchers in the history of baseball's most storied franchise.

Teams:
Philadelphia Athletics AL (1913–1915)
New York Yankees AL (1915–1927; manager: 1930)

Born:
December 4, 1890
Sigel, PA

Died:
December 31, 1980
Syracuse, NY

▷ Batted: RH
▷ Threw: RH
▷ Position: P
▷ MLB Pitching Record: 195–150
▷ ERA: 3.09
▷ Managerial Record: 86–68

Frank Smith

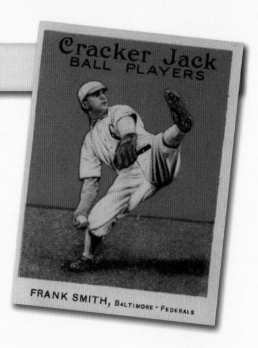

FRANK SMITH, BALTIMORE - FEDERALS

K nown as the "Piano Mover," Frank Smith looked more like a piano. The hefty 5-foot 10-inch, 194-pound Smith credited his offseason work at the family moving business with developing his strength and physique, helping him to become one of the better pitchers in the early part of the century. Smith started with his first pro team in 1900 and moved up through the ranks until he was signed by the White Sox in 1904. With a drop dead curveball and a nasty spitball that he was still perfecting, Smith won an impressive 16 games in his rookie campaign, followed by a 19-win season in 1905. That year, to go along with his excellent record, Smith sported a sweet 2.13 earned-run average, but the highlight of that season came on September 6, when Smith hurled a no-hitter against the Detroit Tigers.

In 1906, the White Sox won the World Series, but Smith was not really a factor. He had developed problems with controlling his pitches, and, some say, controlling the bottle. Smith was a force to be reckoned with in 1907, compiling a 23–10 record. Although his record dipped to 16–17 in 1908, Smith pitched another no-hitter against the Philadelphia Athletics, becoming the first White Sox pitcher to hurl two no-hitters. Now considered one of the premier pitchers in the league, Smith reached his pinnacle in 1909 when he went 25–17, posted a miniscule 1.80 ERA, and led the league with a whopping 365 innings pitched.

Teams:
Chicago White Sox AL (1904–1910)
Boston Red Sox AL (1910–1911)
Cincinnati Reds NL (1911–1912)
Baltimore Terrapins FL (1914–1915)
Brooklyn Tip-Tops FL (1915)

Frank Elmer Smith

Throughout all of this, Smith had several run-ins with Sox owner Charles Comiskey and even jumped the team for several months. His skills started to diminish in 1910, and he was dispatched to the Red Sox. He moved from Boston to Cincinnati and finally jumped to the upstart Federal League. During his last few seasons, Smith pitched adequately, hovering around the .500 mark, but he finally called it quits after the Federal League folded. Smith moved on from baseball to do the logical thing. He returned to the family moving business that had earned him his MLB nickname.

Born:
October 28, 1879
Pittsburgh, PA

Died:
November 3, 1952
Pittsburgh, PA

▷ Batted: RH
▷ Threw: RH
▷ Position: P
▷ MLB Pitching Record: 139–111
▷ ERA: 2.59

George Suggs

Lefty Tyler

George Suggs' 99 wins, two seasons of 20 or more victories, and career 3.11 ERA do not tell the full story of his penchant for getting himself into jams. In limited work during his first two seasons with Detroit, Suggs posted earned-run averages of 1.67 and 2.03, pretty impressive. Unfortunately, as his innings increased, so did his woes. In 1910, he delivered a sterling 20–12 mark for the Cincinnati Reds, but gave up 248 hits in 266 innings pitched. He also hit 14 batters. This trend continued in 1912 when Suggs went 19–16, but surrendered a league-leading 320 hits in 303 innings pitched. And yes, he plunked 11 batters just for good measure.

Suggs was also subject to the gopher ball, giving up six home runs each year in 1910, 1912, 1913 and 1914. That may not seem like much now, but in the Deadball Era, it was a pretty hefty number. In 1915, playing in his second season for the Baltimore Terrapins of the Federal League, Suggs doubled that total, leading the league with 12 homers

George Franklin Suggs

Born:
July 7, 1882
Kinston, NC

Died:
April 4, 1949
Kinston, NC

▷ Batted: RH

▷ Threw: RH

▷ Position: P

▷ MLB Pitching Record: 99–91

▷ ERA: 3.11

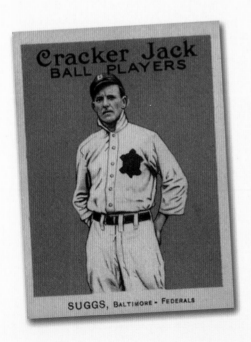

allowed. Suggs' moments of glory were spotty at best, but he did manage to cross paths with some future Hall of Famers. He was a teammate of Ty Cobb with the Tigers, played for Clark Griffith with the Reds, and was on the same staff as Chief Bender with Baltimore. It is clear that George Suggs never attained the excellence of these immortals, but he did have his moments in a gritty eight-year career.

Upon his return home, Suggs helped organize semi-pro league ball in Kinston, North Carolina. He managed two teams in the early 1920s and is credited with designing their stadium, West End Park. He was inducted into the Kinston Professional Baseball Hall of Fame in 1983.

Teams:
Detroit Tigers AL (1908–1909)
Cincinnati Reds NL (1910–1913)
Baltimore Terrapins FL (1914–1915)

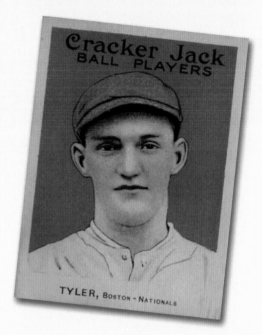

As one of just a few players from New Hampshire, George "Lefty" Tyler made the Granite State proud during his days as a Major League pitcher. A Pinkerton Academy graduate, Tyler came up from the Lowell Tigers of the New England League to make a few brief appearances for the Boston Doves in 1910. Even though the Doves changed their name to the Rustlers in 1911, they did not change their luck, remaining in last place. Tyler got very little run support, and was especially hammered during that 1911 season, leading the league with 22 losses.

As his experience progressed and his team improved, things began to turn around for the young pitcher. His breakout year was in 1914 when he went 16–13 with a 2.69 ERA. Now called the Braves, the team surprised everyone by sweeping the World Series after rising from the ashes of last place that season. Tyler was very consistent over the next several seasons, most notably during the 1916 campaign when he posted a

George Albert Tyler

sparkling 17–9 record with a 2.02 earned-run average. Before the war-shortened 1918 season, Tyler was traded to the Cubs for "Laughing" Larry Doyle, Art Wilson, and $15,000, which was a very pricy transaction at that time. He had a superb season, posting a gaudy 19–8 record with a 2.00 ERA, helping his new team to the pennant. Tyler would surely have won at least 20 games had the season not been cut short due to the conflict overseas. Once again, Tyler got to pitch in the World Series, winning one and losing one, with an outstanding 1.17 ERA.

During the next season, Tyler began to develop shoulder problems and became a .500 pitcher for the balance of his career. After wrapping up his stint in the majors in 1921, Tyler dabbled in the minors. He played for and managed the Lawrence Merry Macks of the New England League in 1926. Tyler then umpired in the minors through 1932, before leaving the game to work in the shoe industry in the mill city of Lowell, Massachusetts.

Teams:
Boston Doves/Rustlers/Braves NL (1910–1917)
Chicago Cubs NL (1918–1921)

Born:
December 14, 1889
Derry, NH

Died:
September 29, 1953
Lowell, MA

▷ Batted: LH
▷ Threw: LH
▷ Position: P
▷ MLB Pitching Record: 127–116
▷ ERA: 2.95

Jeff Tesreau

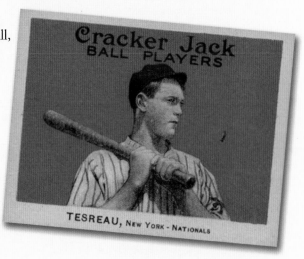

TESREAU, New York - Nationals

Known for his exceptional spitball, Jeff Tesreau wowed National League fans for seven seasons. Over that time he played on three NL Pennant winners, won at least 20 games on two occasions, and led the league in shutouts and ERA. Sports scribes nicknamed him "Jeff" because he resembled heavyweight boxer Jim Jeffries and "The Ozark Bear" because Tesreau once made a comment about bear hunting.

After developing his spitball in the Texas League and the Eastern League, Tesreau made a splash as a rookie with the New York Giants in 1912, compiling a 17–7 record with a 1.96 earned-run average, On September 6, 1912, he pitched a no-hitter against the Phillies, helping to lead the Giants to the pennant. In the World Series matchup against the Boston Red Sox, Tesreau appeared in three games, winning one. He went on to become the go-to guy for the Giants over the next five years. In 1914 he won an impressive 26 games while leading the league with eight shutouts. Tesreau proved to be very durable, piling up over 1,600 innings pitched over his stint with the Giants, but during the 1918 season he had a falling out with manager John McGraw. The fiery manager wanted Tesreau to report on player activities outside of the ballpark. He refused, a feud ensued, and he promptly quit the team never to pitch in the majors again.

Tesreau took a job as baseball coach for Darthmouth College for what he thought would be a brief period. He ended up coaching at the Ivy League school until 1946, compiling a 379–264 record and winning the Eastern League Championship in 1930, 1935, 1936, and

Charles Monroe Tesreau

1938. As a matter of fact, his old nemesis from the 1912 Series, Boston pitcher Smokey Joe Wood, became the coach for Yale University, and it was a special event when the two Ivy teams went head to head. Jeff Tesreau passed away at age 57 following a stroke. Without the spitball who knows how his pro career would have progressed, but during a time when it was perfectly legal, it was his calling card and he used it to his advantage.

Born:
March 5, 1888
Ironton, MO

Died:
September 24, 1946
Hanover, NH

▷ Batted: RH
▷ Threw: RH
▷ Position: P
▷ MLB Pitching Record: 115–72
▷ ERA: 2.43

Team:
New York Giants NL (1912–1918)

Hippo Vaughn

Ed Walsh

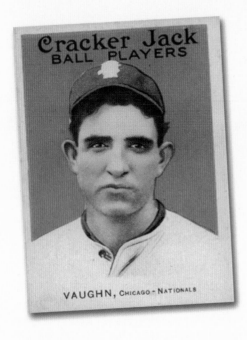

VAUGHN, CHICAGO - NATIONALS

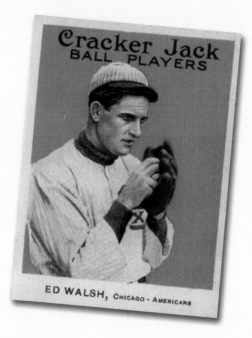

ED WALSH, CHICAGO - AMERICANS

File Hippo Vaughn under the category of late bloomer. The first four years of his big-league career were largely unremarkable. Vaughn had his moments, 13 wins and an ERA of 1.83 with the 1910 Highlanders, but it was not until 1913 that he began to emerge as a top southpaw in the National League. In 1914, Vaughn began a seven-year run in Chicago with at least 17 victories, including five seasons of 20 or more wins. In 1917, he dueled Fred Toney of the Reds in a double no-hitter

through nine innings. He would lose the no-no and the game in the 10th, but it was an historic feat.

Vaughn's watershed season was 1918, when he led the National League in wins, ERA, games started, shutouts, innings pitched, and strikeouts. His brilliance catapulted the Cubs to the World Series against the Red Sox. Vaughn was 1–2 in the Series, but had an ERA of 1.00. He pitched three complete games, struck out 17, and walked just five in 27 innings, but Boston beat the Cubs in six games.

The nickname Hippo was appropriate for a man who stood 6-foot, 4-inches and weighed 215 pounds, but Vaughn was more of a workhorse. In 1919, he logged over 306 innings pitched to again lead the league. The next season, he added another 301 innings. Vaughn flamed out with the Cubs in 1921, going 3–11 and mysteriously bolted from the team. His final record was 178–137, but at his best, Hippo Vaughn was as good as any lefty who ever picked up a rosin bag.

James Leslie Vaughn

Teams:

New York Highlanders AL (1908, 1910–1912)

Washington Senators AL (1912)

Chicago Cubs NL (1913–1921)

Born:
April 9, 1888
Weatherford, TX

Died:
May 29, 1966
Chicago, IL

▷ Batted: Switch

▷ Threw: LH

▷ Position: P

▷ MLB Pitching Record: 178–137

▷ ERA: 2.49

Over a span of six years from 1907 to 1912, "Big Ed" Walsh was as good as or better than any Major League pitcher. During that time, he averaged 25 wins and 374 innings pitched per season, with an average ERA well below 2.00. His overall lifetime earned-run average of 1.82 is still a Major League record. Walsh helped the White Sox to the pennant in 1906 with his 17–13 record and 1.88 ERA. The Sox beat their crosstown rivals, the Cubs, 4–2 in the Series with the support of Walsh's fine pitching. His 2–0 record with a miniscule 0.60 ERA and 17 Ks was a sign of things to come.

In 1908 Walsh led the league with his 40 wins, 42 complete games, 11 shutouts, 6 saves, 464 innings pitched, 269 strikeouts, and .727 win-loss percentage. One point of reference is that Walsh's "out pitch" was the spitter that was later banned from baseball. Although he played a total of 14 seasons in the majors, the years after 1912 were unproductive for Walsh. After that season, his arm was

Edward Augustine Walsh

pretty much burned out, but he managed to stick around for five more years. Ed Walsh certainly left his mark, however. Besides holding the record for the lowest career ERA in MLB history, he led the American League in innings pitched on four occasions; ranks number two all-time in WHIP (1.00), and had a total of five 200-plus strikeout seasons.

Over and above his playing skills and stats, Walsh is credited with helping to design Comiskey Park, which opened in 1910. After his playing days, he coached the White Sox and then managed the team during the 1924 season. Walsh lost nearly everything in the Great Depression and ended up running the baseball school in the Works Progress Administration (WPA) Recreation Department. He later worked for the Meriden, Connecticut, water department and became a golf pro. Ed Walsh was elected to the Hall of Fame in 1946.

Teams:

Chicago White Sox AL (1904–1916; manager: 1924)

Boston Braves NL (1917)

Born:
May 14, 1881
Plains Township, PA

Died:
May 26, 1959
Pompano Beach, FL

▷ Batted: RH

▷ Threw: RH

▷ Position: P

▷ MLB Pitching Record: 195–126

▷ ERA: 1.82

▷ Managerial Record: 1–2

Smokey Joe Wood

Joe Wood

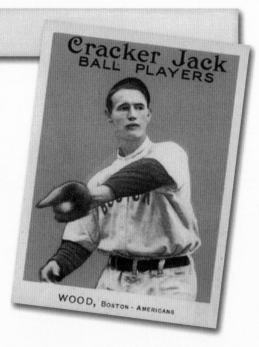

Had it not been for an injury-shortened career, fireballer Smokey Joe Wood would be a lock for the Hall of Fame. The hard-throwing righty had an unbelievable 34–5 record in 1912 with a sparkling 1.91 ERA and led the Red Sox to the World Series Championship. Wood starred in the Series, posting a 3–1 record. He is credited with the win in Game 8, when Giants outfielder Fred Snodgrass dropped the fly ball that ultimately lost the Series for New York. The "Snodgrass Muff" will forever be remembered as one of the biggest blunders in baseball.

The 1912 season also saw Wood participating in one of the most legendary pitching matchups of all time. On September 6, 1912, Smokey Joe Wood faced off with Washington Senators ace and future Hall of Famer, Walter Johnson, at Fenway Park. Wood pitched a masterful two-hitter and the Red Sox won 1–0. Legend has it that Walter Johnson once commented there was no man alive who threw harder than Smokey Joe Wood. Tragically, Wood injured his thumb and arm in 1913, and although he had winning records over the next three seasons, he was never the same pitcher. Wood's 15–5 season in 1915 with a league-leading 1.49 ERA helped lead Boston to another pennant. The Red Sox took the Series but Wood was not a factor in the postseason.

After sitting out the 1916 season due to salary disputes, Wood was sold to Cleveland where he promptly injured his arm again, causing him to miss most of the 1917 season. He converted to the outfield in 1918, stretching out his career for a few more seasons. Wood played in the World Series in 1920, helping the Indians best the Brooklyn Robins to win the Championship. After batting .297 and banging out 150 hits in 1922, the 32-year-old Wood abruptly announced his retirement. He coached at Yale University from 1924 to 1942 and lived to the ripe old age of 95, becoming the last surviving Major League player from the Deadball Era.

Teams:

Boston Red Sox AL (1908–1915)

Cleveland Indians AL (1917–1922)

Born:
October 25, 1889
Kansas City, MO

Died:
July 27, 1985
West Haven, CT

▷ Batted: RH

▷ Threw: RH

▷ Position: P

▷ MLB Pitching Record: 117–57

▷ ERA: 2.03

"Slide, Kelly, Slide!"

"The More You Eat—The More You Want"
Now comes the open season
for baseball fans and good old
Cracker Jack

10

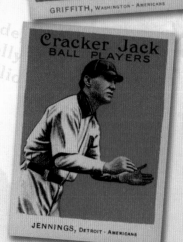

COMISKEY, Owner of White Sox

GRIFFITH, Washington - Americans

THE FRONT OFFICE

W hen it comes down to the final decision in any business, management usually makes the call. It is really no different on the ball field. Managers usually make the decisions on the field, with owners and other management personnel making the decisions regarding just about everything else. Although several other players featured in the Cracker Jack Collection managed at some point during their career, the managers and owners discussed in this chapter were not actively playing during the issue of the 1915 Collection. Each one of these men played the game and each one made decisions that forever changed the game. Some of the choices made by these men even impacted our society as a whole. There are only seven men featured in this chapter, but each in their own way changed the baseball landscape forever.

Meet the owners and managers of the Cracker Jack Front Office.

JENNINGS, Detroit - Americans

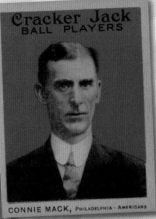

CONNIE MACK, Philadelphia - Americans

McGRAW, New York - Nationals

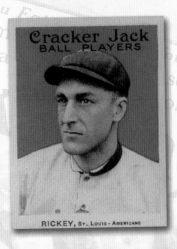

RICKEY, St. Louis - Americans

STALLINGS, Boston - Nationals

Charlie Comiskey

The legend of Charlie Comiskey permeates all aspects of baseball. He played in the 1880s as a speedy number-two hitter with the St. Louis Browns of the American Association. Comiskey had an incredible 117 steals in 1887 and followed that up with season swipes of 72 and 65. Perennially among the league leaders in hits, RBI, and at-bats, he was also a solid first sacker and patient hitter whose at-bats-per-strikeout ratio was outstanding. With Comiskey as player-manager, the Browns made four trips to the postseason and won the American Association title in 1886. In 1890, he jumped to the rival Players League as a player-manager for the Chicago Pirates, but returned to St. Louis in 1891. He culminated his on-field career with the Cincinnati Reds from 1892 until 1894.

For most men, a 13-year playing and managing career would be enough, but Charlie Comiskey was not most men. In 1894, he had a concept to form a professional league of teams in the western part of the country. The Western League was created with Comiskey as the owner of the Sioux City Cornhuskers. Comiskey would move the team to St. Paul and then to Chicago as the White Sox, named after the Chicago White Stockings, the club that Comiskey beat for the title in 1886. The Western League became the American League in 1899 and Comiskey's White Sox flourished, taking five pennants and winning the World Series in 1906 and 1917. He spent lavishly to build Comiskey Park, which opened in 1910 and was home to the Sox for 80 years.

Comiskey was the model of generosity in the Windy City, but was notoriously stingy when it came to players' salaries. This was a key reason behind the 1919 Black Sox scandal, where eight Chicago players took money to throw the World Series. The scandal wrecked Comiskey's team and haunted his reputation until his death in 1931. Despite this, the man they called "The Old Roman" should be remembered as a baseball emperor who helped lay the foundation for today's thriving game. Charles Comiskey was recognized as a baseball pioneer and executive with his induction into the Hall of Fame in 1939.

Teams:

St. Louis Brown Stockings/Browns AA (1882; player-manager: 1883–1889, 1891)

Chicago Pirates PL (player-manager: 1890)

Cincinnati Reds NL (player-manager: 1892–1894)

Chicago White Sox AL (owner: 1895–1931)

For most men, a 13-year playing and managing career would be enough, but Charlie Comiskey was not most men.

Charles Albert Comiskey

Born:
August 15, 1859
Chicago, IL
Died:
October 26, 1931
Eagle River, WI
▷ Batted: RH
▷ Threw: RH
▷ Position: 1B
▷ Career BA: .264
▷ Managerial Record: 840–541

Clark Griffith

Baseball has never seen a more diversely accomplished man than Clark Griffith, a Hall of Famer renowned for his amazing feats as a player, manager, and owner. Griffith won 237 games over a 20-year pitching career for the American Association's St. Louis Browns and Boston Reds, as well as the Chicago Colts/Orphans, White Sox, New York Highlanders, Cincinnati Reds, and Senators. He won more than 20 games for six consecutive seasons with the Colts/Orphans (1894–1899), enjoying his best year as a player in 1898 when he went 24–10 and led the National League with a 1.88 ERA.

In 1900, Griffith spearheaded the Ball Players Protective Association, which essentially led to the establishment of the American League in 1901. That year, as player-manager of the White Sox, he posted a 24-win season and led Chicago to the inaugural AL pennant, his only title as a manager. After stints as player-manager with the Highlanders and Reds, Griffith mortgaged his Montana family ranch in 1911 to purchase a stake in the Senators and become the team's player-manager. Dubbed the "Old Fox" for his shrewd intellect, Griffith would be as influential in Washington as any U.S. President. Of course, Walter Johnson had a little something to do with that, leading the AL in wins five seasons during Griffith's stint as manager.

In 1920, Griffith became the majority owner of the Senators and, in 1924, brought D.C. its only World Championship, beating the Giants in seven games. Washington returned to the Series in 1925, but lost to the Pirates, also in seven games. Griffith played no favorites. He traded his niece's husband, future Hall of Famer Joe Cronin, to the Red Sox in 1934. He also sold his nephew, Sherry Robertson, to the Athletics in 1952. More importantly, Griffith was recognized as a pioneer in bringing dozens of Cuban players to the majors. As health issues mounted, Griffith ceded control of the franchise to his nephew, Calvin Griffith, who would eventually move the team to Minnesota as the Twins in 1961. Clark Griffith died in 1955, but his influence on the game remains very much alive to this day.

> *Dubbed the "Old Fox" for his shrewd intellect, Griffith would be as influential in Washington as any U.S. President.*

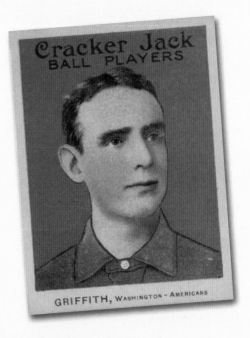

GRIFFITH, WASHINGTON - AMERICANS

Clark Calvin Griffith

Teams:

St. Louis Browns AA (1891)

Boston Reds AA (1891)

Chicago Colts/Orphans NL (1893–1900)

Chicago White Sox AL (player-manager: 1901–1902)

New York Highlanders AL (player-manager: 1903–1907; manager: 1908)

Cincinnati Reds NL (player-manager: 1909; manager: 1910–1911)

Washington Senators AL (player-manager: 1912–1914; manager: 1915–1920; owner: 1920–1955)

Born:
November 20, 1869
Clear Creek, MO

Died:
October 27, 1955
Washington, D.C.

▷ Batted: RH

▷ Threw: RH

▷ Position: P

▷ MLB Pitching Record: 237–146

▷ ERA: 3.31

▷ Managerial Record: 1,491–1,367

Hughie Jennings

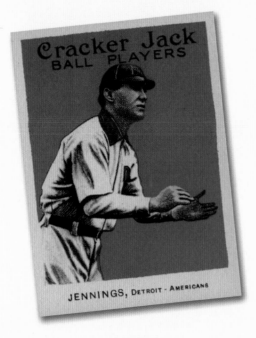

JENNINGS, DETROIT - AMERICANS

Hugh Ambrose Jennings

Born:
April 2, 1869
Pittston, PA

Died:
February 1, 1928
Scranton, PA

▷ Batted: RH

▷ Threw: RH

▷ Position: SS/1B

▷ Career BA: .312

▷ Managerial Record: 1,184–995

Hughie Jennings was considered near or at the top of the list as a strategist and great teacher of fundamentals.

Hughie "Ee-Yah" Jennings goes down as one of the most colorful players and managers who ever stepped onto the field. As a player, Jennings was an outstanding shortstop who had some incredible offensive seasons with the Orioles. He batted over .300 five straight seasons from 1894 to 1898, posting a sensational .401 BA in 1896. That year the tough-as-they-come Jennings was hit by pitches 51 times, setting a National League record. Willing to do whatever it took to get on base, he led the league in HBP five seasons in a row, and his career 287 plunkings are still a Major League record. Also known for his speed, Jennings swiped 70 bases in 1896. Great with the glove, Jennings led the league in putouts on four occasions.

As a manager of the Tigers, he was known for his antics while coaching at third base, and his famous shouts of "Ee-Yah" which soon became his nickname. Hughie Jennings was considered near or at the top of the list as a strategist and

great teacher of fundamentals. He led the Tigers to the American League pennant three consecutive seasons from 1907 to 1909, but also had the challenging task of keeping the fiery Ty Cobb in check and running interference between Cobb and his archenemy and teammate, Sam Crawford. After 13 seasons in Detroit, Jennings moved on to coach and manage for John McGraw's Giants, winning the pennant in 1924.

During the offseason, Jennings was a practicing attorney. He had attended Cornell University and, although he never finished, he passed the bar exam and went into practice in 1905. After winning over 1,184 games as a manager, Jennings concentrated his attention on his thriving law practice. In 1926, Jennings was diagnosed with tuberculosis. He died in 1928 at age 58, just months after he was diagnosed with meningitis. He was elected to the Hall of Fame in 1945.

Teams:

Louisville Colonels AA/NL (1891–1893)

Baltimore Orioles NL (1893–1899)

Brooklyn Superbas NL (1899–1900, 1903)

Philadelphia Phillies NL (1901–1902)

Detroit Tigers AL (player-manager: 1907, 1909, 1912, 1918; manager: 1907–1920)

New York Giants NL (manager: 1924–1925)

Connie Mack

Connie Mack changed the face of our National Pastime.

When it comes to the front office, Connie Mack is at the very front. Although his numbers are a bit deceiving, Cornelius McGillicuddy is considered the greatest manager of all time. His overall won-lost record is actually below .500, but keep in mind that Mack was forced to constantly tweak his teams and replenish his roster because of the organization's financial turmoil. The fact remains that Connie Mack managed five World Series Champions, nine pennant winners, and more games than anyone in baseball history. Some of his Athletics teams were dynasties, and some were plain awful.

As a player, Mack was a good defensive catcher with an average bat. His managing career started in 1894 when he became player-manager of the Pittsburgh Pirates. He managed the Milwaukee Brewers in the Western League from 1897 to 1900, and then made the jump for good with the A's in 1901 as manager and part-owner. Over the course of his managing career, Mack led some of the greatest players to ever don a uniform. Rube Waddell, Eddie Plank, the famous $100,000 infield of Home Run Baker,

Jack Barry, Eddie Collins and Stuffy McInnis, as well as Jimmie Foxx, Mickey Cochrane, Lefty Grove and Al Simmons were some of the greats that played for Mack. Because of poor attendance, World War I, and the Great Depression, Mack had to dismantle several of his teams to maintain fiscal stability. Many of his teams wound up in the American League cellar, but Mack is still considered to be the best.

A gentleman as well as a players' manager, he counseled, mentored, and respected his ballplayers. The "Tall Tactician" was inducted into the Hall of Fame in 1937 but continued on with the A's until 1950, racking up an MLB record 3,731 wins as a manager. At the age of 88, he finally called it quits. New rule changes, player salaries and personalities made it difficult to continue. He could no longer wear his customary suit in the dugout as the new rules mandated that a manager had to wear a uniform, and he was just too old and frail to lead his players. Some say that Connie Mack stayed on too long and the game passed him by. Others say he was the greatest manager of all time. One thing is certain; Connie Mack changed the face of our National Pastime.

Teams:

Washington Nationals NL (1886–1889)

Buffalo Bisons PL (1890)

Pittsburgh Pirates NL (1891–1893; player-manager: 1894–1896)

Philadelphia Athletics AL (manager: 1901–1936, owner-manager: 1937–1950)

Cornelius Alexander Mack

Born: Cornelius Alexander McGillicuddy

Born:
December 22, 1862
East Brookfield, MA

Died:
February 8, 1956
Philadelphia, PA

▷ Batted: RH

▷ Threw: RH

▷ Position: C/1B/OF

▷ Career BA: .244

▷ Managerial Record: 3,731–3948

John McGraw

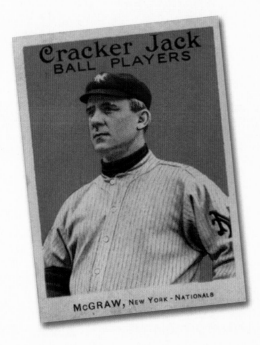

Cracker Jack BALL PLAYERS

McGRAW, NEW YORK - NATIONALS

If you were to build a Mount Rushmore of baseball managers, John McGraw would have to be part of any foursome. McGraw managed the New York Giants from 1902 to 1932, winning ten National League pennants and three World Championships. Along the way, he influenced the game of baseball like no one before or since. At 5-foot, 7-inches, 155 pounds, McGraw was famously known as "Little Napoleon," and the name fit like one of his trademark suits. McGraw was given to violent outbursts toward his players, the opposition, and, of course, umpires. He was not, however, all brimstone and no brains. On the contrary, McGraw brought a cerebral quality to managing, using his mind as much as his mouth.

Overshadowed by his amazing managerial record is the fact that John McGraw was one heck of a ballplayer. Some of his numbers are downright unfathomable. With Baltimore in 1898 and 1899, he led the league in runs scored, with 143 and 140, respectively. He also drew a league-leading 236 walks in those two seasons. McGraw had a ridiculous career on-base percentage of .466, and between 1899 and 1901, his OBP exceeded .500. He was a career .334 hitter, and a smart speedster with outstanding base running skills.

McGraw was as strong of heart as he was of body and mind. Over the course of his life, he overcame the deaths of his mother, three siblings, and later, his wife. As a child, McGraw was physically abused by his father and eventually moved to a neighboring inn. Despite these personal setbacks, McGraw's focus was unshaken. His conservative, buttoned-down veneer aside, McGraw was a worldly sort, performing in Vaudeville shows and investing in pool halls, race tracks, and casinos.

First and foremost, however, McGraw was a winner. In 33 years as a manager with the Orioles and Giants, he won 2,763 games, second only to Connie Mack. Heed the words of the man himself, "In playing or managing, the game of ball is only fun for me when I'm out in front and winning," said McGraw. "I don't give a hill of beans for the rest of the game." Although retired, John McGraw was selected to manage the National League team in the first All-Star game in 1933, and he was inducted into the Hall of Fame in 1937.

Born:
April 7, 1873
Truxton, NY

Died:
February 25, 1934
New Rochelle, NY

▷ Batted: LH

▷ Threw: RH

▷ Position: 3B

▷ Career BA: .334

▷ Managerial Record: 2,763–1,948

Teams:

Baltimore Orioles AA/NL (1891–1898; player-manager: 1899)

St. Louis Cardinals NL (1900)

Baltimore Orioles AL (player-manager: 1901–1902)

New York Giants NL (player-manager: 1902–1906; manager: 1907–1932)

John Joseph McGraw

McGraw was famously known as "Little Napoleon," and the name fit like one of his trademark suits.

Branch Rickey

So there was this guy who played a couple of seasons for the St. Louis Browns and hit a decent .284 in 1906. The next season, with the New York Highlanders, he hit .182 and his playing career was essentially finished save for two at-bats and no hits as the player-manager of the Browns in 1914. This guy managed for 10 seasons and never won a single pennant. In fact, his best finish ever was third place with the Cardinals in both 1921 and 1922. As a manager, he compiled a .473 winning percentage and never won more than 87 games in a season. When you look at his body of work as both a player and a manager, you might think he was average. On the contrary, this guy might just be the single most significant personality that baseball has ever known.

As an executive with the Cardinals, Branch Rickey constructed a team that would win six National League pennants and four World Championships. Rickey also created the modern farm system where teams could grow and develop their own talent. As baseball czar of the Brooklyn Dodgers, Rickey popularized the use of statistics to measure a player's worth. In addition, he spearheaded the movement toward protective batting helmets.

Known as "The Mahatma," Rickey was an expert in seeing a player's physical and mental attributes. It is this gift that led Rickey to the most earth-shattering move of his career. In 1945, he signed Negro Leagues star Jackie Robinson. Two years later, Robinson joined the Dodgers, breaking baseball's ancient color barrier. With Robinson, Brooklyn won six NL pennants and the 1955 World Series. Rickey would be forced out of Brooklyn, but moved on to Pittsburgh, where he masterminded the roster that would win the 1960 World Series. He was inducted into the Hall of Fame in 1967. Leader, innovator, visionary, all of these words apply to Branch Rickey. Simply put, he not only changed a game, he changed a culture.

Wesley Branch Rickey

Leader, innovator, visionary, all these words apply to Branch Rickey.

Teams:

St. Louis Browns AL (1905–1906; player-manager: 1914; manager: 1913, 1915)

New York Highlanders (1907)

St. Louis Cardinals NL (manager: 1919–1925; vice president: 1926–1942)

Brooklyn Dodgers NL (president: 1943–1950)

Pittsburgh Pirates NL (vice president-general manager: 1951–1955)

Born:
December 20, 1881
Flat, OH

Died:
December 9, 1965
Columbia, MO

▷ Batted: LH

▷ Threw: RH

▷ Position: C/OF/1B

▷ Career BA: .239

▷ Managerial Record: 597–664

George Stallings

STALLINGS, BOSTON-NATIONALS

*I*t was one team and one season that stamped his legacy.

Born:
November 17, 1867
Augusta, GA
Died:
May 13, 1929
Haddock, GA

▷ Batted: RH

▷ Threw: RH

▷ Position: C/1B/OF

▷ Career BA: .100

▷ Managerial Record: 879–898

Teams:

Brooklyn Bridegrooms NL (1890)
Philadelphia Phillies NL (player-manager: 1897–1898)
Detroit Tigers AL (manager: 1901)
New York Highlanders AL (manager: 1909–1910)
Boston Braves NL (manager: 1913–1920)

George Tweedy Stallings

George Stallings was a catcher, first baseman and rightfielder who played a total of seven Major League games, first with the Brooklyn Bridegrooms in 1890 and then as player-manager with the Philadelphia Phillies in 1897 and 1898. Stallings had 20 career at-bats, two hits and a .100 average. His meager stats as a player, however, do not tell the full story. Stallings managed in the Major Leagues for 13 seasons and had some decent ball clubs along the way, but it was one team and one season that stamped his legacy.

In 1914, Stallings was in his second season as manager of the Boston Braves. He had already had managerial stops with the Phillies, Tigers and New York Highlanders, never winning more than 78 games in a season. "Gentlemen George," as he was known around the game, was all too gentlemanly to opponents, finishing as high as second place just once. In his first season in Boston, the Braves went 69–82, good—or bad—for fifth in the National League, 31.5 games behind the Giants. Not a single starter hit higher than .281, and one of their two 16-game winners, Lefty Tyler, also lost 17 games.

As the 1914 season began, there was no real cause for optimism. Things got worse as the team found itself in last place at midseason, but Stallings persevered and guided Boston to an astounding 94 wins and the National League pennant. The Braves were led by Joe Connolly and future Hall of Famers Johnny Evers and Rabbit Maranville. They also had two 26-game winners, Dick Rudolph and Bill James. In the World Series, Stallings' club faced the heavily favored Philadelphia Athletics. Manager Connie Mack had won 99 games and his lineup featured the likes of Eddie Collins, Home Run Baker and Stuffy McInnis, all .300 hitters. Incredibly, Boston swept the A's in four games. Stallings was the toast of Beantown, and while he would eventually settle back into mediocrity, for one brief shining season, he lived up to his Augusta, Georgia, roots and was, indeed, a managerial master.

CATALOGUE OF CRACKER JACK PREMIUMS

FORM-E

Rueckheim Bros.
& Eckstein

CRACKER JACK and
CANDY · MAKERS

CHICAGO
U.S.A.

Cracker Jack Riddles

im Bros. & Eckstein

r Jack & Candy Makers~

hicago and BROOKLYN·
U·S·A·

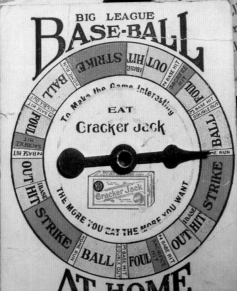

BIG LEAGUE BASE-BALL

To Make the Game Interesting

EAT
Cracker Jack

THE MORE YOU EAT THE MORE YOU WANT

AT HOME

STRIKE · BALL · OUT · HIT · FOUL

11

A TALE OF TWO SETS

The Striking Similarities and Key Differences between the Classic 1914 and 1915 Cracker Jack Sets

In this final chapter, Joe Orlando, president of Professional Sports Authenticator (PSA) and editor of *Sports Market Report* (SMR), discusses just about every aspect of both the 1914 and 1915 Cracker Jack Sets, including the design, distribution, popularity and rarity of certain cards. He also talks about the Cracker Jack card that never was. This chapter takes us full circle on our Cracker Jack journey. Enjoy the rest of the ride.

A Sweet Start

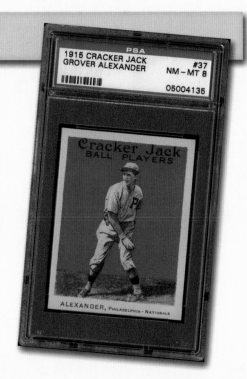

Two years after Cracker Jack® decided to include tiny surprises into packages

of their mouthwatering confection, the company replaced the random prize in 1914 and inserted a lone baseball card from their very first set. Unlike most of the cards produced during the period, namely the various tobacco and candy issues (often referred to as "T" and "E" sets), the Cracker Jack cards were larger and more aesthetically pleasing. Measuring two and one-quarter by three inches, the Cracker Jack cards seem gargantuan compared to most of the more narrowly constructed "T" and "E" cards of the era.

Each card contains an image of the baseball figure on the front against a striking red background. The visual appeal of the Cracker Jack fronts is arguably without peer. While there are certainly a host of other trading card sets that exhibit a much greater combination of color, the simplicity of the Cracker Jack design

and commitment to the consistent, yet bold backdrops give the cards uniform strength. The reverse of each card is split into two fairly distinct sections. One portion contains a brief player biography, while the other is focused on promoting the candy and set.

Astonishingly, cards 1–72 in the 1914 set were printed with the claim that 10 million Cracker Jack cards were issued, while cards 73–144 contain a claim of 15 million total cards. There is some dispute as to whether those numbers were real or simply a product of a marketing ploy. No matter what the original printing numbers were, the only statistic that is relevant today is how many cards survived and in what type of condition. While there is no way to know exactly how many exist, there is no doubt that it is a mere fraction of the number actually printed.

The visual appeal of the Cracker Jack fronts is arguably without peer.

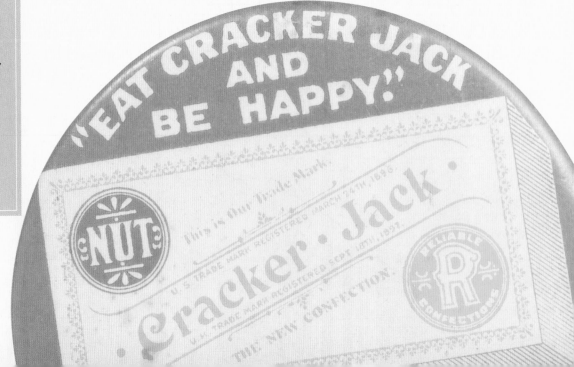

The Cracker Jack Design

Generally speaking, the design of both the 1914 and 1915 Cracker Jack cards

is virtually identical. While almost all of the fronts are mirror images from year to year, the backs are what clearly distinguish one set from the other. The information on the 1914 card backs is printed in a traditional manner, following the position of the card fronts. The 1915 Cracker Jack cards are different in that the text found on the reverse is printed upside down, which is consistent throughout the issue.

In addition, while neither set of Cracker Jack cards was manufactured with the type of thick cardboard stock used for other popular trading card issues, such as the legendary 1909–1911 T206 set, the 1914 Cracker Jack cards were printed on an even thinner paper stock than the 1915 cards were. The difference in card thickness is very subtle, but it does help distinguish the two issues beyond the positioning of the text on the reverse.

Cracker Jack's initial release included a total of 144 cards in 1914.

After a terrific response from the public in year one, Cracker Jack decided to expand the set to 176 subjects in 1915. This enabled the company to include 32 more subjects in the 1915 set; however, there are four subjects that can only be found in the smaller 1914 set. These include cards of Harry Lord, Jay Cashion, Nixey Callahan and Hall of Famer Frank Chance.

Furthermore, Rollie Zeider has two cards in the 1914 set (#60 and #116), but in 1915, his #60 card was replaced by Oscar Dugey. To further the intrigue of the technically smaller 1914 set, there are also a couple of cards that contain different poses than the ones found in 1915. While the 1915 set contains portraits of Del Pratt (#93) and Christy Mathewson (#88), the 1914 Cracker Jack set features both players in a throwing pose.

In 1915, Steve O'Neill replaced Harry Lord (#48), Willie Mitchell replaced Jay Cashion (#62), Hal Chase replaced Frank Chance (#99) and Herbie Moran replaced Nixey Callahan (#111), in addition to

the Dugey/Zeider (#60) swap mentioned earlier. Within the additional 32 subjects, two more Hall of Famers were included in the 1915 Cracker Jack issue. Cards of outfielder Ed Roush (Rousch) (#161) and former pitcher-turned-manager Clark Griffith (#167) are key bonuses in the 1915 set. Information such as team affiliation was also updated on all the cards in 1915.

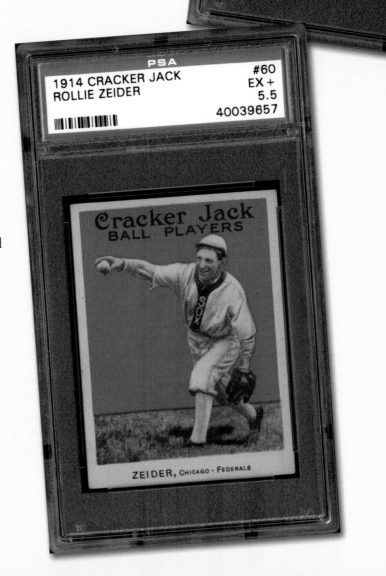

Distribution and Difficulty

While collecting complete sets from either year is tough, there is no question

that the 1914 set is infinitely more difficult to acquire, and it all comes down to the way the cards were distributed. In 1914, the only way you could obtain the cards was through purchasing boxes of the Cracker Jack® treats. There was only one card inserted within each box. In other words, you had to assemble the set one card at a time. Furthermore, the cards you did have access to were subject to the potential pitfalls inherent in rattling around inside a box surrounded by sticky caramel.

That all changed in 1915. The baseball cards were still being included within packages of Cracker Jack; however, now there was an additional way to obtain the cards. As part of a mail-in offer, collectors could receive an entire set of the cards, all 176 of them, in exchange for either 100 coupons or one coupon plus a whopping 25 cents! In addition, for 50 coupons or one coupon plus 10 cents, you could receive a custom album for storage. The reason the backs of the 1915 cards were printed upside down was so the card information could be read while mounted in the specially-designed albums. The albums themselves do not generate a lot of interest in the market today and can be obtained for a relatively low price when they do surface, but this program is the key reason why high-grade copies are much more plentiful from 1915 versus 1914.

On the other hand, you do see quite a few more 1915 cards with back damage

as a result of collectors utilizing these albums. The damage may come in the form of reverse staining from glue or a glue-like substance, as well as stock damage from impressions or tears in the cardboard. Keep in mind that not all collectors used or kept their cards inside albums like the ones distributed by the company, but it is important to note their existence. Despite many of the 1915 cards being subjected to possible album-related condition obstacles, the 1914 cards are many times more difficult to find in top grades or at all.

To illustrate the point, we have taken the latest PSA Population Report figures and placed them in the table on the following page. The PSA Population Report is a census of all the cards graded by the company in our 22-year history, broken down by year, set, card number/player and grade. PSA has graded well over 20,000,000 total collectibles since 1991. This online resource reveals the drastic difference in Cracker Jack difficulty, an obvious result of the 1915 mail-in program. Not only are the overall number of 1914 card submissions much lower, but the percentage of cards graded at the PSA Near Mint 7 level or higher is even more telling.

A good portion of the existing 1915 cards exhibit bolder colors and whiter borders compared to many 1914 examples as a result of the protection afforded by the special offer.

Here is a breakdown of Cracker Jack cards graded PSA NM 7 or higher and the total number of cards graded for each issue.

	PSA NM 7	PSA NM + 7.5	PSA NM-MT 8	PSA NM-MT + 8.5	PSA Mint 9	PSA Gem Mint 10
Total						
1914 Cracker Jack 3,118	113	1	80	1	2	0
1915 Cracker Jack 10,278	1,578	30	2,173	85	290	2

As you can see, more than one-third of the 1915 Cracker Jack cards submitted to PSA have achieved a grade of PSA NM 7 or higher, while only about three percent of the 1914 Cracker Jack cards have reached the same stratosphere. In addition to the difference in technical grades, a good portion of the existing 1915 cards exhibit bolder colors and whiter borders compared to many 1914 examples as a result of the protection afforded by the special offer. Many of the 1915 cards were spared from the tasty but sticky Cracker Jack boxes and preserved in much greater numbers, giving the collectors of today a more feasible goal of completing a quality set.

It would seem logical that the 1914 cards would sell for a significant premium compared to the easier-to-find 1915 cards; however, the price premium isn't as extreme as one might think. Ironically, the difficulty inherent in the 1914 set has actually become a deterrent over time. Many collectors, even advanced ones, have avoided collecting the 1914 set because of its difficulty to assemble, especially in mid-to-high grades. On the other hand, since the 1915 Cracker Jack issue is actually attainable in top grades, this set has generated greater collector interest and overall demand.

The Keys to the Cracker Jack Set

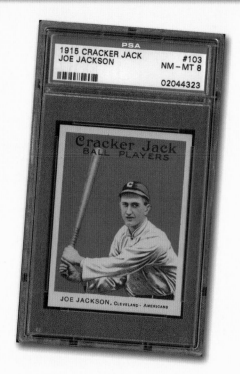

One of the more attractive aspects to both sets is the incredible selection of

recognizable names, including over 30 Hall of Famers. The biggest names in baseball at the time were included, such as Ty Cobb, Walter Johnson, Christy Mathewson and Honus Wagner, to name a few. In addition to the players, key managers were included as well, like Connie Mack, John McGraw and Branch Rickey—the man who would ultimately help end segregation in baseball by signing Jackie Robinson to a Major League contract with the Brooklyn Dodgers in 1947. There is even a card of Chicago White Sox owner Charles Comiskey, wearing his famous hat.

Beyond the men who would ultimately be inducted into the Hall of Fame, there were some infamous figures who were also included. A few members of Chicago's 1919 Black Sox team can also be found here, including three of the scandal's most prominent names in Ed Cicotte, Chick Gandil and Shoeless Joe Jackson. While the first two men admitted guilt at some point in their lives, Jackson denied being part of the fix until his death.

As a result of Jackson's stance, the lack of clear evidence and testimony by some of his teammates exonerating Jackson, the public seems to be split on whether or not Jackson was guilty and a good portion of the public feels he should be enshrined in Cooperstown. Regardless of whether the legendary hitter was guilty or not, Jackson's Cracker Jack card remains the most popular card in the entire set, and

it is arguably his most desirable baseball card ever made despite not being nearly as tough as his 1909 E90-1 American Caramel or 1910 T210 Old Mill issues.

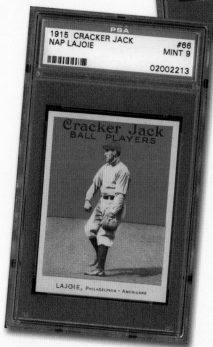

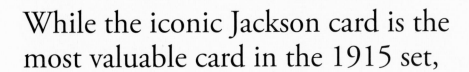

While the iconic Jackson card is the most valuable card in the 1915 set,

it is only the second most valuable Cracker Jack card ever made. That title would go the 1914 Christy Mathewson card. Mathewson's 1915 portrait-style card is one of the more expensive cards in the set, but nothing compared to his 1914 pitching pose, which has been a perceived rarity for a long time. That said, this card may not be quite as tough to find as the hobby once thought, as more examples have been found in recent times.

In 22 years, PSA has graded only 18 examples of the 1914 Mathewson card, with the highest grade achieved being NM 7. Compare that to his 1915 card, a tough card to find in its own right. There are 92 entries into the PSA Population

Report, with six examples reaching PSA Mint 9 status. The 1914 Mathewson is certainly not easy to find, but the legend of its scarcity has taken on a life of its own, much like the 1909–1911 T206 Honus Wagner card, which has fueled the demand even further. Beyond the scarcity, hobbyists have always been intrigued by the 1914 Mathewson card due to the distinct pose. It remains the crown jewel of all Cracker Jack cards.

The Card that Never Was

Throughout hobby history, there have been many trading card sets that failed

to include some major stars for one reason or another. Some star cards were pulled early in production at the specific player's request, as was the case with Honus Wagner and the T206 series, while others were prevented from inclusion as a result of contractual exclusivity with another brand. In 1954 and 1955, Mickey Mantle was noticeably missing from sets issued by Topps, but he was under contract with rival Bowman at the time.

Stan Musial was another legend who was absent from inclusion in Topps issues between 1952–1957, making his debut in 1958 on an All-Star card in the high-number series. Musial had been a mainstay in Bowman releases for years, but interestingly enough he did not appear in any Bowman or Topps issues in 1954 or 1955. Other times, great players

When it comes to the Cracker Jack issue, there is one card that collectors can only dream of owning—the Babe Ruth rookie that never was.

were missing from sets due to things such as military service, like Whitey Ford, who appeared in no Bowman or Topps sets in 1952.

There are countless examples of "missing" cards that carry with them a host of stories, but when it comes to the Cracker Jack issue, there is one card that collectors can only dream of owning— the Babe Ruth rookie that never was. In 1914, Babe Ruth made his debut for the Boston Red Sox. The young left-handed pitcher would soon become one of the best pitchers in baseball before heading to New York in 1920, transforming into the Sultan of Swat.

Technically, Ruth could have been included in the Cracker Jack issue. He was not yet a superstar, but neither were

many other players who appeared in the 176-card issue in 1915. Ruth did appear on a Minor League card as a member of the Baltimore Orioles in 1914, which is exceedingly rare with only 10 examples known at this time. Ruth also appeared in the 1916 M101-5 and M101-4 Sporting News sets as a Major Leaguer.

The Sporting News issue is regarded by most hobbyists as Ruth's true rookie card since it represents his first big-league appearance on cardboard. While the M101-5 set was issued slightly earlier than the M101-4 release, both Ruth cards are highly coveted. If Cracker Jack decided to include Ruth in a set which already contained virtually all the other legends of the period, it would certainly be the most prized card in the set and more valuable than the 1914 Mathewson. Since Ruth never was included, collectors can only imagine what the card would look like. Oh, what could have been.

The Future of Cracker Jack Cards

There aren't too many sets that can compare to the significance, visual

appeal and overall collectability of vintage Cracker Jack cards. As a standalone issue, the set exhibits all of the attributes hobbyists look for, but what takes the issue to another level of importance is the cultural link to the game itself as a result of the set's affiliation with the Cracker Jack confection.

The world of collectibles is filled with fads. Some items go through wildly volatile streaks of "hot" and "cold" in the marketplace, but Cracker Jack cards possess an enduring appeal that should stand the test of time. The

names are recognizable, the aesthetics are unforgettable and the set's place in history can't be denied. It is one of the classic trading card sets that the entire hobby is built upon, one of the mere handful of sets that new collectors ask about as soon as they enter the field.

During the seventh inning of every MLB game, future generations of baseball fans will be exposed to the tune that reminds us of the close tie between the sweet snack and the National Pastime—both American originals.

PLAYER INDEX

ABOUT THE AUTHORS

TOM ZAPPALA is a businessman in the Greater Boston area who is passionate about maintaining the traditions and historical significance of our National Pastime. He is co- author of the award-winning book *The T206 Collection: The Players & Their Stories*, and co-hosts a popular talk radio show broadcast in northern Massachusetts and southern New Hampshire. As co-owner of ATS Communications, a multimedia and consulting company, he handles publicity and personal appearances for several authors and a variety of artists in the entertainment field. He also enjoys collecting vintage baseball and boxing memorabilia, using the simple philosophy of collecting for the love of the sport. He loves spending time with his children and grandchildren, and enjoys a Grey Goose martini with two baseball-sized olives.

ELLEN ZAPPALA is president of ATS Communications, a multimedia marketing and consulting company. Co-author of the award-winning book *The T206 Collection: The Players & Their Stories* and *Nardo: Memoirs of a Boxing Champion*, Zappala was publisher of a group of six newspapers in Massachusetts and New Hampshire for many years and served as president of the New England Press Association. She works closely with various publishing companies on behalf of other authors and handles publicity in both print and electronic media. She especially enjoys bringing the stories of the Deadball Era players to life.

JOE ORLANDO is president of Professional Sports Authenticator and PSA/DNA, the largest trading card and sports memorabilia authentication service in the hobby. Editor of the nationally-distributed *Sports Market Report (SMR)*, a Juris Doctor, and an advanced collector of sportscards and memorabilia, Orlando has authored several collecting guides and dozens of articles for Collectors Universe, Inc. He is the author of *The Top 200 Sportscards in the Hobby* and *Collecting Sports Legends*, and contributed the foreword and last chapter to the award-winning *The T206 Collection: The Players & Their Stories*. As a hobby expert, Orlando has appeared as featured guest on numerous radio and television programs including ESPN's *Outside the Lines* and HBO's *Real Sports*.

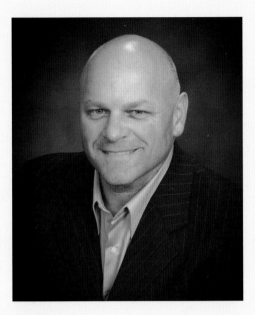

JOHN MOLORI is a columnist for *Boston Baseball Magazine*, *ESPNW.com*, *Patriots Football Weekly*, and *New England Golf Monthly*. A former writer for *Boston Metro*, *Providence Journal*, *Lowell Sun*, and *The Eagle-Tribune*, his radio and television credits include ESPN, Sirius XM, Fox, Comcast, NESN, and NECN. He has lectured on sports media at Emerson College, Boston University, and Curry College, and has been honored with the New England Emmy Award, CableAce, Beacon Award, and the New Hampshire Association of Broadcasters Award. He was inducted into the Methuen Athletic Hall of Fame for his contributions as a sports journalist, alongside former NL Cy Young award winner Steve Bedrosian.

JIM DAVIS is a charter member of the Cracker Jack Collectors Association, and creator of The Cracker Jack Box website for Cracker Jack collecting. His Cracker Jack collection was featured on the Food Network's *Top 5* episode on food premiums, and prizes from his collection have appeared on the NPR, Vintage Non-Sports Cards, and Chow websites. His articles have appeared in *Collectors' Eye*, the *Charmed I'm Sure* newsletter, *Outlaw Biker Tattoo Review*, and CJCA's *The Prize Insider*. A New Orleans resident, he coordinates the Louisiana Book Festival as Director of the Louisiana Center for the Book in the State Library of Louisiana in Baton Rouge.

TONY DUBE, is president of White Point Imaging in Windsor, Connecticut. One of the first to embrace digital photography, he has extensive knowledge of leading-edge equipment and techniques. His images depicted in *The T206 Collection: The Players & Their Stories* received critical acclaim for set design, styling and lighting. In addition to product and collectible photography, Dube works on lifestyle and model photography as well as non-professional subjects. He also enjoys coaching baseball, playing racquetball, inventing products, and working on his photographic series called "Collectographs™: The Art of Collecting."